To Dennis
from Heather
15 August 1982

Wellington's Army

Wellington's Army

In the Peninsula 1808-1814

MICHAEL GLOVER

It is probably the most complete machine
for its numbers now existing in Europe.
Wellington (21 November 1813)

DAVID & CHARLES

NEWTON ABBOT   LONDON   VANCOUVER

ISBN 0 7153 7369 2

Photoset in 11 on 13pt Baskerville
by Trade Linotype Limited Birmingham
and printed in Great Britain
by Redwood Burn Limited, Trowbridge
for David & Charles (Publishers) Limited Brunel House Newton Abbot Devon

Published in Canada
by Douglas David & Charles Limited
1875 Welch Street North Vancouver BC

Contents

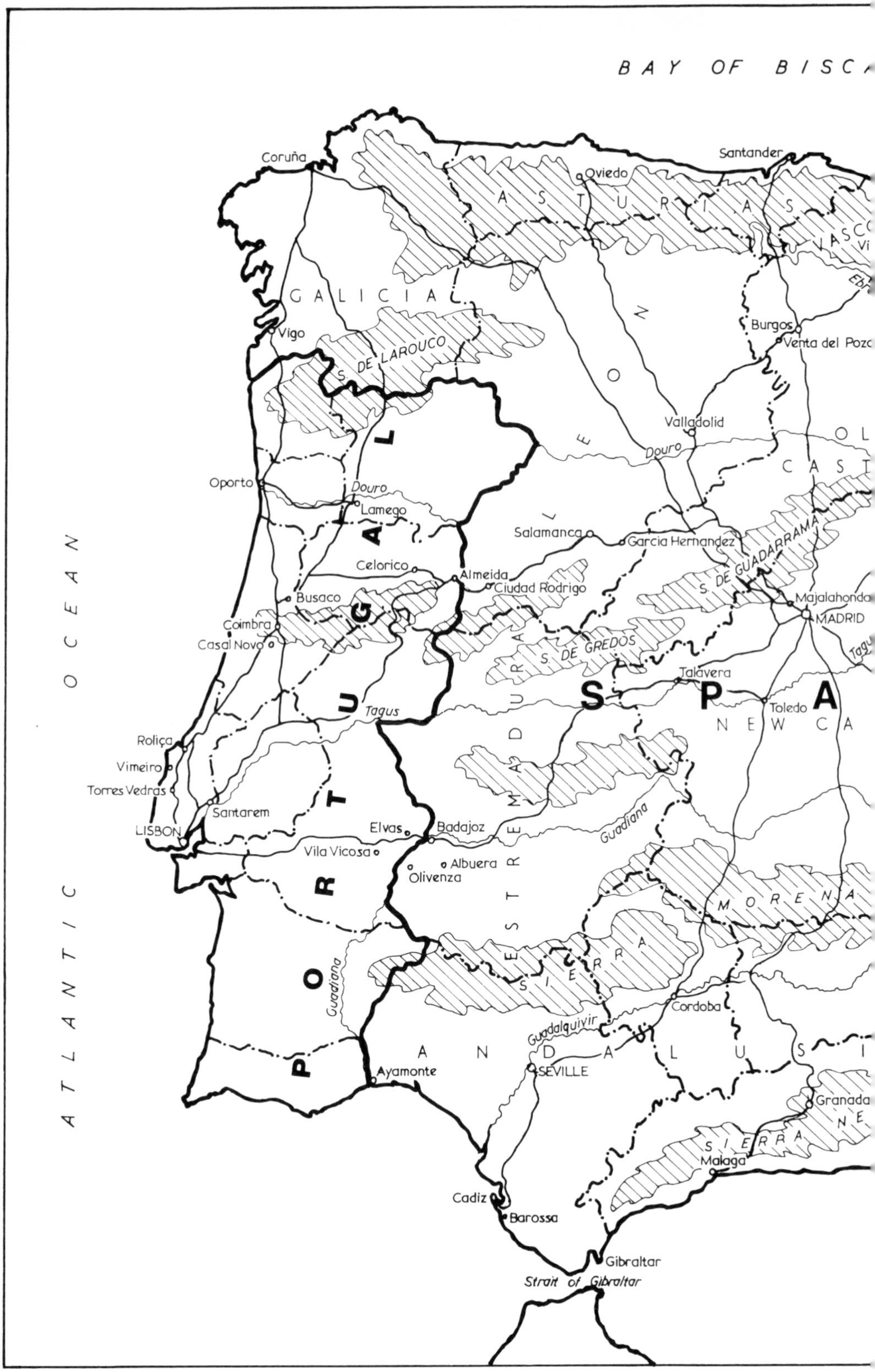

BAY OF BISCA

Coruña

Santander

Oviedo

ASTURIAS

ASCO

Vi

GALICIA

E

Vigo

Burgos

S DE LAROUCO

Venta del Poz

Valladolid

OL

CAST

Douro

Oporto

Douro

Lamego

Salamanca

Garcia Hernandez

S DE GUADARRAMA

Celorico

Ciudad Rodrigo

Almeida

Majalahonda

Busaco

MADRID

Coimbra

S DE GREDOS

Casal Novo

SPA

Tagus

Talavera

Toledo

NEW CA

Roliça

Vimeiro

Torres Vedras

Santarem

Elvas

Badajoz

Guadiana

LISBON

Vila Vicosa

Albuera

Olivenza

MORENA

Guadiana

SIERRA

Cordoba

ANDALUSI

Guadalquivir

Ayamonte

SEVILLE

Granada

SIERRA

NE

Malaga

Cadiz

Barossa

Gibraltar

Strait of Gibraltar

ATLANTIC OCEAN

PORTUGAL

Spain and Portugal
at the time of the
Peninsular War

FRANCE

Adour

sajes
Bayonne   o Orthez
San Marcial
Vera   Roncesvalles
Pamplona
VARRA

PYRENEES

CATALONIA

Saragossa

Ebro

BARCELONA

Tarragona

VALENCIA

N

VALENCIA

RCIA

Alicante

Murcia

Cartagena

N

0   50   100 miles

International boundaries
Provincial boundaries
Main roads
Principal mountain ranges

MEDITERRANEAN   SEA

For
DAPHNE
'All other things to their destruction draw . . .'

Introduction

While it is permissible to write of the armies of Frederick the Great and Napoleon, it is not, strictly speaking, to write of such an organisation as Wellington's army. Constitutionally it was the army of King George III. More immediately it was the army of Frederick, Duke of York, since it was he, more than any other man, who moulded the existing British army into an improved and improving force, part of which was given to Wellington to command in the Peninsula. Even then the Duke of York was responsible only for the infantry and cavalry. Other authorities controlled the artillery and the engineers, the supply services, the transport and the provision of intelligence. The Household Troops were responsible only to the Sovereign. Until 1812 the Colonel of the Royal Horse Guards asserted an absolute and unfettered right to appoint and promote the officers of his regiment.

Wellington's task was 'to do the best I can with the instruments that have been sent to assist me'. He had no say in the way the army was recruited, officered, armed, trained and dressed. It follows, therefore, that much of this book will have to deal with the organisation of the British army as a whole rather than that part of it which served in the Peninsula. Wellington's victory over the French was possible only because he was able to manage the administrative hydra in England.

One preliminary word of caution is necessary. The ideas and events of Wellington's time cannot be judged fairly by the standards of the last quarter of the twentieth century. Society was far more stratified then than it is now, and this state of affairs was all but universally accepted. Literacy was confined to a small proportion of the population, and was a great, almost impassable, social divider. Savage punishments, corporal and capital, were believed by all classes in society to be not only essential but desirable. Unless allowance is made for these and similar facts, the picture will be seen through a distorting glass.

The classic work on this subject is Sir Charles Oman's *Wellington's Army*, first published in 1912. Some of his judgements were questioned by Godfrey Davies in his *Wellington and His Army* (1954). More than 60 years have passed since Oman's work was published, and much new evidence has become available in that time. It should also be noticed that *Wellington's Army* appeared at a time when Oman had completed only four of the seven volumes of his splendid *History of the Peninsular War*, bringing the story down only to the end of 1811. Eighteen years were to pass before he completed his work on the subject.

Oman's book has stood the test of time very well, but there are some points where his judgement is open to dispute and others where new information is available. There are also some points which he ignored. One example is that in none of his works (or, in fact, those of Sir John Fortescue) is there any information on one extremely relevant point — the effective range of the artillery of Wellington's day. On only one point is this book in total disagreement with Oman, and that is on the system under which officers were appointed and promoted.

This book does not, of course, set out to recount the campaigns of the Peninsular War. These can best be followed by reading Oman's seven-volume history, mentioned above. Those who have not the time or the opportunity to attempt this massive but very readable work could do worse than try my *The Peninsular War: A Concise Military History*, published in 1974. Four other books are particularly valuable for the background. These are S. G. P. Ward's *Wellington's Headquarters* (1957), Richard Glover's *Peninsular Preparation* (1963), Antony Brett-James's *Life in Wellington's Army* (1972) and Major-General B. P. Hughes's *British Smooth Bore Artillery* (1969).

One or two matters of nomenclature need to be clarified. I have used the title Wellington for the Commander of the Forces throughout the book, although he was, in fact, the Hon Sir Arthur Wellesley until 4 September 1809. The office of the Commander-in-Chief in London is referred to as the Horse Guards, as was the practice at the time. The regiment now usually known by that title is called the Royal Horse Guards or the Blues. The contemporary titles for artillery units were particularly cumbersome and confusing. I have used the modern term 'field artillery' for what was known as Foot (as opposed to Horse) Artillery or, more formally, as the Marching Battalions of Artillery. The tactical unit of this arm was a *company* of gunners who manned a *brigade* of guns and howitzers. To make the matter even more confusing, the brigade of guns was divided into three divisions. I have replaced the term *company/brigade* with the modern *battery*, although, in Wellington's day, a battery was a fortification, permanent or temporary, into which artillery pieces were put. Less easy to circumvent is the early nineteenth-century use of the word *corps*. This was given its literal sense as a body of men. Thus it was used for any sized body of troops from a group of several divisions down to a battalion, or occasionally a small detachment.

PROLOGUE

1

The System

The other shape
If shape it might be call'd that shape had none.
John Milton *Paradise Lost,* ii, 666

There was no love lost between Britain and her army in the eighteenth century. Edmund Burke maintained that any 'armed and disciplined body' was dangerous to liberty. Dean Swift claimed that 'it is no part of our business to be a warlike nation, otherwise than by our fleets. In foreign wars we have no concern further than in allies, whom we may either assist by sea or by foreign troops paid with our money.' In other words, Britain would fight to the last Hessian.

The belief that the army was 'dangerous to liberty' had worn thin by 1800 but the national dislike for the army continued. The rich disliked it because it swelled the amount they had to pay in taxes. The poor mistrusted it because, in the absence of police or an efficient preventative service, troops were used to quell riots and prevent smuggling. Troops were obtrusive since they were billetted in inns, spread over large tracts of the countryside for all to see. An eighteenth century member of Parliament considered it 'one of the tacit obligations of a member to keep the place he represented as free as he could from being pestered [sic] and burthend with soldiers.' It was bad enough to have to pay taxes to support the navy and the navy at least won their battles. The army had acquired the habit of losing theirs.

An elaborate system of controls had evolved to prevent the army from menacing civil liberty. They would have made any kind of military coup very difficult. They made any operation against a foreign enemy almost impossible. In constitutional theory the King was head of the army but only Parliament could keep the army in being by passing the annual Mutiny Act and, more important, by providing the money needed to pay the soldiers. Since the loss of the American War, not a soldier could be moved without the authorisation of a minister responsible to Parliament — the Secretary at War.

The Secretary at War had originally been the King's personal secretary for military business. This had entailed preparing the army estimates and presenting them to Parliament. He also kept the register of commissions and had, over the decades, developed a responsibility for seeing that the money voted by Parliament for the army was spent on the activities for which it was provided. He had no responsibility for what the army did, provided that they did it according to the regulations. Burke's reforms, although they did not change his duties, made him responsible to Parliament. Secretaries at War were seldom members of the cabinet but they always had the cabinet minister's right of direct access to the King 'in his closet'. This was not because his business was important but because he was the channel by which the Sovereign issued his orders to his Foot Guards who, in matters of internal administration, were not subject to the Commander-in-Chief.

The task of the Commander-in-Chief was to supervise the training and discipline of the infantry and cavalry of the line; he was also responsible for the appointment and promotion of the officers in those regiments, for the provision of staff officers at home and abroad and for the appointment of general officers to all posts except those of commanders-in-chief overseas. In the event of a foreign invasion he would have commanded the defending forces but he had no direct power over expeditionary forces or garrisons overseas. He was likely to be consulted about the destination of overseas expeditions but it sometimes happened that he was merely asked whether he could provide a given number of troops for 'a particular service'.

Since only the Commander-in-Chief could order troops to move, and only the Secretary at War could authorise them to do so, there was bound to be friction between these two officials. In fact, this friction occurred only in wartime as, as a matter of economy, the post of Commander-in-Chief was usually left vacant in peacetime. This had a deleterious effect on the army's training but left the large and influential patronage of the army in the hands of the Secretary at War, who used it not for military ends but to further the political ends of the government of the day.

The complaints of both Lord North and Lord Rockingham demonstrated that George III deprived them of the use of military patronage which they needed to cement the hold of their governments in the two houses of Parliament but Burke's reform, while diminishing the power of the Crown over military appointments greatly increased that of the government, made the army a political convenience. For most of the period between the end of the American War and the outbreak of the French Revolutionary War there was no Commander-in-Chief and the Secretary at War was Sir George Yonge, a thorough-going politician, who used the patronage ruthlessly for political ends.

Yonge's misrule was not checked by the appointment of a Commander-in-Chief on the outbreak of war in 1793. The officer appointed was Lord Amherst who was seventy-six years old and who had made his reputation in the Seven Years' War more than 30 years earlier. He had the advantage of having held the post before, between 1778 and 1782, but even then he was, according to Horace Walpole, 'found out, and allowed to be, a man totally devoid of parts [who suffered from] immoderate self-interest and obstinacy (the latter of which proceeded from his extreme slowness of conception, and fear of changing his opinion on what he had at last understood for another which he should be as long in comprehending).' Amherst was no match for Yonge. He could not even prevent his own aide-de-camp, whose accelerated promotion he had refused on three occasions, from obtaining promotion from Sir George.

In less than two years it was clear that Amherst, a popular and revered figure, was worse than useless and, on the recommendation of Pitt, the Duke of York, the King's second and favourite son was appointed Commander-in-Chief. He held the post, with one short break, from 1795 until his death in 1827 and raised it from the slough into which it had sunk after the twin disasters of defeat in the American War and the administration of Sir George Yonge until it became, in Wellington's words, 'the most complete machine for its numbers now existing in Europe'.

The Duke of York's reforms were many but three are pre-eminent. He standardised the training of the infantry and cavalry, which previously had been left, effectively if not officially, to the whims of commanding officers; he took a firm grip of the military patronage at all ranks, working through a Military Secretary who replaced the elderly clerk (paid 10/- a day) who had done the work for Yonge; he set out to rid the army of the useless and incompetent officers with whom Yonge had flooded it.

As Commander-in-Chief, the Duke's powers were limited. His direct authority extended only to the infantry and cavalry of the line. Any authority he had over the Foot Guards arose coincidentally from the fact that he was colonel of a regiment of Guards. He could not give orders to the Household Cavalry except through the King and the colonels of the Life and Horse Guards. He had no control over the artillery, the engineers, the militia, the volunteers, the yeomanry or the supply services. Transport by sea or on land was under other departments and he had no funds for the collection of intelligence.

There was a second Commander-in-Chief in the person of the Master General of the Ordnance. The troops he commanded were not large, consisting only of the Royal Artillery, the Royal Engineers and their supporting services but his influence was widespread. Unlike the Commander-in-Chief, he was a member of the government and its principal military adviser. His responsibilities included manufacturing and supplying cannon for both the Royal Navy and the army; supplying the infantry and cavalry with arms, ammunition and a number of other military stores, including greatcoats, surveying the United Kingdom and providing maps. Nevertheless, it was not considered a full-time occupation. Lord Cornwallis had not resigned from it when he spent three years in Ireland as Lord Lieutenant (1798--1801) and Lord Mulgrave was appointed to it in 1811 because he was 'too old and ill' to continue at the Admiralty.

Some improvements, notably the raising of the Royal Horse Artillery and the replacement of hired peasants as artillery drivers by the Corps of Artillery Drivers, had been effected in the Ordnance organisation since 1793 but it remained an inefficient body. As late as 1814 the most competent artillery officer of his generation was complaining from America that 'with respect to our ammunition and stores, great quantities of articles have been sent that are perfectly unnecessary and have never been demanded, whereas others greatly required have never been sent although demanded in the most urgent fashion.'

Neither the army of the Commander-in-Chief nor that of the Master General of the Ordnance could undertake even the simplest operation without the active cooperation of the Treasury, which was responsible for supplying food, forage and fuel. This was no arduous task in peacetime when the troops were in static quarters. Long term contracts were made with civilian merchants, who supplied what was necessary subject to a superficial inspection for quality. This meant that no peacetime Commissariat was required and that, at the outbreak of war, the whole supply service had to be improvised.

Having hastily recruited a staff, the Treasury expected its officials to accompany the army overseas and procure supplies as if they were negotiating at a garrison town in England. The Chief Commissary accompanying an expedition was

Wellington in 1812, by Juan Bauzit (NPG)

instructed 'to take a written voucher for the due payment of all articles purchased by you, with a certificate of two reputable merchants annexed thereto that the same were bought at the market-price of the time, and on payment thereof, the receipt of the party is to be attested by at least one witness.' Such instructions were admirably calculated to protect the taxpayer but they were scarcely adequate to ensure a regular supply of food, forage and fuel to a large army engaged in a war of manoeuvre in Egypt or the plains of Leon where reputable merchants were not in plentiful supply.

Further efforts on the Treasury's part were necessary before the army could move on land. The army had no vehicles except the forge waggons of the cavalry. The Ordnance corps had only the limbers of the artillery. All other transport had to be hired in the theatre of war—if they were available. The Duke of York succeeded in raising a modest Waggon Train which was independent of direct Treasury control but it was the target of bitter hostility in the House of Commons. In 1810 General Tarleton, a senile hero of the American war, said that 'Let the British army go where it may, it will always get waggons enough'; and William Huskisson, whose experience of transport amounted to becoming, in 1830, the first man to be killed by a railway engine, declared that 'The Waggon Train is an annoyance on foreign service and useless at home.' The House insisted that the Train be cut from twelve troops to seven, and Wellington, already desperately short of transport, was ordered to sent two troops home for disbandment. He ignored the order.

To get an expeditionary force in motion was a task of great intricacy. The Commander-in-Chief and the Master General had to detail troops from their respective armies. The Treasury had to appoint a Commissariat staff and provide them with cash or credit for the purchase of supplies. The Sovereign had to give any orders necessary to get the Household Troops in motion. The movement of all troops to their port of embarkation required the warrant of the Secretary at War and their movement by sea was the charge of the Transport Board, a semi-independent offshoot of the Admiralty. The Joint Paymasters General, junior members of the government, had to find cash to pay the troops; the Medical Board provided hospital staff; the Apothecary General medicines and hospital supplies. Tentage came from a thinly disguised commercial firm, operating under the title of the Storekeeper General's Department. Intelligence about the theatre of war must come from the Foreign Office and the Admiralty had to provide escort for the troop convoy.

Compared to the complications arising from any attempt to launch an expeditionary force, the business of deciding where it should go was, in theory, simple. Since 1794 there had been a Secretary for War whose task was to direct grand strategy. His task was to select the Commander-in-Chief, to give him his objective and to tell him what troops and supplies were, or would shortly be, available to him.

In practice things were less simple. With the possible exception of the Lord Chancellor, every member of the cabinet felt entitled to have a finger in the strategic pie. The Prime Minister, who bore the supreme responsibility for the government, naturally believed that he had the right to make his views felt. The Master General had naturally to be consulted. The Chancellor of the Exchequer was responsible for the Commissariat and the Foreign Secetary had an obvious interest in the destination of the expedition. The Home Secretary, who was the titular head of the home defence forces—the militia, the volunteers and the yeomanry—must be consulted if the regular force in the kingdom was to be reduced; he depended on the regulars not only to repel invasion but to maintain the civil peace. The same concern applied, even more strongly, to the Lord Lieutenant of Ireland.

The First Lord of the Admiralty was a prime mover in any strategic discussion. Only he could get the troops to their destination and sustain them after their arrival. It was largely due to pressure from the Navy, intent on securing the all-weather harbour of Lisbon, that the British base during the Peninsular War was set in Lisbon. The civilian ministers were unanimous in wishing the army to operate from Cadiz.

As might be expected the orders emerging from such committee deliberations were far from definite. In 1811 Wellington complained to his brother that 'I have never been able to obtain any specific instructions, or even a statement of object. You have seen the only instructions which I have, which are to save the British army; and that is the only object officially stated to me for keeping the army in the Peninsula.'

If the machinery for the control of the army was complex and confused, the organisation at a lower level was almost non-existent. There was no formation with any permanent existence larger than the regiment. Over each regiment was the colonel, almost always a general officer, who was, for most purposes the proprietor. In addition to the pay as colonel (22s6d a day in the infantry, 32s10d in the cavalry), he could draw the basic pay (i.e. exclusive of ration money) of one non-existent man in each troop or company in the regiment. He was also responsible for providing the soldiers with uniform, except greatcoats. For this purpose a lump sum was made over to him annually. It was possible to make a handsome profit on the clothing account but very few colonels did so. Wellington, when colonel of the Thirty Third, believed that it was 'a losing concern'.

A colonelcy was intended to be a well-paid reward for military services rendered to the country. The payment for the non-existent 'warrant men' and the possible profit on the clothing account would have appeared less anomalous if they had been expressed as an increase in the colonel's pay but parliament would not sanction an increase in officers' pay. Except for subalterns, the rates had been unchanged since the reign of Queen Anne.

The other outstanding anomaly was the way in which some of the officers purchased their commissions and their promotions. This, like the additional payments to the colonels of regiments, stemmed from parliamentary parsimony. Regiments had been raised by farming out recruiting to the colonels who had to collect a given number of men in return for a set sum of money. This amount was usually inadequate: Thomas Graham, who raised the Ninetieth Foot in 1794, spent £10,000 of his own money. In consequence, colonels sub-contracted the raising of companies to captains and the captains sub-contracted further to their subalterns.

While this system saved the taxpayer the cost of a recruiting service and raised more men than the amount of 'levy money' regularly supplied would have produced, it did leave the officers with a financial investment in the ranks they held. If Parliament was not prepared to buy out the officers, to recompense them for their investment, there was no alternative to letting them sell their commissions.

As will be shown in Chapters 3 and 6, the extent to which purchase dominated

William Carr Beresford, by Thomas Heaphy (NPG)

the appointment and promotion of officers has been greatly exaggerated. The fact that a commission was not heritable property and that it was customary for newly-created commissions to be awarded free should have meant that purchased commissions would have died out during the long wars between 1793 and 1815. In the early years of the war Pitt's unwise attempt to conquer France by filching sugar islands dealt a savage blow to the number of old commissions. The Thirteenth Light Dragoons spent 30 months in the West Indies in the 1790s and nineteen of their officers died of disease. The Seventeenth Foot lost two-thirds of their officers in five months in 1804. Those who had purchased commissions in regiments stationed in the Caribbean found themselves unable to sell them. In 1796 an officer of the Eighty First wrote: 'To give you an idea of what people think of the West Indies, my company has been on sale for £1,200 [£300 less than the regulation price] ever since I came home [a year ago] and no offers to purchase, in fact they are glad to give commissions of all descriptions to any that will venture out'.

It is true that those who had not purchased their rank were permitted to sell it after 20 years of satisfactory service, to compensate themselves for the fact that there were no pensions except for disabling wounds. Such cases did not come near balancing the number of purchased commissions which lapsed through the death of the holder.

Unfortunately Sir George Yonge was selling new commissions at an unprecedented rate in Britain. He authorised new regiments in all directions. In 1792 there had been seventeen regiments of cavalry of the line and seventy seven of infantry. Before Yonge left the War Office in 1794 there existed, on paper, the Thirty Third Regiment of Dragoons and the Hundred and Thirty Fifth Foot, apart from a collection of unnumbered units. Most of these new bodies never existed in anything but the most skeletal form, but Yonge allowed their officers to purchase rank at any speed up to lieutenant-colonel, usually on the unfulfilled promise of bringing in recruits.

The result was a chaotic scramble for rank. Anyone with money or credit could purchase any regimental rank he fancied. Andrew Gammell became an ensign on 24 December 1793. On 18 September of the following year he was lieutenant-colonel of the Hundred and Fourth Foot. There was no minimum age. George Landman met an ensign of the Sixty Fourth aged seven. Francis Hastings Doyle became a captain in the Hundred and Sixth a month before his twelfth birthday.

When the Duke of York became Commander-in-Chief, one of his most daunting tasks was to restore order, discipline and justice to the officers, an operation he started by relegating most of Yonge's overpromoted youngsters to half-pay where some of them remained a charge to the taxpayers for sixty years and more. The Duke would have preferred to have abolished purchase. When asked to suggest how the promotion structure of the East India Company's army could best be organised, he recommended that there should be no purchase but that 'the promotion [of British officers] in the native troops should, I think, go on progressively in regimental seniority, but not beyond the rank of captain . . . but above that rank, the promotion may be made by his Majesty generally throughout the native army. You will thereby not only effectually prevent one corps obtaining a more rapid share of promotion than another, but you will be enabled to select such efficient men for the important station of field officers as may have distinguished themselves from the generality of senior captains of the respective corps.. It appears to me that this arrangement tends much to the encouragement of the good officers as it does to the advantage of the public service.'

The impossibility of abolishing purchase and Yonge's great increase in the number of purchased commissions, made the adoption of this plan unthinkable in the British army. The Duke, therefore, did his best to make the existing system work as smoothly and equitably as possible. He laid down that no subaltern could become a captain until he had completed two years' service and that no captain could advance to field rank with less than six years' service. He instituted confidential reports, to be submitted annually, on each officer by the commander of his battalion or regiment. No officer could be promoted without a satisfactory annual report. He adhered rigidly to these rules. He would not be moved from them even by a personal appeal from the Prince Regent trying to oblige a friend.

The principle of purchase is so foreign to twentieth-century ideas that it is easy to believe that it was an indisputable evil which can be held responsible for all the army's shortcomings. This is certainly not the case. Purchase officers, who during the Peninsular War, accounted for only about a fifth of the army's officers, were at least as good as those who rose in other ways, and had the advantage in the senior ranks, that they were usually younger. The purchase system was certainly no worse than that practised at the same time in the Royal Navy. There, once an officer had got his first commission as a lieutenant, the equivalent of a captain in the army, his further promotion depended entirely on the amount of influence he could command. Admiral Lord Rodney succeeded in getting his son made post-captain, equivalent to lieutenant-colonel, before he was sixteen. His career was broken by a court martial. Christopher Parker, son of Admiral Sir Peter Parker, was a captain at seventeen.

It is instructive to compare the early promotion of the outstanding figures in the two services. Both men had merit on the grand scale, but Nelson's uncle was Comptroller to the Navy while Wellington had to make do with an influential brother who, if he was always in debt, could command large sums of money. Nelson became a lieutenant at eighteen and a half; Wellington reached the equivalent rank at twenty two. Nelson was made post-captain at twenty years and eight months; Wellington became a lieutenant-colonel when he was twenty four and five months. Both his majority and his lieutenant-colonelcy were bought during Yonge's free-for-all. It should be noted that the command of a 'post' ship, a frigate or ship of the line, was a very much greater responsibility than the command of a battalion of infantry.

Both Nelson and Wellington reached high rank by means that would today be considered scandalous. Both leaped over the heads of hundreds of deserving officers. In both cases their rapid advancement was abundantly justified. It would not be difficult to point to cases where bad officers rose to high rank in both services but it is even easier to point out much larger numbers whose 'accelerated promotion' more than justified the use of wealth or influence to reach their high rank. The system was patently inequitable but it achieved results, and was surprisingly little resented by those who were left behind.

Part I

THE RAW MATERIAL

2

Recruiting the Ranks

Wellington has often been taken to task for describing his soldiers as 'the scum of the earth', but his proud addition, 'it is really wonderful that we should have made them the fine fellows they are', is seldom quoted. It is quite certain that Wellington was extremely proud of his soldiers. Nothing proves this more conclusively than his encouragement to a timid subordinate in 1812: 'His Majesty and the public have a right to expect from us that we should place a reasonable confidence in the gallantry and discipline of the troops under our command; and I have the satisfaction of reflecting that, having tried them frequently, they have never failed me.'

The phrase about 'the scum of the earth' referred not to the soldiers but to the men who enlisted. It was a recognition that conditions in the ranks were so deplorable that only 'the very worst members of society' could be persuaded to volunteer. Wellington said: 'I have often been induced to attribute the frequency and enormity of the crimes committed by the soldiers to our having so many men who have left their families to starve for the inducement of a few guineas to get drunk.' He said that the French army was 'certainly a wonderful machine; but if we are to form such a one, we must compose our army of soldiers drawn from all classes of the population of the country; from the good and middling, as well in rank as in education, as from the bad, and not, as we in particular do, from the bad only.'

The evidence is clear that, with rare exceptions, those who joined the army were 'the very worst members of society'. A witness from the ranks of the Third Guards wrote: 'Of those who voluntarily enlist, some few are driven by poverty . . . Some have disgraced themselves in their situation or employment, many have committed misdemeanours which expose them to the penalties of the law of the land, and most are confirmed drunkards.' A sergeant of the Ninety Fourth complained that, after he had enlisted,

> . . . there were few with whom I could associate, that had an idea beyond the situation they were in: Those who had, were afraid to shew they possessed any more knowledge than their comrades, for fear of being laughed at by fellows who, in any other circumstances, they would have despised. If he did not join in their ribald obscenities and nonsense, if he did not curse and swear, he was a Quaker, if he did not drink most of his pay, he was called a miser, a mean scab, and the generality of his comrades would join in execrating him.

These voices from the ranks confirm Wellington's belief that the army was recruited from 'the scum of the earth' as no more than the truth. As a regimental officer of unquestionable humanity remarked, 'The system of recruiting is so defective and so radically bad that in every regiment there are from 50 to 100 bad characters that neither punishment nor any kind of discipline can restrain.'

When Wellington said that 'English soldiers are fellows who have enlisted for drink — that is the plain fact — they have all enlisted for drink,' statistics suggest that he was not greatly exaggerating. After 1808 it was possible for a recruit to choose whether he would engage for life or for a term of seven years with the option of renewing his service. Should he sign for life, his bounty was increased by 5 guineas. Three-quarters of those enlisting chose to sign their lives away for an extra 5 guineas. Of 3,143 who signed on in 1814, only 772 took the prudent course of limiting their service. It was noticeable that, while 29 per cent of the English and 26 per cent of the Scots signed for seven years, among the Irish, traditionally the thirstiest and most shiftless of recruits, only one out of 566 thought it worthwhile to limit his engagement.

Ireland always provided a high proportion of the soldiers for the British infantry. Naturally the thirteen specifically Irish battalions were almost wholly recruited from Ireland, but the Irish also provided a large and growing proportion of the strength of English battalions. In 1809 34 per cent of the ranks of the Fifty Seventh (West Middlesex) were Irish. In the Twenty Ninth (Worcestershire) there were only 19 per cent, but this rose to 37 per cent in the next two years. The Scottish regiments (except the Royal Scots) had a lower proportion of Irish, but even there it was rising. The Gordon Highlanders had 3 per cent of Irishmen in 1807 and 6 per cent in 1813. The percentage of English in that regiment fell from 6 per cent to 3 per cent over the same period.

There was little to tempt a man to enlist. *Dulce et decorum est pro patria mori*, but there was nothing attractive to the most romantically minded patriot in dying in a fever-stricken island in the Caribbean without an enemy in sight. Nothing made recruiting more difficult than Pitt's policy of winning the war in the West Indies. During the 15 months of the Grenada campaign, the Twenty Fifth Foot lost '11 officers, 30 sergeants, 15 drummers and upwards of 500 rank and file from disease alone'. In one of their companies, Captain Wade's, every man except the captain and one drummer died. In the four years up to 1797, 80,000 British soldiers died or were permanently disabled in the West Indies, the vast majority of them as the result of disease. At the time of the Peninsular War there were still twenty-one British battalions stationed in the Caribbean, and even the thirstiest Irishman would be reluctant to risk being sent to one of them, whatever the inducements.

In all the British army's stations, battle casualties represented only a small proportion of its total deaths. In 1811, a very bloody year, with the battles of Fuentes de Oñoro and Albuera, the unsuccessful siege of Badajoz and a host of minor actions, the total loss to the army was 22,953. Of these, only 6,066 died in the Peninsula, of which only some 1,500 were returned as killed in action and about 500 more would have died of wounds. In the rest of the world the only battle casualties were less than 100 men killed in the Java campaign. Thus, some 4,000 men in the Peninsula and more than 15,000 men in the rest of the world died or were disabled through disease. Although most garrisons in the West Indies had been turned over to indigenous troops, or to Dutchmen and Germans, one man in eleven throughout the army would die or be invalided out of the service every year, but less than one man in a hundred would die as the result of battle.

If, despite these prospects, a man was rash enough to enlist, he would be paid at the rate of a shilling a day in the infantry, 1s1d in the Foot Guards or 1s3d in the cavalry of the line. In the Life Guards privates were paid 1s11¾d; in the Blues 1s8¼d a day. It is true that civil wages were low. A farm labourer could expect to get 14s6d a week, and a 'domestic artificer' about 30s0d. In 1814 a bricklayer could expect to get 5s6d a day. Civilians, of course, had to house and feed themselves and their families. A soldier did not have to house himself, though he might be billeted on an unwilling publican who would do his best to cheat him out of his meagre entitlement. He would, more probably, be accommodated in insanitary jerry-built barracks in which his allocation of space would be only 400cu ft, less than half the allocation for a convict. His sleeping space would be a wooden crib, which he had to share with three of his comrades.

Soldiers, with few exceptions, were not expected to have families. The *Rules and Regulations for the Cavalry* laid down that 'marriage is to be discouraged as much as possible. Officers must explain to the men the many miseries that women are exposed to, and by every sort of persuasion they must prevent their marrying if possible.' In each company of 100 men six wives were permitted to accompany the troops, draw half rations, and sleep, with such privacy as they could devise, in the overcrowded barrack rooms. Naturally, despite every discouragement, more than six men in every company did marry but, when the regiment was ordered overseas, the surplus wives had to be left behind. Each of these unfortunate women was given a pass entitling her to accommodation and meals from parish authorities as she walked back to her native village. Once she had reached it, no further provision was made for her. Even if her husband could manage to save some of his pay, there was no official arrangement whereby such savings could be transmitted to her, although in good regiments the officers would arrange to pass money to her through private channels. Every time a unit went overseas, there were heartrending scenes. When the Ninety Fourth were ordered to Portugal,

> . . . it was ordered that the wives should draw lots to see who should remain. The proportionate number of tickets were made with "to go" or "not to go" written on them. They were then placed in a hat, and the women called by their seniority to draw their ticket. The sergeant stood in the middle with the hat in his hand, the women stood around him, with their hearts palpitating, and anxiety and suspense in every countenance . . . The barracks for the rest of the day was one continual scene of lamentation.

If the soldier did not have to provide his own housing, it was still believed that he should pay for his own food. From his shilling a day, sixpence was deducted towards the cost of his rations. In return he was provided with a daily pound of meat (including a proportion of bone), a pound and a half of bread and a quart of beer. Nothing else was provided, and there were no cooks. Each man took his turn at preparing the two daily meals — one in the morning, one at midday. Inevitably both consisted of either a thin stew or a watery soup. Wellington pointed out from the

Peninsula that 'the rations of the soldier are not sufficient for his subsistence for any great length of time', but nothing was done to improve the rations.

Ration money was not the only deduction made from the soldier's pay. Every week he was mulcted of fourpence so that his washing could be done by the 'wives on the strength'. Each year he had to pay 4s4d for whitening and pipeclay, 1s3d for three shoe brushes at 5d each, 2s0d for blackball and 4s0d for having his boots soled and heeled. Every second year he had to pay an additional 1s0d for a clothes brush. A further sum was demanded for the upkeep of his 'necessaries' and, like every other member of the army, he had to contribute one day's pay each year to maintain the hospitals for old and incapacitated soldiers at Chelsea and Kilmainham. Naturally he had to pay for any items of clothing and equipment lost by neglect.

Few men would join the army unless they were bribed to do so. The bribe was called a bounty, and the amount was determined by the urgency of the need for men. In 1803 £7 12s 6d was being offered and very few recruits were coming in. Two years later the bounty was up to 12 guineas. This was not the whole cost to the taxpayer. For every recruit obtained the recruiting officer received 16s0d, the recruiting party 15s6d and the bringer of the recruit, usually a publican, £2 12s 6d. The total cost to the state was 16 guineas. By 1812 it had risen to £23 17s 6d for each recruit for life service and £18 12s 6d for limited service. Not that the recruiting party made much money out of the service. As one recruiting sergeant put it, 'Our money didn't do much good—it all went on raking and drinking.' When James Smithies offered himself for the Royal Dragoons in 1804, the sergeant was so low in funds that 'finding he had not a shilling in his pocket, went upstairs, awoke his mother to borrow one, with which he enlisted me.'

According to his own account, Smithies was an exceptional recruit, since he was sober when he took the King's shilling. Sir Frederick Robinson, when he was an Inspecting Field Officer of a Recruiting District, observed that 'Almost all recruits are invited into the service in a public house, and generally by the publican'. The recruiting sergeant put the same idea in different words. If the potential recruit could not be persuaded in any other way,

> . . . your last recourse was to get him drunk, and then slip a shilling in his pocket, get him home to your billet, and next morning swear he enlisted, bring all your party to prove it, get him persuaded to pass the doctor. Should he pass, you must try every means in your power to get him to drink, blow him up with a fine story, get him inveigled to the magistrates, in some shape or other, and get him attested; but by no means let him out of your hands.

Weavers, the sergeant said, were the easiest to enlist:

> You could scarcely ever catch a weaver contented. They are always complain- ing. Ask him how a clever handsome-looking fellow like him could waste his time hanging see-saw between heaven and earth in a damp unwholesome shop, when he could breathe the pure air of heaven and have little or nothing to do if he enlisted for a soldier. Ploughboys had to be hooked in a different way. When you got into conversation with them, tell how many recruits had been

George Murray, by Thomas Heaphy (NPG)

made sergeants, when they enlisted — how many were now officers. If you saw an officer pass while you were speaking, no matter whether you knew him or not, tell him he was only a recruit a year ago; but now he's so proud he won't speak to you. If this won't do, don't give up the chase — keep after him — tell him that in the place your *gallant honourable* regiment is lying, everything may be had for almost nothing. As you find him to have stomach, strengthen the dose, and he must be overcome at last. You must keep him drinking — don't let him go to the door without one of your party with him, until he is passed the doctor and attested.

Once the recruits were attested, the problem was to keep them. They had been drunk when they enlisted and, on attestation, they would be given the first instalment of their bounty, a sum larger than any of them would ever have held in their hands at one time. Many would repent their bargain as soon as they were sober and would do their best to get away. Some made a practice of 'bounty-jumping', taking the money, deserting, and then repeating the process with another regiment. A man had been hanged in Ipswich in 1787 who 'made the extraordinary confession that he had enlisted forty nine times and had had three hundred and ninety seven guineas as bounty money thereby.'

Once more the recruiting party relied on drink to stop the men changing their minds. When John Harris joined the Rifles at Cashell, he was the only Englishman among a party of Irish recruits. They were

as reckless and dare-devil a set of men as ever I beheld before or since. Being joined by a sergeant of the 92nd Highlanders and a Highland piper of the same regiment, we started on our journey from the Royal Oak; the whole lot of us three sheets to the wind. When we paraded before the door, the landlord and landlady of the inn, who were quite as lively, came reeling forth with two decanters of whisky which they thrust into the fists of the sergeants. The piper struck up, the sergeants flourished their decanters, and the whole commenced a terrible yell. We then all began to dance through the town, every now and then stopping for another pull at the decanters. Thus we kept it up till we had danced, drunk, shouted and piped thirteen Irish miles from Cashell to Clonmell and on arriving we were as glorious as any soldier in Christendom need wish to be.

When they joined their regiment the recruits had an unpleasant shock. They had been promised a bounty of 12 guineas, but few recruiters ever bothered to explain to them that £2 14s 0d of this had to be given back to the army in payment for their 'necessaries'. These comprised one pair of black cloth gaiters, two pairs of shoes, one pair of stockings (or two pairs of socks), two shirts, a foraging cap, a pair of worsted mittens and a knapsack. It was an unsusual recruit who had not drunk his bounty by the time he made this discovery, so that most started their regimental soldiering in debt.

The wiles of the recruiting sergeants and the publicans were aided in many areas by the Justices of the Peace, who were always ready to release minor offenders on condition that they enlisted. Convicted criminals seldom, if ever, went into the regiments of the line but were sometimes allowed to commute their sentences by volunteering for the Royal African Corps or the Royal West Indian Rangers. Ordinary recruiting, however, never kept up with the drain of casualties. The annual loss to the army through death, discharge of the unfit and desertion never fell below 16,071 (in 1806), and it reached a peak of 25,498 in 1812. Ordinary recruiting in the British Isles never exceeded 15,308 (in 1807), and in 1810 it fell to 7,367. The traditional resource of hiring German mercenaries was not available, since Germany was under Napoleon's control. Eight regiments of West Indians and four of Sinhalese made up some of the deficiency. From 1805 the recruitment of boys of fourteen or more was permitted and these were put into holding units until they were sufficiently mature to take their place in the line. This added 1,500 potential soldiers annually. Nevertheless many more British and Irish soldiers were necessary if the army was to keep up its strength, to say nothing of expansion. In fact, between 1804 and 1813 the army increased from 150,593 to 260,279, the number born in the British Isles increasing from 133,500 to 207,000.

The reason for the constant shortfall in regular recruiting was that Britain was maintaining a third army. Apart from the independent armies of the Commander-in-Chief and the Master General of the Ordnance, there was a third army composed entirely of infantry who were compelled to serve but could not be sent out of the British Isles. This was the Militia, the 'constitutional' home defence force. It was supervised by the Home Office and its officers were appointed by the Lords Lieutenant of counties. At the time that Wellington first landed in Portugal there were 86,788 men in the Militia. By Act of Parliament any militiaman who joined the regular army was liable to six months' imprisonment.

The Ballot Act of 1802 laid down that all men between eighteen and forty years of age were liable to be drafted into the Militia. Exemption was given only to clergymen, registered teachers, articled clerks, apprentices, seafaring men, employees of the Royal Dockyards and Arsenals, Freemen of the Company of Watermen and those worth less than £100 a year who had one or more legitimate children. Also exempted were those who had enlisted and were reported as efficient in the Volunteers and Yeomanry, two other home defence forces. A man who was drawn in the ballot had to take an oath that he had no rupture, was not subject to fits and was not lame. Neither unfitness nor being less than the regulation height of 5ft 4in, nor being a doctor prevented a man from being drafted. Any man could, however, procure a substitute, thereby securing immunity for life. Alternately, he could pay a fine of £15 which secured immunity for five years.

The effect was that the type of man who might be expected to join the regular army could do better for himself by taking service as a substitute in the Militia. In 1803, the first year in which the ballot was held, the regulars were offering a bounty of £7 12s 6d, whereas a Militia substitute could command £25 from a private individual. In theory substitutes had to be men, having not more than one child born in lawful wedlock, 'from the same county, riding or from some adjoining county or place' as the men they replaced. In practice enquiries were seldom made into the origins of those who offered themselves and those who were prepared to act as substitutes could offer their services in the best paying market.

This would seem to be an arrangement that favoured the rich at the expense of all but the poorest of the poor, but this was not so. The sons of the rich were already widely engaged in serving as officers in the regular army or navy, or in the Militia. Many more were in the church and immune in any case. Since Britain was largely an agricultural country, the landowners were far from pleased if their labourers were conscripted into the Militia. Responsibility for the ballot and for filling the quotas was given to the parish authorities, and it was worth the while of the squire and the other substantial farmers to organise and finance the provision of substitutes for their labour force. Naturally, unsatisfactory labourers and such undesirables as poachers, and 'those who have increased the population of the parish without permission of the clergy' would be strongly encouraged to volunteer, and would not be provided with substitutes, should they be unfortunate enough to be drawn in the ballot.

In the country the parish authority was the squire, who could be counted upon to look after his own people, but in the teeming slums of the newly industrialised towns and cities the parish authority was little more than a name and a memory. Few were capable of organising a ballot among their unregistered, uncounted populations. For men with some funds there were insurance clubs that undertook to provide substitutes for any member who was drawn. In 1803 the club at Lichfield gave cover for as little as 5s0d, scarcely beyond the reach of the poorest. In the same year at Blackburn the premium was a pound. The organisers made a handsome profit, the substitutes were well paid and those who were drafted escaped at a moderate cost. Thus everyone was happy, except the recruiting parties of the regular army, who lost tens of thousands of potential recruits.

Service in the Militia had many attractions compared with joining the line. There was no question of being sent to the West Indies. The Militia could only be posted to places in the British Isles, including the Channel Islands. For the conscientious married man the choice was an easy one. If he joined the Militia, his wife and children would be supported by the parish; if he joined the regulars, they would be left to shift for themselves. The government's attitude was made absolutely clear. The punishment for a substitute who deserted was that he should be compulsorily enrolled in the regulars.

To try to find a way out of this constitutional cul-de-sac, the government passed the Additional Forces Act of 1803. This created yet another army, the Army of Reserve, which was intended to consist of 50,000 infantry with service limited, like that of the Militia, to the British Isles. The units of the Army of Reserve were designated as second battalions of regular regiments, and it was hoped that the men would volunteer to transfer to unlimited service in the first battalions. As an inducement, they were offered a bounty of 10 guineas (less the cost of 'necessaries'). Like the Militia, the Army of Reserve was raised by a ballot administered by the parish authorities. It was, however, a quite distinct operation, and the fact that a man had bought immunity or provided a substitute for the Militia did not affect his chance of being drafted into the new force. This was not unnaturally regarded as governmental sharp practice and the Army of Reserve was intensely unpopular. The main result was to raise the price of Militia substitutes and to make regular recruiting even more difficult.

SIR JAMES McGRIGOR, BART.
1771-1858

James McGrigor, by Thomas Heaphy (NPG)

The first ballot for the Army of Reserve raised 45,492 men, of whom 41,198 were substitutes; 5,651 deserted in the first ten months, and 17,307 agreed to transfer into the line. A second ballot in the following year was intended to raise a further 29,000 men but brought in only 7,683; 3,041 more men deserted and another 8,562 transferred to the line. The scheme was then dropped, and the remaining men were formed into Garrison battalions, most of which formed part of the army of occupation in Ireland, although one served in the Channel Islands. As the number of Army of Reserve men dwindled, these battalions were made up with boy soldiers, and eventually one Garrison battalion went out to Malta and five companies of another to Bermuda.

Finally the government had to face the fact that the army could not be recruited without drawing men from the Militia. After 1805 limited periods were set aside during which the regulars were permitted to call for volunteers from the Militia. Recruiting parties were enjoined to 'be careful not to disturb the discipline' of the Militia, meaning that they should not reduce whole battalions to alcoholic stupor. Substantial numbers of militiamen were quite ready to volunteer. The Militia had been embodied since 1803 and there was no prospect of its members being released until the war ended; many of the younger men felt that, if they had to be soldier, they might as well be real soldiers rather than train indefinitely to repel an invasion which never came and which, after Trafalgar, appeared unlikely ever to come. Certainly regiments going to the Peninsula could always count on volunteers from the Militia. To ease the transfer, a bounty of 10 guineas was offered, and this was later increased to £14 for life enlistment and £11 for limited service.

A good deal of pressure was put on militiamen to encourage them to volunteer. According to one account,

> The Militia would be drawn up in line, and the officers or non-commissioned officers from the regiments requiring volunteers would give a glowing description of their several regiments, describing the victories they had gained and the honours they had acquired, and conclude by offering a bounty. If these inducements were not effectual in getting men then coercive measures were adopted; heavy and long drills and field exercises were forced upon them; which became so oppressive that, to escape them, the men would embrace the alternative and join the regulars.

Militiamen could choose the regular regiment they joined and naturally avoided volunteering for those that were serving in unhealthy climates. Since Miltia units had been serving alongside regular units in Britain and Ireland for years, potential volunteers would have far more chance of discovering which regiments had good reputations and which bad, than a discontented weaver or a bemused ploughboy. Some regiments had such a high reputation that volunteering for them had to be halted. The militiamen of Cambridgeshire asserted that if they could not join the Ninety Fifth Rifles, they would only volunteer for the Royal Marines. The Rifles were so popular that they raised a second battalion in 1805, only three years after they had been included in the regiments of the line. In 1809, when they

Edward Pakenham, by Thomas Heaphy (NPG)

appealed for 350 recruits to make up their losses on the Coruña campaign, 1,282 volunteers immediately offered themselves from the English Militia alone. A third battalion was added before the Horse Guards forbade further volunteering for the regiment.

Once transfers from the Militia were permitted, good regiments were seldom short of volunteers, particularly if they were serving in the Peninsula. Volunteering was also encouraged when the Duke of York offered a regular ensign's commission to any Militia officer who could induce forty of his men to go with him to the regulars. This again worked almost entirely to the benefit of regiments with good reputations, and had the side effect of weakening the links the authorities were trying to build between regiments and counties. It was quite rare for militiamen to volunteer for their own county regiment. If the regiment was a good one, there would not be vacancies in it; if it had a poor reputation, potential volunteers would go elsewhere. When the Seventy Seventh (East Middlesex) was made up to strength before sailing to Lisbon, it received all the men it needed from the Militia regiments of West Yorks, Mayo, Northampton and South Lincoln before any Middlesex men had a chance to join. William Wheeler volunteered from the Royal Surrey Militia into the Fifty First (West Riding) Foot. On joining he wrote: 'We are about eight hundred strong, about one hundred and fifty of this number are old soldiers, the remainder being voluntiers [sic] from the Stafford, South Gloucester, 1st & 2nd Surry [sic] together with some half dozen Irish regiments.'

In 1805, the first year in which volunteering from the Militia was sanctioned, 13,580 men took advantage of the opportunity. Only 10,180 men and 1,497 boys enlisted through ordinary recruiting. In subsequent years volunteering provided half the total of all recruits. Between January and September 1809 the army raised 112,103 recruits from the British Isles. Of these, 54,299 (48 per cent) came from the Militia. No doubt there were many bad characters among them but, considered as a whole, they were a steadier class of man than the army usually managed to obtain. They were, in fact, the men that the army should have enlisted if they had not been swept compulsorily into the Militia.

It was this increase in strength that made it possible for the army to find the men to fight the Peninsular campaigns. It is no coincidence that on 30 September 1813 the strength of Wellington's army was 54,945. This number was almost precisely the same as the number of militiamen who had volunteered since the army had first landed in Portugal. Nevertheless, the Act of 1802 had not been repealed and, had not Parliament indemnified them, a number of former militiamen equal to the strength of Wellington's army in Spain would have been liable to six months' imprisonment each for having enlisted.

3

Officer Material

Under the stresses of the Napoleonic war almost any young man who wished to serve and was literate would have little difficulty in obtaining a commission. The peacetime officer corps was largely a self-perpetuating body composed of the sons of officers, with a leavening of the aristocracy and the landed gentry. The vast expansion of the army between 1793 and 1814 wholly altered this picture. In the last year of peace there had been 3,107 officers. By 1814 there were 10,590 on full pay exclusive of foreign regiments and veteran battalions. In the same period the officers of the Ordnance corps increased from 361 to 912. Simultaneously there was a heavy wastage. During the Peninsular War the requirement for new officers was running at about 1,000 a year. In 1813, for example, some 300 officers were required for new and expanded units, and 792 left the army — 426 died, 307 retired or resigned and 59 left as a consequence of disciplinary action. The traditional sources could no longer supply the need.

The formal qualifications for a commission were sparse and simple:-

No person is considered eligible for a commission until he has attained the age of sixteen years.
All recommendations shall certify the eligibility of the person recommended in respect of character, education and bodily health, and that he is prepared immediately to join any regiment to which he may be appointed. His Christian names and place of address must also be particularly stated.

The letter of recommendation had to be signed by someone who held the rank of major or above and a suggested form for it was:

I beg leave to recommend Mr A.B. as a gentleman fully qualified to hold a cornetcy/ensigncy in his Majesty's . . . regiment of Dragoons/Foot.

The Duke of York did his best to do away with the practice of giving commissions to children although the fact that births were not officially registered made it difficult to ensure that a proportion of fifteen year olds were not admitted. After the Peace of Amiens half the army's new officers were commissioned at under eighteen, the largest single group being sixteen. Before that Peace one officer in five had been less than fifteen when gazetted.

The fathers of regimental officers covered a wide social range, from the Duke of Beaufort, who had five sons and two grandsons on the active list, to Private Babington Nolan, Thirteenth Light Dragoons, whose son was given an ensigncy in the Sixty First Foot (and whose grandson was to carry the order that launched the Light Brigade at Balaclava). The morganatic son of HRH the Duke of Sussex was a lieutenant in the Royal Fusiliers. The son of a sergeant major in the Royal Scots Fusiliers died commanding the Scots Greys at Waterloo. Lieutenant Edward Fox Fitzgerald, Tenth Hussars, was the son of Lord Edward Fitzgerald, the Irish rebel; and Colonel John Elley, Royal Horse Guards, was the son of an eating-house keeper in Holborn.

Clerics, lawyers, doctors, playwrights, painters, architects and scientists all contributed their quotas. Naval officers fathered a strong contingent of military sons, and quite a number of officers had served as midshipmen before joining the army. The largest single category of fathers remained army officers but the commonest description of an officer's father was 'gentleman'. This could mean anything from the proprietor of huge landed estates to a 'gentleman in trade' — a shopkeeper. The term was often used to conceal the fact that the father, though a professional man, was in one of the less highly regarded branches of his profession — a surgeon rather than a physician, a solicitor rather than a barrister.

A twentieth-century American historian who referred to the officers of Wellington's army as being 'aristocratic' and coming 'almost entirely from the landed gentry' is very wide of the mark. A Peninsular officer regretted that 'we had but a slender sprinkling of the aristocracy among us'. The fact was that there were only about 450 peers (including the peers of Scotland and Ireland), and it was inconceivable that they could have provided a preponderant numbers of officers for the army while contributing many of their sons to the Royal Navy (to which, according to Professor Michael Lewis, they provided 7.3 per cent of the officers), the Militia, the Church of England and the two Houses of Parliament. In 1809 there were 140 regimental officers on full pay who were either peers or the sons of peers. By the time Waterloo had been won, one in five of this group of 140 had died on active service.

It is difficult to estimate the extent to which the untitled landed gentry sent their sons into the army. It is probable that the fathers of the majority of officers had some land, but most of them were by no means large landed proprietors. Many were no more than substantial farmers or professional men with a few fields attached to their house. Most had nothing except the prospect of half pay, a meagre allowance amounting to only 5s a day for a captain. After all deductions had been made the actual issue of half pay for a captain would be £86 13s 9d a year.

It was not wealth or land that restricted the choice of officers, but literacy. This was the great social dividing line in the days before education had been extended to the whole population. The basic ability to read and write was the all-important qualification for a commission. By and large, the officers did not acquire it at the the great public schools, which contributed surprisingly small numbers. In 1809 only 127 Old Etonians held full pay regimental commissions. Westminster came next with sixty one, followed by Harrow with fifty seven and Rugby with thirty eight. The contribution of Winchester is hard to assess but there were eleven Winchester scholars on the active list. That four out of the five most notable schools in Britain should provide only 283 out of 10,000 strongly suggests that it was not the rich and privileged who dominated the officer corps. Although a few of the aristocratic officers were educated by private tutors, the majority of officers had attended local grammar schools. Very few indeed had been to universities.

Education was far more widespread in Scotland than in the rest of the United Kingdom, and this was reflected in the very large number of Scots officers. In the infantry of the line, where most Scots served, one officer in every sixteen bore one of the following fifteen Scots surnames:- Anderson, Cameron, Campbell, Fraser (Frazer), Henderson, Macdonald, MacKenzie, Mackay, Maclean, Macleod, Morison, Reid, Ross, Scott and Stewart (Stuart). In the infantry there were 119 Campbells, twelve of them in the Ninety First. It is hardly surprising when young Colin Macliver, son of a Glasgow carpenter, was introduced to the Duke of York by his maternal uncle, Colonel John Campbell, the Duke assumed he was another of the clan and gave him an ensigncy under the name of Colin Campbell. So named, he worked his way up to the rank of Field Marshal and died as Lord Clyde, the hero of the Indian Mutiny.

Although the Protestant Ascendancy in Ireland was very strongly represented, the 'native Irish' were numerically weak among the officers. In the Guards, infantry and cavalry there were, in 1809, only twenty four Kellys, seven Sullivans and five Murphys. This was due largely to the low standard of Irish education. It was not the result of the legal bars against Roman Catholics. According to the solicitors to the Ordnance:

Commissions are constantly given to persons who profess the Roman Catholic religion; no enquiries are made into the religion of officers and although [Catholics] might *possibly* subject themselves to penalties in accepting commissions, yet experience shows that no inconvenience ever results from the practice. The Indemnifying Act which is passed every session of Parliament, extends the time for taking oaths from year to year, so as to render the Test Act in large measure nugatory.

A sizeable number of officers were born outside the United Kingdom, particularly loyalist Americans, headed by General Samuel Auchmuty, who conquered Java in 1811, and including Colonel William Delancey, who was mortally wounded at the head of the Quartermaster General's department at Waterloo. French Canada supplied the three Baby brothers, and almost certainly many more whose names are hard to distinguish from those of the French *emigrés* who served in British regiments, apart from providing officers for their own corps, the *Chasseurs Britanniques*. Captain Paul St Pol (or St Paul), who died with the Royal Fusiliers at Badajoz, was the son of the Duke of Orleans. German names are common enough, although many of their holders were British subjects, sons of German officers in the Sixtieth (Royal American) Foot. Perhaps the most unexpected officer was Prince Castelcicala, later Neapolitan Minister to the Court of St James. He fought at Waterloo in the Sixth (Inniskilling) Dragoons as Lieutenant Paul Ruffo.

One officer in twenty (5.42 per cent) had risen from the ranks, apart from the ensigns of Veteran battalions who were almost always former non-commissioned officers. Most of these promotions were for long and steady service. Some were the reward for specific acts of gallantry, such as that of Sergeant Masterson of the Eighty Seventh, who captured a French eagle at Barossa in 1811. Sergeant William Newman, Forty Third, distinguished himself by rallying a knot of stragglers on the retreat to Coruña, who beat off repeated attacks by French cavalry and returned to their units. Newman was given an ensigncy and, as was usual with men commissioned from the ranks, received a grant of £50 for his initial expenses from the Royal Patriotic Fund.

Sometimes the promotion was a compliment to a regiment rather than specifically to an individual. Sergeant Donald McIntosh, of the Cameron Highlanders, was made an ensign in the Connaught Rangers to mark Wellington's 'sense of the good conduct of the 79th during the late engagement [Fuentes de Oñoro]'.

Clearly those promoted from the ranks were older than those who joined straight from school. One of the youngest was Sergeant John Fraser, Seventy First, who was commissioned at twenty four. Sergeant-Major John Macdermott of the Queen's was commissioned at forty four, but survived to become a lieutenant-colonel by brevet at the age of sixty three. Many of them became adjutants of the battalions they joined. This had a double purpose: the adjutant was responsible for training the unit in drill, and an experienced sergeant would naturally have much experience in drilling; it also had the advantage that it secured him a higher rate of pay, the adjutant getting 8s6d a day in the infantry compared with 5s3d for an ensign.

One small and unique group, which should be included among those promoted from the ranks, comprised twenty three ensigns in the Portuguese army who received British commissions. These were former sergeants from British regiments who had been lent to Marshal Beresford to help in training the Portuguese.

Another group with service in the ranks and accounting for 4½ per cent of new officers were the Volunteers. These were young gentlemen who, with the permission of a colonel, went on active service with a battalion. They carried muskets and took their places in the ranks, but they messed with the officers. They continued in this way until death created a vacancy when they were appointed to the resulting ensigncy.

The junior department of the Royal Military College had been established in 1802 to train aspirants for commissions. Its contribution was small, less than one in twenty five of all first commissions (3.9 per cent). The college could accommodate 100 cadets, of whom twenty were nominated by the East India Company, in whose army they later served. Of the remaining eighty, thirty were the sons of 'officers who had died or been maimed in his Majesty's service.' They received their education, board and clothing free. Twenty were the sons of officers actually in the army, and paid £40 a year. The remaining thirty were the sons of 'noblemen and gentlemen'. They, like the EICo cadets, paid £90 a year.

Applicants had to be between thirteen and fifteen years of age and, on arrival, had to pass an examination to show that they were 'well grounded in a knowledge of grammar and common arithmetic.' Edward Fitzgerald, straight from Eton, found the College 'a very disagreeable place for a person who has been used to a public school. The hardships are *nothing*, but one has no time to oneself; nothing but sauntering and idling about, the little time one has; hardly anything but *study*. Our beds are good and very clean. Our food very good and plain.'

One in five (19 per cent) of new officers came from the Militia and, since that force had been embodied since 1803, they must have learnt at least the rudiments of their profession by the time they transferred. These were officers who obtained their commissions by persuading forty of their men to transfer to the regulars. In the interests of recruiting such ensigns were 'borne, if necessary, as supernumeraries upon the establishment of their battalions, till vacancies occur.'

The remainder of the newly commissioned officers, sixty-five in every hundred,

Wellington and his staff, from the Prussian dinner service at Apsley House
(Wellington Museum)

joined their regiments with no training of any kind. How much training they subsequently received depended on the unit they joined. Ralph Heathcote, a new cornet in the Royals wrote:

About nine o'clock the trumpets sound for foot parade, when the different troops being formed before the stable doors march towards the centre of the barrack yard, and after being formed in line are examined by the major (viz. their dress and arms are inspected); then the sergeant major exercises the regiment, with which we have nothing to do. At ten o'clock I breakfast

with some others in the mess-room, many officers preferring to breakfast in their own rooms. At eleven o'clock all the subalterns are to go to the riding school, but if you don't go, no notice is taken of it, excepting you were perhaps to stay away for weeks together, and at twelve the same subalterns have to attend foot drill, and then your business is done for the day.'

Other regiments were more conscientious. William Bell, a new ensign in the Eighty Ninth, wrote: 'I have been out at six o'clock in the morning for some time past—since I joined the regiment. We are drilled with the men exactly the same as the private soldiers. We began with the facings and went through all the different steps and evolutions of the marching squads. We were then exercised with the firelock.' In the Forty Third, a young officer was 'not considered clear of the adjutant, until he could put a company through all the evolutions by a word of command, which he had already learned in the ranks. It generally took him six months in summer, at four times a day (an hour to each period) to perfect him in all he had to learn.'

Drill was not the only instruction which the young officer needed. Military administration was complicated and obscure: for example 'In Gibraltar, officers bearing brevets, receive rations according to the rank they hold in the army; but do not in any other part of the British dominions'; and 'When troops march into either of the university towns of Oxford or Cambridge, the commanding officer must wait upon the vice-chancellor to communicate to him the nature of the route.' The compliments paid to senior officers were minutely defined: 'To Governors who have not commissions as general officers, all guards within their garrison turn out with presented arms, and beat one ruffle. The main guard turns out with presented arms every time they pass, yet they give the compliment of the drum but once a day; all other guards beat as often as the Governor passes them.'

There were a number of useful manuals which the new officer could acquire all the recondite information he needed. One of them, *The Regimental Companion*, gave the unlikely warning that 'Prostitutes living in barracks have been known to drive four of the best troop horses four in hand.' They would not have done so when young Colonel Wellesley commanded the Thirty Third in Calcutta. In his Standing Orders, issued in 1798, he laid down that 'The soldiers are not to bring into barracks any common prostitute. If they do so the sergeant must turn them out and confine the man; however if any man wishes to keep a native woman and obtains his captain's permission to do so, there is no objection to her being in barracks.'

It could not be said that junior officers were overpaid. An infantry ensign received 5s3d a day and one in the Guards 5s10d. In the cavalry of the line cornets had 8s0d a day and those in the Life Guards 8s6d. Before they could even receive their commissions they had to pay a fee varying from £4 11s 10d in the infantry to £8 0s 10d in the Blues. From these fees, and the steadily increasing ones that they paid when they received promotion, the salaries of the War Office clerks were provided until 1808. Deductions were made from his pay for poundage, agency and income tax. One day's pay each year was withheld for the expenses of the Royal Hospital at Chelsea. An infantry ensign actually received about 4s a day. John Patterson of the Fiftieth estimated his expenses as follows:

Dinner at the mess	2s0d	Nett pay per day	4s6d
Wine at ditto	1s0d		
Servant & sundries	0s6d		
Breakfast	0s6d		
Washing & mending	0s6d		
	4s6d		4s6d

Balance left for pocket money & dress, £0 0s 0d.

Out of this balance the officer had to provide and maintain his uniform and equipment. When Charles Booth joined the Fifty Second his expenses for his uniform, including his sword (£4 4s), spy-glass and compass were £57 18s 6d. Robert Knowles went to the Royal Fusiliers but had his militia coat cut down for a service jacket. His uniform cost his father £43 15s 0d.

A cavalry officer's expenses would be greater. A regimental enquiry in the Fifteenth Light Dragoons put the cost of equipping a cornet for active service in 1804 at £458 1s 6d.

This was broken down into:

Horses and Horse Furniture	£151	19s	6d
Camp equipage	£50	5s	6d
Dress (ie uniform)	£169	10s	0d
Arms & Accoutrements	£61	4s	0d
Sundries	£25	2s	6d

John Luard, who was commissioned into the Third Dragoons in 1809, estimated his initial expenses for horses and uniform at £500.

When Ralph Heathcote was thinking of a cornetcy in the Blues, he was told that 'no officer was permitted to spend more than £150 p.a. above his pay, but that it was very easy to live merely upon that'. Cornets of the Blues, however, were paid 14s0d a day, £255 10s 0d a year. A cornet of the line received only £146 a year gross, and the Fifteenth's board of enquiry calculated that he would need £381 in addition to his pay, even supposing that he drank only a pint of wine a day and did not have a civilian servant.

Life was cheaper for an infantry officer. In 1804 Sir John Moore wrote that 'it is difficult in these times for a subaltern to live on his pay. There are some few who do it, but it requires a degree of attention which few young men, at starting, are equal to. I should recommend an allowance of not less than £50, nor above £100.' Among the few who did manage to live on their pay was Second Lieutenant George Simmons of the Ninety Fifth. From time to time he even managed to send money to his indigent parents. In 1811, for example, he sent home a draft for £23 9s 0d, almost four months' net pay, to help equip his younger brother, who was sailing to Portugal as a Volunteer in the Sixty Sixth.

There was one other heavy expense a new officer might incur, although it was entirely optional. He might buy his commission. The Regulations laid down that an ensigncy in a 'marching regiment of foot' cost £400. In regiments which had second lieutenants—the Scots and Welsh Fusiliers and the Ninety Fifth Rifles—the price was £450. An ensigncy in the Foot Guards cost £600 and a cornetcy of dragoons

£735. In the Blues a cornetcy was worth £1,050 and in the Life Guards, where the rank was 'cornet and sub-brigadier', the price was £1,600.

There was no need to buy a commission; the demand for young officers was such that there was no difficulty in obtaining one free. One of the main reasons why young men laid out such large sums was as a method of ensuring that they went to the regiments of their choice. Any officer applying for a free commission had to declare that he was 'prepared immediately to join any regiment to which he may be appointed'. This was not a very serious obstacle, as most officers seem to have got to the regiment of their choice even without purchasing but, if a man was determined to go into, say, the Tenth Hussars, he could, by waiting until a cornetcy became available, go into that regiment, and nothing but disciplinary action could move him to another. In fact there was little difficulty in obtaining a cornetcy by purchase. In some regiments they were very difficult to sell. In the Twenty Fourth Light Dragoons, Arthur Macan was promoted to lieutenant on 29 February 1804, but did not succeed in selling his cornetcy until 30 May 1811, more than seven years later.

During the Peninsular War purchase accounted for less than one in five first commissions (19.5 per cent). Almost no ensigncies were sold in the colonial and garrison regiments, and in the infantry of the line the proportion was less than 17 per cent. It was only in the cavalry (47 per cent) and the Foot Guards (44 per cent) that purchase was a major factor. In the Guards purchase was spread fairly evenly between the three regiments, but in the cavalry the percentage was forced upwards by the high level of purchase in the Household regiments and the four hussar regiments.

If any parts of the army could be described as 'aristocratic' they were the cavalry and the Foot Guards. Of the 140 officers from the peerage in 1809 (see p 37), thirty six were in the cavalry and forty three in the Guards. Twenty out of the thirty six aristocratic cavalrymen were concentrated in five regiments—Seventh and Tenth Hussars, Fourteenth, Sixteenth and Twenty Third Light Dragoons. Similarly, the 283 officers from Eton, Harrow, Westminster and Rugby tended to gravitate to the Guards (eighty) and the cavalry (ninety six). Only Rugby of the four schools had more of its former students in the infantry of the line than in either the Guards or the cavalry.

There were only fifty aristocratic officers in the infantry of the line, and they were spread over thirty five regiments. Only in the Fifty Second and the Ninety Fifth Rifles, both regiments with a low level of purchase, were there as many as four in each. Eighty three public school officers were spread over fifty eight infantry regiments, the Fifty Second again having the highest number—six. It was moreover commanded from July 1811 until after Waterloo by a scholar of Winchester. It may not be a coincidence that it was indisputably one of the two best regiments in the army.

The young officers of the army were a very mixed lot. Almost the only thing they had in common was that they started with an almost total ignorance of their profession. When a general in the Portuguese service asked permission to have an ensign as his aide-de-camp, Wellington replied, 'An English ensign can be of little use to him, or to anybody else.'

4

Weapons and Tactics

At the beginning of the nineteenth century the art of war was in transition. European war in the eighteenth century had been a limited affair fought by small professional armies. The prizes to be won were also limited — fortresses, frontier provinces or tropical islands. To compel the unconditional surrender of an enemy would have been considered both impracticable and undesirable. As a German authority laid down in the middle of the century, 'A great general shows his mastery by attaining the object of his campaign by sagacious and sure manoeuvres, without incurring any risk.'

The French Revolution changed the rules. The *levée en masse*, the concept of a nation in arms, of vast conscripted armies, brought with it the possibility of overwhelming an enemy. Huge armies posed their own problems. How were they to be fed? It had been hard enough to feed an eighteenth-century army, and the bankrupt France of the 1790s would have starved if she attempted to provide rations for one half of her soldiers from her own territories. The answer had to be annexation, the quartering of her armies on foreign territory. Overwhelming victory became theoretically possible and logistically essential.

Napoleon's genius, aided by the incompetence of his opponents, enabled France to annex her smaller neighbours and mulct her larger enemies of huge fertile territories. Austria was forced to cede Belgium and North Italy, the Netherlands were made a French province; Prussia surrendered her Westphalian lands; the King of England had to relinquish his Hanoverian electorate; Russian Poland became a granary for the French armies.

The brilliant run of victories ended at Jena in 1806. Napoleon won many more battles but he never again achieved total victory. Thereafter, at Eylau, Friedland, Wagram, Borodino and in lesser battles his enemy always managed to extract an army in being' with which to continue the fight. Up to the destruction of the Prussian army at Jena, Napoleon had been able to achieve complete success partly because he outgeneralled his elderly and frequently disunited opponents, and partly because he had organised his army with a flexibility previously unknown. His later continental opponents, though never able to rival his tactical brilliance, at least reorganised their armies sufficiently to be able to ride, if not to avoid, the blows Napoleon struck at them. Flexibility, however, remained the key to French success. Wasteful though he often was of the lives of his soldiers, Napoleon always set out to outmanoeuvre his opponents rather than attempt to crush them in a slogging match. He knew that the weapons of the day were inadequate to allow one side to crush another army of equally well disciplined troops. Napoleon's final tragedy was that he forgot this truth on 18 June 1815 and, disdaining all manoeuvre, committed his last army to a frontal attack up the gentle slopes of Mont St Jean against an enemy as well trained and well armed as his own.

Artillery, which will be dealt with in Chapter 7, was little more than a minor hazard against well deployed troops at a range of more than 300yd. What counted on the battlefield was the musket, a weapon of remarkable inefficiency, and one that differed only slightly in design and performance in all the major armies. As a Peninsular subaltern commented, 'Both [sides] were so badly armed that I wonder we killed each other at all, but the distance was very short at times.'

The standard musket of the Peninsular army was the 'India pattern', designed for the East India Company, whose stocks were appropriated by the government in 1794 and whose design was copied for most of the weapons produced during the long wars that followed. The barrel was 39in long and the piece weighed 9lb 1oz.

The French equivalent, the musket of year IX, was less well made but fractionally lighter, although it had a longer barrel of 44.72in. It threw a ball of 15.34 drams, a smaller projectile than the British, which weighed 18.9 drams. This meant that the British could, in an emergency, use French musket balls in their weapons, but the British ball could not be put down French barrels. This was made more possible because the French ball fitted the barrel much more tightly than the British. The musket of year IX had a barrel diameter of 0.69in and the ball's was 0.65in, whereas the British barrels' were 0.75in and the balls' 0.681in. Thus the 'windage', the amount of play between the ball and the barrel, was 0.04in in the French and 0.069in in the British. This should have meant that the French musket was the more accurate of the two, but the evidence is that it was not. After Busaco Baron Marbot, never a man liable to give unnecessary credit to his opponents, commented that the British 'firing was far more accurate than that of any other infantry'. The only identifiable effect of the greater windage was that it made the British musket easier, and therefore quicker, to load.

In emergencies a musket could fire five or six rounds in a minute, but the highest practicable rate of fire was three rounds a minute. Even this seems remarkably high when the complicated process of loading is considered. Merely to prime and load required seven motions:

1   The firelock is by the left hand dropped to within two inches of the ground, the butt feeling the calf of the leg, the cartridge is brought to the muzzle & emptied by turning the back of the hand inward with the thumb on the ramrod.
2   The right hand strikes the muzzle and immediately seizes the ramrod between the joint of the forefinger and thumb.
3   The ramrod is half drawn and caught close by the muzzle with the back of the hand drawn inward.
4   The ramrod is quite drawn, turned over the elbow and placed about an inch into the barrel.
5   The cartridge is rammed down half way by bringing the thumb close to the muzzle, holding the ramrod between the thumb and two forefingers.
6   The hand slides to the top of the ramrod, binding it with the forefinger.
7   When the cartridge is rammed down, the ramrod is quickly returned, the left hand raises the firelock two inches from the ground, and the muzzle is brought

Light Dragoon, by J. A. Atkinson (1807) (NAM)

close to the shoulder by the right hand, holding the ramrod between the fore-finger and thumb. At the motion, the right hand quits after slightly striking the top of the muzzle, the left flings the piece upwards and catches it firmly by the heel.

In all, twenty drill movements were necessary to fire each round. If a young soldier, flurried by the noise of battle, should fire his ramrod away, he could take no further part in the proceedings.

Even after this complex process it was far from certain that the musket would fire. Tests showed that the British musket was likely to misfire twice in thirteen rounds, even if the weather was dry. Heavy rain would stop all shooting, since the flintlock depended on a spark igniting a pinch of powder in a flashpan that was far from weatherproof. Here again the British had a distinct advantage. Their flints were of better quality, their gunpowder was more efficient and their muskets better made. As a French authority admitted, 'The locks of the British musquets are of better workmanship than those hitherto manufactured by any other nation in Europe. They will less frequently misfire upon a given number of rounds than all the rest.'

Assuming the musket did fire, its range was limited. A writer in 1814 commented that 'A soldier's musket, if not exceedingly ill-bored (as many are), will strike a figure of a man at 80 yards; it may even at a hundred; but a soldier must be very unfortunate indeed who shall be wounded by a common musket at 150 yards, provided his opponent aims at him.' The writer was referring to aimed rounds, fired in the comparative tranquillity of a range. In battle, when the firer was himself under fire and hurried, accuracy would inevitably suffer. Moreover, except in the light infantry, British muskets were not supplied with backsights. The rest of the troops were expected to aim by pointing the barrel with the aid of a vestigial foresight.

The musket was not the infantryman's only weapon. He was also provided with a 17in triangular bayonet to attach to the muzzle of his musket. Hand to hand bayonet fighting was very rare in the Peninsula, but the bayonet was a vital piece of a soldier's equipment, since it was his only effective defence against cavalry.

Cavalry were very poorly armed. Their principal weapon was the sabre. British light cavalry (light dragoons and hussars) carried a broad-bladed curved weapon, measuring 33in from hilt to point, which was an excellent slashing weapon, although it left the swordsman's hand dangerously unprotected. The heavy cavalry (dragoons, dragoon guards and Household Cavalry) had a sabre with the broad, straight blade 35in long. This was poorly balanced and was of no use for thrusting; in fact it was of little use for anything but the most unscientific slashing, being more of a chopper than a sabre.

Neither of these sabres were of the slightest use against steady infantry, closely formed and presenting a continuous hedge, three or four ranks deep, of 17in bayonets on the ends of long muskets. No horse in the world would ride up to the points of the bayonets. The only cavalry weapon that had a chance against bayonets was the lance, a weapon the British did not use until after Waterloo, although the French used it successfully in 1813 against formed Austrians at Dresden and

Privates, 1st Guards, by Charles Hamilton Smith (NAM)

Prussians at Katzbach. The British official view was that the lance 'required a man to be covered with heavy armour, and was incompatible with the closeness and vigour of the charge in which the strength of cavalry is allowed to consist.' The disadvantage of the lance was that it left the lancer defenceless once the point of the weapon had been turned. After the first time British cavalry met lancers, at Carpio in September 1811, a light dragoon officer wrote: 'The lancers looked well and formidable before they were broken and closed by our men, and then their lances were an encumbrance.' A few months earlier, at Albuera, Marshal Beresford had unhorsed a lancer with his bare hands. Turning the point with one hand, he had seized the lancer by the collar with the other and thrown him to the ground. But on the same day British infantry discovered how effective the lance could be when Colborne's brigade, unwisely extended by William Stewart, was caught and massacred by a Polish lancer unit.

Colborne's brigade was very unfortunate, in that the men were taken by surprise by lancers charging out of a thick mist. Had they had a few more seconds to prepare, they could have followed the drill laid down for these occasions. Any officer or NCO would have given the order 'Form Rallying Square', while standing facing the enemy. Such men as were within reach would immediately have run to him. 'The first two who join on his right and left, facing outwards. The next three place themselves in front of those posted, and three others to the rear, facing to the rear, thus forming a square of three. [The next four men who come up will] take post at the several angles; and the others as they come up will complete the different faces between these angles, which will form a square of five.' Such an improvised square could be extended until it contained eighty or more men and gave absolute security, since the men were packed in solidly, back to back, presenting an unbroken hedge of bayonets.

Cavalry were also armed with carbines, shortened muskets with barrels 26in long in the heavy cavalry and 16in long in the light. These were too inaccurate to be useful, except for arming sentries. In 1813 Stapleton Cotton, who commanded Wellington's cavalry, reported: 'I have ordered the carbines of the three regiments of Household Cavalry to be collected (except six per troop) and put into regimental store. These troops can never be called upon to skirmish, and the horses have already a sufficient load to carry.'

Infantry formed in line had nothing to fear from cavalry attacking from the front, but would be vulnerable from the flanks if these were not covered by other troops or some natural obstacle. The rear was almost certain to be exposed, although an attack there was dealt with uniquely by the Twenty Eighth at Alexandria. They were engaged by horsemen in front, when they found cavalry charging at their rear; but the rear rank was turned about and drove the assailants off with volleys. The more usual procedure would have been to form square, although, since British battalions consisted of ten companies, squares were always oblong, having three companies on each of two faces and two companies on the remainder.

Squares for resisting the charge of cavalry were formed four deep, except when guarding baggage, when they were formed two deep. To form a battalion into square was a drill movement that required a high standard of drill from the soldiers and great precision in giving orders by officers of all ranks. Any fault in the timing could result in gaps being left in the square through which the enemy might penetrate. The manoeuvre could be started from line (on any given company) or from column at full, half or quarter distance. Each of these variations required different orders, different timings and different turns.

To make certain that no horseman could penetrate between the bayonets, the men had to be packed shoulder to shoulder. The need for this was reinforced by the inaccuracy of the musket. The chances of hitting anything with a single shot were so small that results could only be achieved by firing volleys. If a company or half a battalion loosed off their muskets at the same time, it was reasonably certain that some kind of fire-effect would be produced on the enemy; and the closer the men firing were packed in their ranks, the thicker would be the cloud of bullets in front of them when they fired. The drill book laid down that 'Each soldier, when in his true position under arms and in rank, must just feel with his elbow the touch of the neighbour to whom he dresses; nor in any situation of movement in front must he ever relinguish such touch.' The files should be 'lightly touching, but without crouding [sic]; each man will then occupy a space of 22 inches'. As for ranks, 'There are two distances of ranks, open and close; when open they are three paces asunder; when close, they are one pace [30in]; and when the body is halted and ready to fire they are still closer locked up. Close order is the constant and habitual order at which troops are at all times formed and move. Open order is only an occasional exception made in situations of parade.' Thus, when the line was formed two deep, there were two muskets bearing on the enemy to every 22in of the front.

In order to bring the maximum of fire to bear on the enemy it was desirable to have the troops formed in a long line. This, however, is a very difficult formation in which to move. Anyone who has taken part in a ceremonial parade where a battalion line has advanced in review order will appreciate the difficulty of keeping the dressing for a limited number of paces over the smooth surface of a parade ground. How much greater must have been the problems of a line of two, three or four battalions over uneven ground while under the fire of enemy musketry and cannon. As the *Rules and Regulations for the Formations, Field Exercise and Movements of His Majesty's Forces* of 1803 observes,

The march of the battalion in line, either to the front or rear, being the most important and most difficult of all movements, every exertion of the commanding officer, and every attention of officers and men, become peculiarly necessary to attain this end. The great and indispensable requisites of this operation are, the direction of the march being perpendicular to the front of the battalion as then standing; the perfect squareness of the shoulders and body of each individual; the light touch of the files; the accurate equality of the cadence, and length of step given by the advanced sergeants whom the battalion, in every respect, covers, follows and complies with. If these are not observed its direction will be lost; opening, closing, floating will take place, and disorder will arise, in whatever line it makes a part of, at a time when the remedy is so difficult, and perfect order so essential.

The most essential lesson taught to the recruit was the absolute regularity of his marching pace. This was drilled into him with a precision that would astonish the twentieth-century soldier. A French observer noted:

In spots destined for the exercises of recruits, the precise length of the species of pace is carefully marked off on the ground, in order to accustom the soldier

Sergeant and Privates, 87th Foot, by Charles Hamilton Smith (NAM)

always to complete the same distance in the same number of paces. Such care is bestowed upon the regularity of movement of the soldier that I have seen recruits taught to march, in the depots in England, by marking the time to the motion of a pendulum that mathematical accuracy might be ensured.

To ensure this mathematical accuracy, all marching had to be very slow. Ordinary time was laid down to be seventy-five 30in paces in a minute. Quick time was 108 paces and 'quickest time' (or double quick) 120 paces a minute. 'All marching in the alignment must be made in ordinary time . . . To march with accuracy in an alignment in quick time, so as to be ready to wheel up into line, and (without any considerable pause) to move on, is an operation hardly to be expected, and seldom to be required.' Double quick 'applied chiefly to the purpose of wheeling'.

The French used a shorter pace of 25.6in and took seventy-six paces a minute in ordinary time and 100 in quick time. Thus, in theory, the British should have marched faster — 3,750yd an hour compared to 3,243yd an hour for the French. In practice the reverse was true. Wellington admitted that 'the French troops march better than ours', and a member of his staff wrote, after Vitoria, 'In marching, our men have no chance at all with the French. The latter beat them hollow'.

Owing to the difficulty of manoeuvring in line, the troops were normally moved in column and deployed into line just before they encountered the enemy. The drill manoeuvre for doing this was at least as complicated as that for forming square, and the decision when to deploy was one which called for the nicest judgement by the general commanding a brigade or division. To cut down the time taken in approaching the enemy under the fire of his guns, the move should be made as late as possible. On the other hand, it was best done out of effective musket shot, so that the drill movements could be carried out as calmly as possible. Normally it was done at the halt, but at Salamanca, when Pakenham fell on the French left, he deployed the Third Division on the march, the mounted officers dressing the ranks as they continued unchecked. This bold and successful manoeuvre did not even appear in the drill books.

The French had solved this dilemma by not deploying at all. Their drill book, like the British, called for a fighting formation in a three-deep line. Napoleon's armies had found that, if there was a considerable artillery preparation and if the advance of the main body was shrouded in a thick cloud of skirmishers, they could break through any line composed of less than perfectly trained soldiers while maintaining their formation in column. It was in column that Napoleon ordered forward the Imperial Guard in their last attack. Earlier, on the same day, D'Erlon's divisions had delayed their deployment too long and were shattered by the volleys of Picton's division at close range while still packed in their columns. As Wellington remarked, 'I do not desire better sport than to meet one of their columns *en masse* with our line.'

Tactical discussion in Britain centred round the thickness of the fighting line. Standard practice, as in every European army, was to form the line three deep. Experience in the American War of Independence, however, had encouraged officers to adopt a thinner, two-deep line which, in America, had frequently been

Officer and Privates, 52nd L.I., by Charles Hamilton Smith (NAM)

drawn out to such a length as to resemble a chain of skirmishers. This technique, which had proved successful in America, where the British won most of the battles even if they lost the war, was viewed with great suspicion by traditionally minded tacticians, who could point out that the colonial troops, although brave and determined, were not highly trained, were not supplied with much artillery and were totally deficient in heavy cavalry.

General David Dundas, the dominant military theorist of the first years of the nineteenth century, was firm against

> ...our very thin and extended order to make more show—an affected quickness on all occasions—the running of one movement into another, without those necessary pauses which tend to show their propriety and justness of execution—the system of central dressing, filing and forming on almost all occasions the single person attempting to direct the battalion, and its parts, in every situation, in order to beget a false precision—the forming and breaking on the move, the easier to conceal and cover lost distances and accidental lines, which otherwise would be apparent—the several methods of wheeling established—the different and false composition of columns, which each battalion at pleasure adopts—the chance movements of the line in front, regulated on no fixed principle.

He laid down in the *Rules and Regulations* for 1792 that

> The fundamental order of the infantry, in which they should always form and act, and in which all their various operations are calculated, is in three ranks; the formation in two ranks is to be regarded as an occasional exception, that may be made from it, where an extended and covered front is to be occupied, or where an irregular enemy, who deals only in fire, is to be opposed ....In no service is the fire and consistency of the third rank given up; it serves to fill up the vacancies made in the others in action; without it the battalion would soon be in single rank.

Dundas was both right and wrong. The very loose formation learned in America would undoubtedly have exposed the British to disaster when opposed to Napoleon's army and, indeed, to any steady European army fighting in the old three-deep line and supported by plentiful cavalry. In any case, he deserved the army's gratitude by imposing on it, with the Duke of York's backing, a uniform system of manoeuvre. Dundas was wrong, however, because the French were not playing the game according to the old rules. By staking everything on shock action, the breakthrough by the undeployed column, they had sacrificed firepower. A French division of 5,000 men would attack on a two-company front showing 170 men, each of whom would have twenty-three others ranked behind him. Only the first two ranks could fire at their enemy, so that, imposing as the advancing column might look, it could only bring 340 muskets to bear—less than the firepower of three and a half companies drawn up two deep. It was this that caused Wellington, before he sailed for Portugal in 1808, to remark: 'If what I hear about [the French] system of manoeuvre is true, I think it is a false one against steady stroops. I suspect all the continental armies were more than half beaten before the battle was begun. I, at least, will not be frightened beforehand.'

The technique Wellington employed to defeat the French was a compromise between the lessons learned in America and the more formal teachings, based on European warfare, of Dundas. Relying on the steadiness of his infantry, which never failed him, he normally deployed them in two ranks but closed up the files as tightly as Dundas could have wished. The drill was as precise as that called for in the *Rules and Regulations*, but the 'occasional exception' became the usual practice. Thus, from the American school he took the firepower of two ranks while not sacrificing the steadiness and 'consistency' of the traditionalists. As to Dundas's objection to the two-rank formation, that there was no third rank from which to fill 'the vacancies made in action', this was overcome by the line closing on the centre (or in certain cases to a flank) as gaps appeared.

Wellington was not the first commander in the French wars to use the two-deep line. Abercromby used it at Alexandria, Moore at Coruña, but it was Wellington who demonstrated conclusively that, given an adequate supply of reliable infantry, the employment of massive firepower could stop the French columns in their tracks. He had the advantage that the British infantry had the finest musketry in the world. As a Frenchman reported,

By a general regulation, all the corps of infantry receive in each year the following quantity of ammunition:

	Line	Light Infantry	Riflemen
Ball Cartridge	30	50	60
Blank Cartridge	70	60	60
Flints	3	3	3

The British are not satisfied with merely supplying their troops with the means of firing a great number of rounds for instruction, or to maintain them in practice. They use every exertion to render the fire of the soldier efficient; and in place of expending nearly the whole of their powder in discharging volleys by platoons or battalions, where the sole aim of the officer is to cause the whole body to fire at the same moment, or to preserve a continuous running volley, they rather endeavour to instruct the soldier in the true principles at a small, moderate and great distance. He is frequently practised in shooting at a target; and it is an object never lost sight of that the value of musquetry is not the compactness or regularity of its sound, but in the murderous execution produced by steady aim.

Battles in which the column attacked the line directly were uncommon. Between the two would be their respective screens of skirmishers. Their task in battle would be to shroud the main formations, to gall the opposing force and, if possible, to draw from it the first, the most carefully loaded, volley. Between battles

Riflemen, 60th and 95th, by Charles Hamilton Smith (NAM)

the same troops would hold the outposts and would head every advance and cover every retreat. As the recruiting poster of one skirmishing corps proclaimed: 'The bloody, fighting Ninety Fifth — the first into the field and the last out.'

After the Seven Years' War Britain had the finest light troops of any European army. She disbanded them and forgot their hard-learned skills before she went to war again in 1775. By the end of the American War she again had expert skirmishers, but ten years later she went to war with France with no more than one light infantry company in each infantry battalion, and no complete light infantry battalions. Light infantry was under a cloud and Dundas, although he admitted that they had their place in warfare, deprecated 'the showy exercises, the airy dress, the independent modes which they have adopted'.

In the early campaigns of the French wars Britain relied entirely on foreign regiments to cover the front of the army, and it was not until 1798 that a battalion of the line consisting entirely of light troops was added to the establishment. This was the fifth battalion of the Sixtieth (Royal American) Foot. It was armed with rifles, and the ranks were filled entirely with Germans, Austrians, Dutch and Swiss. Two years later an Experimental Corps of Riflemen was formed as a temporary measure from detachments from various British regiments. This became, in 1802, a regular regiment under the style of the Ninety Fifth Regiment of Foot (Riflemen). The first light infantry battalions were formed in the following year from the Forty Third and Fifty Second Foot, and between then and Waterloo four further regiments were converted to light infantry.

The British technique, as it emerged in the early years of the nineteenth century, was to graft the skills of the light infantryman on to the discipline and order of the line. As Sir John Moore, the brightest ornament of the British light service, wrote:

> Light infantry in the British service is a species of troops different from the light troops of every other nation. These seldom act in line. Out light infantry, on the contrary, are not only employed as Yägers, but act in line, and are selected to head attacks when enterprise, activity and courage are particularly required. They are, in fact, a mixture of the Yäger and the Grenadier . . . Their first drill and instruction should, I conceive, be the same as that of other infantry — they should be confirmed in the exercise and movements of regular battalions before they are taught any other.

They were taught to fight in extended order but, by modern standards, that order was not very extended — a mere two paces between the files. They invariably worked in pairs, so that one man would always have a loaded musket. They moved more quickly than ordinary infantry, but not very quickly. 'All movements of the light [troops] except when firing, advancing or retreating are to be in quick time [108 paces to the minute]. They are never to run unless particularly directed, and in that case, they are only to run at that pace in which they can preserve their order.' Their weapon, when on active service, was the same as that used by the infantry of the line, except that it was fitted with a backsight.

The fifth battalion of the Sixtieth and the three battalions of the Ninety Fifth were armed with rifles. The British had done a good deal of work on military rifles during the American War, but it was all forgotten after the peace, and in 1798 the rifle battalion of the Sixtieth had to be given German weapons even though most of Germany was enemy-occupied territory. However, when the Experimental Corps was raised, the Board of Ordnance, acting with uncharacteristic speed, assembled and tested forty different models and selected one made by a London gunmaker, Ezekiel Baker. The Baker rifle eventually issued to the troops had only a 30in barrel, and this meant that, unlike the musket, it could be loaded by a man lying down. It weighed, however, 9lb 0.5oz, only half an ounce less than the India

Ensign with colour, 9th Foot, by Charles Hamilton Smith (NAM)

pattern musket, and the rifleman's load was actually greater, since he was equipped with a 23in sword bayonet. This great length of sword was to make it possible for Riflemen to stand in square between men armed with muskets without the hedge of bayonets varying in length.

The Baker was an excellent weapon, almost as robust as the musket and accurate at three times the range. The French commentator quoted above noted that 'To exercise Riflemen, they are first made to fire at a circular target about five or six feet in diameter, with coloured circles to mark different distances from the centre. The target is first placed about fifty yards from the men, and gradually removed farther and farther, until it is about three hundred yards from them.'

Nevertheless, the Baker rifle had its weaknesses. As a flintlock, it was as likely as a musket to misfire, but in addition it was extremely slow to load. As it was a muzzle-loader, the ball had to be forced down the grooves in the barrel, having first been placed on a greased patch. This meant that even a skilled Rifleman was hard put to it to get off as many as two rounds a minute. This made it quite unsuitable to be the main weapon of the infantry of the line, where weight of fire was quite as important as minute accuracy. It was, however, the most effective single weapon used on either side during the war, and its supremacy was highlighted in 1807, when Napoleon ordered the withdrawal of all rifles from the French army because they were so slow to load. From that time onward the British had a permanent advantage in skirmishing.

One other factor contributed to British victories in the Peninsula. This was entirely a personal contribution from their general. Wellington seems to have been the only general who realised that troops drawn up on a reverse slope were immune from all musketry and most artillery fire. Even Blücher at Ligny and Napoleon at Waterloo had failed to grasp this simple truth. Both drew up their armies on the forward slope and suffered heavy casualties from their opponent's artillery. No line of British infantry was ever unnecessarily exposed to fire when Wellington commanded them.

Part II

THE COMPONENT PARTS

5

Rank and File

Life in the ranks of the army was compounded of discomfort and boredom. The soldier's uniform was distinctive and, from a distance, impressive, but it was far from comfortable, being designed for show rather than utility. Sergeant Cooper of the Seventh Foot wrote:

> Take for example, one of the 7th Fusiliers full dressed. On his head he wore a cap covered with heel-ball, polished like a mirror. On the cap, under a varnished rosette, stood a tuft of wool, six inches long, neatly trimmed. This weighty cap, or rather helmet, had nothing attached to it to prevent it falling off. When it did, it took hours to repair the damage.
>
> All his hair, except a little piece on the sides and front, was tightly bound round a piece of lead behind. The hair on the sides was rubbed round till matted, then greased and powdered with flour. The whiskers were greased, set up and also powdered. About his neck he wore a stock of stiff leather, four inches broad, well varnished. This thing was a real nuisance.
>
> Projecting two inches from his breast, he had a neatly crimped ruffle. On his shoulders were two wings made of cloth and wool, neatly combed and trimmed. The wings were useful in keeping on the crossbelts.
>
> His jacket fitted far too tightly; his buttons were bright as silver; and the lace on his breast and cuffs was as white as pipeclay could make it.
>
> His breeches were of white cloth, and reached a little below the knee; his long gaiters were black, and both breeches and gaiters were tight, of course.
>
> To bring all parts of his dress and accoutrements into close contact, there were loops, loops, loops; loops to the gaiters; braces to the breeches; loops to the jacket; loops to the cross belts; loops to the wings, etc., etc. Should he try to reach the ground, it would be fatal to some article of his set-off. Nothing could be worse contrived for real service.

As the Peninsular War progressed, these inconveniences were, to some extent, lessened. The hair clubbed into a pigtail was abandoned almost as soon as the troops landed in Portugal. This not only increased the cleanliness of the men's hair but avoided the trouble incurred by a soldier of the Seventy First who, in 1808, found his pigtail frozen to the ground after spending a December night asleep in a field. The white breeches gave way to baggy blue-grey overalls worn with short canvas gaiters. Wellington did not care how his men were dressed provided they were 'forced to keep themselves clean and smart as a soldier ought to be'.

Nevertheless, many of the inconveniences remained, not least the constricting

Royal Horse Guards, by Charles Hamilton Smith (NAM)

cross belts and the cruel leather stock, which was not abandoned until 1854. The great weight of the cap was reduced in 1812, but its impressive height was retained by means of a false front. The Highlanders, however, kept their top-heavy bonnets, so unwieldy that when, at Fuentes de Oñoro, they charged at the 'double-quick', they carried their bonnets in their hands.

One discomfort Sergeant Cooper did not mention, perhaps because it did not occur to him that things could be otherwise. The boots issued (which were known as shoes to distinguish them from the thigh boots worn by heavy cavalry) were the same for the right and left feet. The soldier was instructed to wear them alternately on different feet to equalise the wear. Nor were these boots issued with eyelet holes for the laces, the wearer being expected to punch his own as best suited his feet. Two pairs were issued to each man as part of the necessaries he paid for himself. The price in 1809 was 6s6d a pair. Carefully soled and heeled (for which he paid 4s0d a year), these would last the soldier for a year, after which two new pairs would be issued. This rate of wear took into account only normal use. Long marches over rough roads would destroy the boots in a much shorter time, and an extended move in bad weather, such as the retreat to Coruña, would leave many men, and officers, barefoot without the chance of obtaining replacements. On these occasions it was usual for a special free issue to be made:

In consideration of the bad weather in which the troops have carried on their operations during the winter, and the consequent wear and tear of shoes, the Commander of the Forces has determined that each non-commissioned officer and soldier of the infantry who was present with his regiment between the 8th and 14th December [1813], between the 2nd and 8th of January, or between the 14th of February and the 24th of March [1814], shall receive from the Commissariat a pair of shoes gratis.

Such additional calls on the Commissariat sometimes meant that the supply of boots from England ran dry. This entailed the issue of locally made boots, which were seldom satisfactory. When the Fourth Division were ordered to Badajoz in the spring of 1811, they halted at Portalegre where, according to a private in the Enniskillens, they 'were served out with a kind of shoe made in the country. They were very clumsy, and of a dirty buff colour; and as many of us were without stockings, their rough seams made their wearers hobble like so many cripples.'

Even when his feet were comfortable, the soldier had a great weight to carry. According to Sergeant Cooper,

The government should have sent us new backbones to bear the weight. The following is a list of the articles carried by each man during the march:-

1 fusee [musket] and bayonet	14lbs.
1 pouch & 60 rounds of bullets	6
1 canteen [waterbottle] & belt	1
1 mess tin	1
1 knapsack, frame & belts	3
1 blanket	4

1 greatcoat	4
1 dress coat	3
1 white [fatigue] jacket	0½
2 shirts & 3 breasts	2½
2 pairs shoes	3
1 pair gaiters	0¼
2 pairs stockings	1
4 brushes, button stick, comb	3
2 cross belts	1
Pen, ink & paper	0¼
Pipeclay, chalk, etc.	1
2 tent pegs	0½
Whole weight of kit without provisions	51lbs (sic)
Extra weight for marching:-	
Three days' bread	3
Two days' beef	2
Water in our canteens	3
	59lbs

Beside this weight, the orderly sergeant of each company had to carry the orderly book, the weight of which was perhaps 2lbs; and in turn the regimental colours.

When not on active service, the soldier was 'forced from bed at five o'clock each morning to get all things ready for drill; then drilled for three hours with the utmost vigour'.

To be tolerably fit for parade required three hours work. His pouch, magazine and bayonet scabbard were covered with heel-bore like his cap. The barrel of his musket, the outside and inside of the lock, the bayonet and ramrod must be polished like a razor. In addition to the above, he had to clean white leather gloves, cap and breast plate; his great coat must be neatly rolled up, and be exactly eighteen inches long. When blankets were issued, they had to be folded to suit the square of the knapsack. Many other things required polishing besides those already mentioned, such as the gun brasses, picker and brush, and the bayonet [scabbard] tip.

Between the first cleaning period and the drill period the soldier had his first meal, usually consisting of a pint of beef broth with some bread. After the three-hour drill he had his second and last meal of the day, beef stew, which could be distinguished from the beef broth because it contained fragments of bone. Then, if he was detailed for guard, he would have another three-hour cleaning period. Otherwise there was nothing further for him to do until tattoo. He had the choice between lounging about in a foetid barrack room and lounging about an unwelcoming town. Most public parks refused to admit soldiers off duty. Most public houses disliked serving soldiers and many refused to do so. In any case few soldiers had any of their meagre pay to spare. When they did, and when they found a broadminded publican, they usually got drunk. In good regiments the officers would arrange sports and other diversions for the men's spare time. In some there were regimental schools, but such units were in a small minority.

On active service conditions were less comfortable but more tolerable. The Spanish and Portuguese took a more friendly view of the redcoats than did their own compatriots, despite the fact that some of the troops, by their plundering, violence and drunkenness, showed that they were unworthy of such kindness. Accommodating as the people of the Peninsula usually were, all ranks received an even warmer and more personal welcome from the fleas with which most of their billets were infested.

On the march conditions varied greatly. Bivouacking in fine weather could be as idyllic as experience as a soldier was ever likely to enjoy. In heavy rain he might even think kindly of his squalid barrack room in England. After the retreat to Torres Vedras in 1810, one soldier recalled:

> For five nights I had never been in bed and, during a good part of that time, it had rained hard. We were upon ploughed land which was rendered so soft that we sank over the shoes at every step. The manner in which I passed the night was thus: I placed my canteen upon the ground, put my knapsack above, and sat upon it, supporting my head upon my hands; my musket between my knees, resting upon my shoulders, and my blanket over all—ready to start in a moment at the least alarm. The nights were chill; indeed, in the morning I was so stiff I could not move with ease for some time; my legs were benumbed to the knees. I was completely wet three nights out of five.

Things were somewhat better in the campaign of 1813, when tents were issued, but since only three tents could be carried for each company, 'the number in each [bell] tent was generally above twenty. When these were all laid, none could turn without general consent, and the word "turn" given.' Nevertheless, 'a great change was felt in the way of comfort.'

The soldier's food when campaigning was no better and no worse than in barracks at home, although there was always the chance of acquiring, probably illegally, some vegetables to relieve the eternal soup and stew. Sometimes the rations failed to arrive. On the 1812 retreat from Salamanca nothing but live beef was available, but it could not be cooked. 'Our attempts to kindle fires with wet wood were quite abortive. Sometimes, indeed, we managed to raise a smoke, and numbers gathered round, in the vain hope of getting themselves warmed, but the fire would extinguish in spite of all their efforts.' That was the most uncomfortable period of the whole war. 'Our camp or resting place would soon be reduced to mud, ankle deep, on which we must lie or sleep for the night. Our blankets were so wet that every morning before we could put them in our knapsacks they were obliged to be wrung. The roads were so cut up that it was with the greatest difficulty that the hardiest soldier could march. Provisions were scarce, shoes failed and many were barefoot.'

Faced with such discomfort, to say nothing of the hazards of battle, it is not surprising that the soldier found refuge in drink. Many drank themselves to death:

Private, 3rd Dragoons, by Charles Hamilton Smith (NAM)

Mr Barstow, Hospital Mate, states that on the 24th of May [1812] he was called to see the deceased Henry Ralphs of the 52nd Regiment, and on arrival at the house found him dead; and further says, that in a few hours after, he was called to see the deceased James Fairfield, 52nd Regiment, and on arrival at the house found him likewise dead. The evidence further states, that it is his opinion that their deaths were caused by excessive drinking. The Commander of the Forces is concerned to add that this is not the first instance that has come to his knowledge of soldiers dying drunk; and that he trusts that the knowledge of the immediate fatal effects of excessive drinking will induce the soldiers of the army to be a little more moderate.

Many fell into the hands of the French through being incapably drunk. A sergeant on the retreat from Burgos wrote:

. . . the conduct of some men would have disgraced savages, drunkenness prevailed to such a frightful extent that I have often wondered how it was that a great part of the army was not cut off. It was no infrequent thing to see a long string of mules carrying drunken soldiers to prevent them falling into the hands of the enemy. The new wine was in tanks particularly about Valladolid and the men ran mad. I remember seeing a soldier lying fully accoutred with his knapsack on in a large tank, he had either fallen in or had been pushed in by his comrades, there he lay. I saw a dragoon fire his pistol into a large vat containing thousands of gallons; in a few minutes we were up to our knees in wine, fighting like tigers for it.

The soldier's capacity for wine was prodigious. Brigadier Robinson wrote home that in a single day the Fifty Ninth Foot, then about 750 strong, 'drank four pipes during one day's stay', more than half a gallon a man. That particular wine cost only 'about three halfpence a bottle', but a soldier's pay was too small to keep pace with his thirst. Many men did not allow this to deter them. 'No soldier' wrote Wellington, 'can withstand the temptation of wine. This is constantly before their eyes in this country, and they are constantly intoxicated when absent from their regiments, and there is no crime they will not commit to obtain it; or if they cannot get money, to obtain it by force.'

This was a hard saying but the accounts of men in the ranks and the reports of courts martial show that it had an uncomfortable measure of truth in it. It was the inevitable corollary of recruiting 'the scum of the earth', of making the conditions such that self-respecting men were loathe to enlist. To try to curb excesses there was a savage code of discipline, but one no more savage than that of civilian life where a man could still be hanged for stealing 40s. Flogging with the cat o'nine tails was a barbarous business but in the army the lashes were inflicted by the drummers, barely more than boys, whereas in the Royal Navy it was the bosun who wielded the cat.

The steadier soldiers were unanimous in believing that crimes should be publicly and brutally punished. A soldier in the Black Watch wrote:

Philanthropists who decry the lash ought to consider in what manner the good men — the deserving exemplary soldiers — are to be protected; if no coercive measures are to be resorted to on purpose to prevent ruthless villains from insulting with impunity the temperate, the well-inclined and the orderly-disposed, the good must be left to the mercy of the pauper . . . The good soldier thanks you not for such philanthropy; the incorrigible laughs at your humanity, despises your clemency and meditates only how to gratify his naturally vicious propensities.

Sergeant Stevenson, who served 21 years in the Guards, wrote,

'They talk of the lash. I was never more afraid of the lash than I was of the gibbet. No man ever comes to that but through his own conduct.' In what is probably the only surviving autobiographical record of a man who was flogged, William Lawrence of the Fortieth, said, 'Perhaps it is a good thing for me as could then have happened, as it prevented me from committing greater crimes, which must at last have brought me to my ruin.'

The amount of flogging varied greatly between units. In the Light Division it was scarcely used at all and in the Fifty First Foot, Colonel Mainwaring, an eccentric and a martinet, so loathed the punishment that it was said of him that 'if he could not stand fire better than witness flogging he would be the worst soldier in the army'. At the other extreme was the Thirty Fourth where 'corporal punishment was going on all the year'. In one battery of artillery, with a complement of 136 rank and file, fifty seven men were flogged within twelve months.

In the more enlightened regiments petty crimes were nipped in the bud by company courts. The *Regulations for the Rifle Corps* laid down the following:

For the trial of corporals who may have committed misdemeanours, a court may assemble composed of three sergeants and two corporals, by a written order of the captain. For the trial of private Riflemen and Buglers the court will consist of a corporal, a chosen man [lance corporal] and three privates . . . All extra duties, confinement to barracks, turned coats, fines for the benefit of messes and cobbing [striking the buttocks with a flat instrument] are permitted as punishments.

Regimental courts martial could award up to three hundred lashes. Serious crimes — desertion, robbery with violence, mutiny, striking a superior, murder, rape and sodomy — were dealt with by a general court martial presided over by a general officer or a full colonel. The chances of being acquitted, except in the clearest cases, seem to have been very fair but once men had been found guilty their sentences were very severe. The maximum number of lashes that could be awarded was 1,200 but this was very rare. Three privates were sentenced to that number in May 1812 for robbery with violence and the next award of the same size was in April 1813 when Private John Fay, Eighty Seventh Foot, was found guilty of robbery with violence, drunkenness, violent and mutinous conduct towards an officer. A

Officer, 14th Light Dragoons, by Charles Hamilton Smith (NAM)

sentence of 1,000 lashes was not uncommon. Such a punishment usually had to be inflicted in instalments, but one gunner received 1,000 at one parade and had 'recovered from his late punishment' within two weeks.

Gaol sentences were rare, as there were no military prisons in the Peninsula. Only two appear in the court martial records. One was for six months for the manslaughter of a comrade, the other, a year's confinement to the guard, for the manslaughter of an unfaithful wife. General courts martial could also give sentences of transportation, usually to New South Wales, or of service for life in either the Royal African Corps or the Royal West India Rangers. Such sentences required the confirmation of the Commander-in-Chief in London. Between 1809 and 1814 courts martial in the Peninsula awarded about 120 death sentences. The largest number were for 'desertion towards the enemy'. When there was no intention of going over to the enemy, the sentence was usually either transportation or flogging. Wellington on occasions pardoned deserters and once offered a convicted man to the Royal Navy, telling the admiral that 'He is a stout man and has not been guilty of any crime which renders him infamous'.

Of course, the number of deserters who were sentenced represented only the unsuccessful ones, a small proportion of the whole. Desertion cost the Peninsular army about 500 men a year, about a third of whom were enlisted foreigners (other than Portuguese). There was a sharp increase in the numbers in 1813, when the army reached the French frontier and many foreigners who had been enlisted from the prisoner-of-war camps ran for it.

Deserters and mutineers were shot. For other capital crimes the punishment was hanging. The most common of these was robbing the local inhabitants with violence, but soldiers were also hanged for murder, pilfering stores under the culprit's own charge, offering violence to a superior and, in one case, sodomy. In 1810, a fairly average year, general courts martial passed twenty one death sentences that were confirmed; three were for murder, six for desertion, eleven for robbery with violence and one for desertion and robbery. 1813 was the year with the highest number of confirmed death sentences — thirty five. In addition there were occasional instances of the provost marshal exercising his traditional right of executing summarily men caught in the commission of a capital crime. One dragoon (and one Portuguese) were summarily hanged for looting on the retreat to Torres Vedras, and four or five suffered the same fate when an orgy of looting broke out on the army's crossing the French frontier after the battle of the Nivelle. A gallows was erected in Badajoz after the sack, but although one man had the noose round his neck, no one was actually hanged.

One question inevitably occurs. Why should an army that was recruited from the desperate rather than the patriotic, which was consistently neglected and scurvily treated by government, Parliament and people, and where life was harsh and punishment harsher, fight so consistently well? There is no doubt that the British soldier, with all his faults, was at least the equal of any in Europe. It was not the fear of the lash that kept the Fusiliers in line as they forced their way to the crest of 'that fatal hill' at Albuera. It was not dread of the firing squad that sent the Light Division back into the blood-soaked breach at Badajoz with as much unconcern 'as if nothing had happened'. One reason was the confidence they felt in Wellington's

Private, 18th Hussars, by Charles Hamilton Smith (NAM)

leadership, but the deciding factor was the pride they felt in their regiments. Most of the men who enlisted were social outcasts before they joined, and the regiment took the place of a family. It gave them a sense of security and stability which they were most unlikely to find elsewhere. Even the worst of the 'fifty to one hundred bad characters' in every battalion could be counted upon to defend the reputation of their regiment in anything from a public house brawl to a major action, even if their own brutality and drunkenness frequently besmirched that reputation when there was no fighting to be done. In all the squalid tales of crime in the General Orders of the Peninsular army there is no court martial on a charge of cowardice against a man in the ranks.

In the long run the quality of the regiments depended on the officers and on the relation between the officers and men. There was undoubtedly a minority of very bad officers. After the battle of the Nive two lieutenant-colonels were dismissed the service accused of cowardice. Sergeant Donaldson, Ninety Fourth, writes of a temporary commander of his regiment, Captain James Craig, who,

> having neither the education nor the breeding of a gentleman, felt jealous in the company of officers, and lived in a retired and sullen manner. He generally passed his time in gossiping with his barber and his cook, or indeed any of the men, with an affectation of entering into their concerns. By this and eaves-dropping he became acquainted with little circumstances which another commanding officer would have disdained to listen to, and which he made bad use of. The full extent of his malevolent disposition was not known, however, until he got command of the regiment, when he introduced flogging for every trivial excuse.

In the Sixty Eighth there was a Major Champion de Crespigny. When he was a captain, his name had appeared in General Orders as 'having absented himself without leave [and] is to be put into arrest by the Commanding Officer of any station through which he may pass'. He must have had some explanation for his absence, but he exchanged into another regiment, only to reappear six months later in the Sixty Eighth with a purchased majority. When he was killed in July 1813, 'joy was seen on every countenance and', wrote Private Green, 'I verily thought we should have had three cheers, for several of our men began to cry "Hip! Hip!" which was always the signal for cheering. He was a cruel man to us, and his death was considered a happy release.'

To set against the small number of bad officers, there are a vast number of examples of the devotion of the troops to their officers. Major General Robert Craufurd was one of the strictest disciplinarians in the army, subject to outbursts of uncontrollable rage. His severity was widely resented by the officers but his soldiers idolised him. When he died, Private Harris of the Rifles wrote, 'I do not think I ever admired any man who wore the British uniform more than I did General Craufurd.'

The ideal relation between officers and men was that laid down in the *Regulations for the Rifle Corps*, which was practised in that and many other of the best regiments:

Officer, Royal Horse Artillery, by C. Verney (NAM)

Every inferior, whether officer or soldier, shall receive the lawful commands of his senior with deference and respect, and shall execute them to the best of his power. Every superior in his turn, whether he be an officer or a non-commissioned officer, shall give his orders in the language of moderation and of regard to the feelings of the individual under his command; abuse, bad language and blows being positively forbid in the regiment.

One of Napoleon's best divisional commanders wrote, five days after Waterloo, that British officers were '*les plus braves et les plus patriotes de l'Europe*'. He might have added that they had a multitude of faults. As Wellington had constantly to remind them,

The Commander of the Forces is always concerned to be observing upon the conduct of officers who have invariably conducted themselves well in the field: but the officers of the army must recollect that to perform their duty with gallantry in the field is but a small part of what is required of them; and that obedience to orders, accuracy in the performance, and discipline are necessary to keep any military body together and to perform any military operation with advantage to their country or service to themselves.

The officers had one virtue equal to their gallantry. They seem, almost without exception, to have understood the art of leadership. How else could they have welded the drunken plundering collection of social misfits they commanded into 'the most complete machine for its numbers now existing in Europe.'

6

Regimental Officers

Once a man received his first commission, there were three methods by which he might rise to the rank of lieutenant-colonel. At each step he could advance by purchase, by seniority or by patronage.

If he was in a position to purchase, his first step was to have his name noted on the 'list for purchase' of his regiment and to deposit the price of the next rank with the regimental agent. The prices were fixed by the Commander-in-Chief and, leaving aside the very expensive commissions in the Household Cavalry, were, during the Peninsular campaigns, as follows:

	Cavalry of the Line	Foot Guards	Infantry of the Line
Lieutenant-Colonel	£4,982 10s	£6,700	£3,500
Major	£3,882 10s	£6,300	£2,600
Captain	£2,782 10s	£3,500	£1,500
Lieutenant	£997 10s	£1,500	£550

Despite the fact that every officer concerned in purchase had to declare on his honour that no additional payment was being made, it was widely believed that there was a black market in commissions. Not unnaturally, little evidence exists of such underhand transactions, and it seems clear that in peacetime, when the number of commissions was very limited, some over-payment was made. In wartime, when death and the expansion of the army made abundant vacancies, illicit dealings were few and confined largely to a small number of fashionable cavalry regiments. In many regiments commissions for cornets, ensigns and lieutenants were hard to sell.

The worst abuses of the purchase system were curbed by the Duke of York's regulation that no officer could acquire a captaincy until he had served two years as a subaltern, and that he must have six years commissioned service before becoming a major. In 1809 he extended this ruling so that 'No officer shall be promoted to the rank of captain until he has been three years a subaltern. No officer shall be promoted to the rank of major until he has been seven years in the service, of which he shall have been at least two years a captain; and no major shall be appointed to the rank of lieutenant-colonel until he shall have been nine years in the service.'

Names appeared on the regimental 'list for purchase' in order of regimental seniority. These lists were sent every quarter to the Military Secretary at the Horse Guards, who correlated them for the whole army. A purchase vacancy would normally go to the senior officer on the list, but it was open to the Commander-in-

Chief to offer it to an officer in another regiment, provided he had more seniority in the army than the first officer for purchase in the regiment concerned. The Duke of York did not hesitate to use this power if he considered the first officer for purchase to be unsuitable, or if the regiment seemed to be in need of new blood.

Promotion by seniority was a simple process. An officer, irrespective of past service, joined a regiment as the junior of his rank. As those above him died, were promoted or transferred to other regiments, he rose in his rank. When he reached the top of the ensign's list, he would automatically succeed to the next non-purchase vacancy for a lieutenancy and so on through the ranks. To reach the top required luck, health and longevity. Jacob Brunt enlisted in 1770 and was commissioned as ensign and adjutant of the Fifty Fifth Foot in 1793. In the expansion of the army at that time, he was promoted to a lieutenancy in the newly raised Eighty Third four months later. He stayed in that regiment for the rest of his active career, rising slowly but steadily by seniority alone. On 13 July 1811, forty one years and seven months after he had enlisted, he became a lieutenant-colonel.

Some things did interfere with promotion by seniority. If an officer became a prisoner-of-war, his rank was frozen. When he regained his liberty, he would, if his conduct had not been discreditable, be promoted to the rank and seniority he would have reached had he not been captured. Being 'noted on the invalid list' would also delay promotion, although it is not clear how seriously disabled a man had to be for him to be 'noted' in this way. Captain Matthew Sutton, Ninety Seventh, was promoted to major in 1813 although he had been totally blind for three years. An adverse confidential report could delay promotion, and so could the sentence of a court martial. On 2 November 1813 Lieutenant Robert Robertson, Seventy Fourth, was found guilty of 'disobedience to orders in not answering official letters'. He was sentenced to be 'suspended from rank and pay for the space of three months and to be publicly and severely reprimanded'. This was unfortunate for him, since he was senior lieutenant and a death vacancy for a captain had just occurred. He was passed over and had to wait six months until another captain's vacancy arose.

Promotion by seniority depended on regimental seniority; but every officer also had army rank, which might not be the same as his regimental rank. If he transferred to another regiment, his regimental rank dated from the day he was posted, but his army seniority dated from the time he first attained his rank. This gave him no claim to seniority in his new unit, but might give him a claim in the army as a whole. Sufficient army seniority would eventually entitle him to promotion in another regiment through the Commander-in-Chief's patronage.

Under the patronage the Commander-in-Chief had the right to appoint to all vacancies but, by a long-standing custom, those caused by death in battle were filled by regimental seniority. These, however, formed only a small proportion of the whole. In 1813 three officers died from sickness, shipwreck or other accident for every one that died in battle. In addition, the Commander-in-Chief had the disposal of vacancies arising from the creation of new units, the augmentation of existing regiments and the removal of officers by courts martial. He could also appoint to vacancies occurring by officers being promoted to major-general, thus becoming ineffective regimentally although, as was usual, retaining their

Hussars and Infantry, Brunswick Oels Corps, by Charles Hamilton Smith (NAM)

regimental commission (see Chapter 12). This meant that, had he chosen to do so the Commander-in-Chief could have filled five out of every six non-purchase vacancies with officers of his own choosing.

The Duke of York was most reluctant to use his powers of patronage. He had bitter memories of the havoc caused by Sir George Yonge's abuse of these powers. His reluctance was increased in 1809 when a parliamentary enquiry established that his mistress, Mary Anne Clarke, had been accepting money for using her influence with him to secure promotion for various officers. There was no evidence that the Duke knew of these transactions and it is most unlikely that he did. Nevertheless he resigned his post but was reinstated in 1811. His interim successor, Sir David Dundas, could hardly be persuaded to use the patronage at all.

It was not only fear of censure that made the Horse Guards reluctant to use the patronage. Both the Duke and Sir David were well aware that to promote, for example, a lieutenant into another regiment would deprive the senior subaltern of that regiment of a step of which he had justified expectations. Almost all the lieutenants whom they did promote by patronage had very long service. In two sample periods there were 197 occasions on which the patronage could have been used to promote lieutenants from other regiments to the command of companies without filling vacancies due to death from *all* causes. Only seventy-six of these 197 opportunities were used and on sixty-one occasions the promotions went to lieutenants of above-average seniority. Only fifteen of these promotions went to lieutenants as a reward for merit or gallantry, and in none of these cases are there suspicions that the patronage was used on any ground but strictly military ones.

Wellington remarked in 1813 that 'Nothing is more difficult that to promote an officer, excepting one of very long standing, to a troop or company without purchase. Since I have commanded this army I have not been able to promote more than two or three in this way.' Even allowing for some exaggeration in this statement, it is true that Wellington's recommendations were seldom attended to and that when they were, the captaincies were usually granted in undesirable colonial regiments stationed in climates where death vacancies were common and promotion, for the survivors, quick.

The Duke of York's reluctance to use the patronage did not extend to vacancies caused by disciplinary action. He regarded the fact that an officer had been cashiered as being a slur on the whole regiment. The vacancy was therefore best filled from outside. The most drastic case was that of the Eighty Fifth (Bucks Volunteers). Before the regiment went to Portugal in 1811 one captain had been cashiered and another shot in a duel. The commanding officer was listless and there were some unsatisfactory junior officers. Wellington sent the regiment home after eight months in the Peninsula, and once it reached England, its condition deteriorated rapidly. The senior major was brought before a court martial on six charges fabricated by the regimental paymaster, and when they were dismissed, the paymaster brought two more changes alleging fraud. Since he could bring 'not a particle of evidence to support them', the major was again acquitted and the pay-master himself charged, found guilty and dismissed. Meanwhile a captain and a lieutenant were charged with 'conduct highly unbecoming an officer', including an assertion that the adjutant 'had had his nose pulled and his posterior kicked, or words to that effect'. Both were found guilty and dismissed the service. No sooner was that case finished than another lieutenant was tried for 'entering into personal contest with Mr Henry Knight (then an ensign in the regiment) by repeatedly striking and receiving blows with a horse whip at the New Inn, New Romsey'. He escaped with a plea of self-defence, and another subaltern was acquitted of two more of the paymster's fraud charges. A captain was dismissed for asserting that the junior lieutenant-colonel was 'a coward and drunk on duty', and finally the adjutant was charged with describing one of the captains as 'a blackguard and damned insolent'. He admitted the charge, but since the captain concerned had already been dismissed for insulting him, the adjutant escaped with a reprimand.

At this stage the Duke of York intervened. The commanding officer was publicly given 'an intimation of the expediency of his retirement from the service', and it was ordained that 'every officer without exception who has joined the Eighty Fifth shall be removed or exchanged to different corps'. The opportunity was taken to restock the regiment with talented young officers, mostly on promotion after service in the Peninsula. The regiment returned to Spain and distinguished itself both there and in America under the nickname of 'The Elegant Extracts'.

The deplorable state of the Eighty Fifth gave the Duke of York the opportunity to promote nine deserving lieutenants to captaincies at one stroke. In less unusual circumstances the only certain way in which a lieutenant could ensure promotion for himself without purchase was to command a 'Forlorn Hope', the leading group of the storming party at a successful siege. He had also to survive the experience. The leader of the Light Division's Forlorn Hope at Ciudad Rodrigo was John Gurwood, the thirty-third Lieutenant in the Fifty Second, and he was rewarded with a captaincy in the Royal African Corps. The leader of the Third Division's party died of wounds, and none of the leaders survived from any of the divisional Forlorn Hopes at Badajoz. At San Sebastian the losses were so heavy that a captaincy was given to 'the only surviving officer of the advance', the only one to come out alive from the whole storming party.

Once a man had achieved a captaincy, he was eligible for promotion in the army, brevet rank, irrespective of his regimental rank. This could make him a lieutenant-colonel, but beyond that only seniority counted for promotion. No amount of merit could make a man a full colonel, since 'the Commander-in-Chief is unwilling to make a precedent of giving an officer the rank of colonel by brevet as a reward for service'. Nevertheless, two rapid promotions could make a great difference to a man who had no money behind him. One such was George Scovell, Wellington's cipher expert. After 13 years' service he was only eighth captain in the Fifty Seventh; then, in the summer of 1811 he was made brevet major and, 15 months later, lieutenant-colonel by brevet. Thus he leapfrogged many of the captains and all the majors in the army at a rate that no purchase officer could not hope to emulate.

Financially, brevet promotion made no great difference — only 2s0d a day and that only in the infantry of the line and the colonial corps — but it did set a man's foot on the ladder that led to general's rank and, more immediately, gave the officer a claim to regimental promotion by patronage in a unit other than his own.

Most brevet promotions were given for long service. The brevet for the King's Birthday in 1813 included all the full-pay captains in the army whose seniority dated between 1 January 1801 (the end of the last brevet) and 31 December 1802. Including Royal Marines, there were seventy-one of them. In 1814 there was a victory brevet encompassing 400 captains of long service. This, however, was little more than a gesture, since many of them immediately went on half-pay, which was calculable only on regimental rank.

A much smaller proportion went to officers of merit. From May 1811, when Wellington was allowed to recommend six majors and twelve captains, every victory was celebrated by a brevet promotion, culminating in the Waterloo brevet, which included fifty-two majors and thirty-seven captains. In addition, by a long tradition, brevet promotion was given to the aide-de-camp who carried to London despatches announcing a victory. Even on these occasions the Duke of York's regulations were meticulously observed. When Captain Ulysses Burgh brought home the despatch announcing the victory at Busaco, his promotion to major was duly gazetted only to be cancelled when it was realised that his length of service fell

King's German Legion; (left to right)
Infantry; Light Infantry; 3rd Hussars (NAM)

short of the minimum prescribed. It was reinstated in the following year, when his qualifying period was complete. Since brevet promotion did not apply to subalterns, two lieutenants who brought back victory despatches received no promotion, although they were both the sons of dukes.

There was one other move an officer could make which, although not promotion, could be part of a manoeuvre to obtain it. This was exchange. Any two officers of equal regimental rank, whether purchased or not, could agree to change places with each other provided that their colonels and the Commander-in-Chief agreed. It should be noticed that although they could exchange ranks, they could not exchange seniorities, and both had to go to the bottom of the seniority list in their new units. There were many reasons why officers wished to exchange — some wished to go on active service, some wished to avoid it, many wished to avoid service in the West Indies, some could not afford to stay in England. Others wished to be in the same regiment as their brothers or friends.

One quite common reason was to obtain promotion without changing regiments. The thinking behind this seeming contradiction was that in good regiments it was very difficult to purchase promotion. The number of purchasable commissions had been much eroded by death, and those who held the remainder were unwilling to part with them. There were, however, some units in which it was hard to sell, and it was not impossible to persuade an elderly non-purchase officer in one's own, good, regiment to exchange into the less-sought-after unit. It made no difference to him in which he ended his career. Such a manoeuvre was carried out by Charles Kinloch, who was a young and efficient officer in the Fifty Second. After five years as a lieutenant he was still six places from a captaincy, and none had been sold in the regiment for more than four years. He therefore bought a captaincy in the Ninety Ninth in March 1813 and immediately exchanged with an elderly captain in the Fifty Second who was on the point of leaving the army and had nothing to lose by resigning from a less famous regiment. Kinloch was thus posted back to the Fifty Second before he actually left it. As it happened, he would have succeeded to a company five months later by seniority, but this could not have been foreseen.

There is no way of telling whether Kinloch gave any financial inducement to his elderly colleague. Both would have had to sign a certificate that 'upon my word of honour as an officer and a gentleman I will not, either now or at any future time, give or receive, by any means or in any shape whatever, directly, any consideration', but there is little doubt that such 'clandestine bargains' did occur and were winked at by the authorities. Wellington's brother-in-law admitted that 'I have offered Burton [Major, 7th Foot] £1,000 to exchange with a relation of mine', but nothing came of this proposition.

Taking the army as a whole, including the Guards, the colonial corps and the Garrison battalions (but excluding the foreign regiments, the Veteran battalions, the artillery and the engineers, where there was no purchase), only two promotions in ten were decided by purchase. Seven went by seniority and one by patronage. The proportions at each step in the infantry, cavalry and colonial corps are shown in Table 1. The Foot Guards were a special case and will be considered later.

TABLE A.   *The Amount of Purchase.*

This table is compiled from all the promotions appearing in the London Gazette between September 1810 and August 1811, and between March 1812 and February 1813. The Foot Guards and Garrison Battalions are omitted.

	INFANTRY		CAVALRY (incl Household)		COLONIAL	
	Total promotions	Percentage by purchase	Total promotions	Percentage by purchase	Total promotions	Percentage by purchase
Ens to Lieut	975	12.3	206	42.7	111	0.9
Lieut to Capt	407	22.3	85	60.0	43	9.3
Capt to Major	126	30.9	22	31.9	12	16.3
Maj to Lieut-Col	50	18.0	13	7.7	9	0.0
Total	1,558	17.7	326	45.1	175	3.4

It will be seen from the table that the proportion of purchase was very much higher in the cavalry up to the crucial rank of captain. This disproportion would have been smaller if it had not been for the very high rate of purchase in some of mounted regiments, particularly the Household Cavalry and the four hussar regiments. One of the remarkable facets of purchase is that there was much of it in the more sought-after cavalry regiments and correspondingly less in the crack infantry regiments. Two facts account for this—death and promotion for merit. The death rate in good infantry regiments was much higher than in their cavalry opposite numbers. The Sixteenth Light Dragoons was the most experienced British cavalry unit in the Peninsula, but between 1809 and 1814 they suffered only five officer deaths, the senior being a captain. By contrast the Fifty Second Foot lost in the same period one lieutenant-colonel, eight captains, eight lieutenants and one ensign. The difference is striking, even allowing for the fact that the Fifty Second, being a two-battalion regiment, had twice as many officers as the Sixteenth. Similarly, with patronage promotion, the Fifty Second had, excluding ensigns, a dozen officers promoted for merit, nine of them lieutenants; but the Sixteenth had only three similarly promoted.

It is easy to exaggerate the time that could be gained by purchasing promotion. Thanks largely to the Duke of York's regulations and partly to the shrinking number of commissions available for purchase, it was by no means easy to buy rapid promotion. Table 2 shows the average time needed to get promotion by seniority and purchase in the various arms of the service. In the cavalry it took six years and one month to purchase promotion from cornet to captain, only a year and ten months quicker than it took to gain the same two steps by seniority. In the cavalry of the German Legion, where there was no purchase, the same rise would take two months longer than it would by seniority in the British cavalry; and in the infantry of the Legion the difference was twice as long.

Paradoxically the effect of the purchase system was to accelerate, in many cases, the promotion of officers who did not purchase. This was because an officer purchasing or exchanging into a regiment went to the bottom of the seniority list for his rank. The more of the seniors on a list who purchased, the faster the officers on the list would rise to the top. The most extreme case was that of Adjutant Samuel Bromley of the Tenth Hussars, a regiment with a very high rate of purchase. He became a lieutenant by seniority on 27 September 1810, when there were eleven lieutenants ahead of him. Three of them retired, two bought captaincies in other regiments and exchanged back to the Tenth, and the remaining six all obtained troops by purchase or seniority within the regiment. When there was an augmentation of two troops for service in the Peninsula in 1813, Bromley was senior subaltern and succeeded to one of them. He had made the step from lieutenant to captain by seniority in two years eleven months, a time seldom achieved by even the richest purchase officer.

The times shown in Table 2 are only averages. There were wide variations between regiments, owing to the amount of active service they saw and the healthiness of their station. In the Twenty Ninth Foot the average time to rise from lieutenant to captain by seniority was only five years and one month: Thomas Langton achieved it in three years and one month. In the Forty Ninth the average

TABLE B.   *Time taken to obtain promotion by purchase & seniority.*

Based on the average time taken by all the officers on full pay who appeared in the Army List for 1809 in the cavalry (incl the Household Cavalry), the infantry of the line and the colonial corps.
The table takes into account only those who were promoted within their own regiments up to April 1814. Officers promoted into regiments other than their own would, except for a small minority of merit promotions, have more seniority than the officers who would have filled the same vacancies from within the regiments.

	INFANTRY		CAVALRY (incl Household)		COLONIAL	
	By Seniority Yrs Mths	By Purchase Yrs Mths	By Seniority Yrs Mths	By Purchase Yrs Mths	By Seniority Yrs Mths	By Purchase Yrs Mths
Ens &c to Lieut	2.1	1.7	2.5	1.6	1.7	(0.4)*
Lieut to Capt	7.0	4.4	6.6	4.7	5.11	(2.11)*
Capt to Maj	9.3	6.4	9.3	7.2	7.5	—
Maj to Lieut-Col	6.4	5.1	5.8	3.2	4.0	—

*The sample in these two cases was too small to be reliable.

4th Portuguese Caçadores, by Denis Dighton (HM)

was nine and a half years. The cavalry regiments that remained in England throughout the war were almost entirely stagnant. In the Scots Greys the four senior subalterns of 1809 were in the same position in 1814. In the Seventh Dragoon Guards only one subaltern became a captain in the same period. He had been a lieutenant for 10½ years.

Regimental majorities were particularly hard to obtain. The Royal Fusiliers had a high turnover of field officers, including four death vacancies and three caused by patronage promotion in the years 1809-14. Despite this, no captain succeeded to a majority by seniority in less than six years, and the only captain who purchased a majority had to wait six years and two months. Even this was quick compared to the Seventh Dragoon Guards, where Captain Francis Dunne waited only a month less than seventeen years for promotion to major. By the time he achieved it, he was a lieutenant-colonel by brevet, owing to the length of his service.

Table 2 shows that the time for promotion by seniority in the colonial regiments was markedly lower than in either the infantry or the cavalry. There was also a very low rate of purchase. The reason was that no one wished to serve in the unhealthy climates in which these regiments were usually stationed. Those who did join them, especially the Royal African Corps, had a high death rate from the climate, not infrequently abetted by a high consumption of liquor. Because of the comparatively rapid rate of promotion, the Horse Guards frequently used these vacancies for patronage promotion, although the officers who obtained the vacancies seldom joined the regiments, usually exchanging with some officer in Europe who was anxious to escape his creditors. Of 111 promotions to captain in the colonial corps between 1809 and 1814, thirteen went by purchase, fifty-five by seniority and forty-three by patronage.

The Brigade of Guards is not shown on either Table 1 or Table 2 because special considerations applied to the three regiments. In the first place every officer of the Guards (except ensigns, who did not obtain the same privilege until after Waterloo) automatically held a higher rank in the army than he did in his regiment. Since 1687 captains in the Guards had ranked as lieutenant-colonels in the army and since 1691, lieutenants had ranked as captains. This 'Privilege of the Guards' gave the officers a theoretical advantage over officers of the line, since it enabled a captain of the Guards to exchange into a line regiment as a lieutenant-colonel (which a line captain who was a lieutenant-colonel by brevet could not do). As it happened, promotion in the Guards was so slow that this advantage was always completely nullified, and, in any case, Guards officers showed very little inclination to move into the line.

Essentially the Guards were regiments for rich men. Their uniform was as expensive as all but the most gorgeous of the hussars, their mess bills were high and the fact that an officer was likely to spend at least half his service in London or at Windsor all contributed to the need for a substantial private income. It is not surprising, therefore, that the rate of purchase was the highest in the army. Half of all promotions were bought, compared to 17.7 per cent in the infantry of the line. On the other hand, purchase made very little difference, especially in the two junior regiments of the Brigade. Those who were ensigns in the Third Guards in 1809 achieved their lieutenancies in their precise order of seniority irrespective of

10th Portuguese Cavalry, by Denis Dighton (HM)

whether they purchased or not. The shortest time any of these officers took to gain the step was four years and seven months, and that was done by seniority. Although there were a few exceptions in the First Guards (where promotion for junior officers moved with agonising slowness), the difference made by purchase was so slight that it seems probable that all the officers had their names on the 'list for purchase' and considered promotion by seniority as an uncovenanted bonus.

Promotion throughout the Brigade was very slow. Of the seventy-five ensigns listed in the three regiments at the beginning of 1809, only eighteen (eleven of them in the Coldstream) became lieutenants (and captains) in less than five years. In the Coldstream and Third Guards a lieutenant could expect to become a captain (and lieutenant-colonel) in nine and a half years, whether he purchased or not. In the First Guards purchasing lieutenants averaged nine years and eleven months in getting their companies. Those who had to wait for seniority to get them their step took eleven years five months.

20th Portuguese Infantry, by Denis Dighton (HM)

This slow promotion meant that captains in the Guards were older than the average captain of the line. The prospect of further regimental promotion was small. W. H. Clinton, who bought a majority in the First Guards in 1813, had been a captain for more than 18 years then and was already a major-general. By 1814 that regiment's lieutenant-colonel and one of its majors were lieutenant-generals. The other two majors were major-generals, and of the thirty-five captains, one was a lieutenant-general, seven were major-generals and six were colonels by brevet. This plethora of senior officers meant that the establishment of ensigns had to be higher than in the line, and that Guards battalions always fought under the command of an officer who was, regimentally speaking, a junior captain. At Salamanca, for example, both the Coldstream and the Third Guards went into action commanded by their eleventh captains.

It will be seen that promotion in any branch of the army was something of a lottery. In some regiments it stagnated, in others it was very fluid. Any regiment that saw plenty of hard fighting had a brisk rate of promotion — for the survivors. In wartime purchase played a relatively minor role. Patronage, or 'interest'. was even less influential.

Ensign Bell of the Thirty Fourth wrote, long after the war, that Peninsular officers 'were entirely neglected by the influence of cold aristocratic pride, injustice and partiality. Promotion went too often by favour, *court* influence, political intrigue or Horse Guards influence.' This verdict is wholly unsupported by the facts. It would be truer to say that 'Horse Guards influence' was used insufficiently, that too often seniority was considered of more importance than merit. It is certainly true that Peninsular officers did not get as much promotion as they thought they deserved. They did not get as much as Wellington tried to get for them. As he wrote angrily in 1810, 'I, who command the largest British army that has ever been employed against the enemy, and who have on my hands certainly the most extensive and difficult concern that was ever imposed upon any British officer, have not the power of making even a corporal.'

The fact was that the pendulum had swung too far back. The reaction against the excesses of the eighteenth century, especially those of Sir George Yonge, inhibited the Horse Guards from using the patronage as much as was either necessary or just. When it was used, Peninsular officers received their fair share, but there was far from being enough to reward all who deserved it.

7

The Ordnance Corps

The two corps for which the Master General of the Ordnance was responsible — the Royal Engineers and the Royal Artillery — trained their officers before giving them commissions. The Royal Military Academy at Woolwich had been established in 1741, and cadets were admitted to it on the recommendation of the Master General.

No cadet to be admitted under fourteen or above sixteen years of age, or below the height of four feet nine inches. [He must be] well grounded in vulgar fractions, write a good round hand, and have gone through the Latin grammar . . . It is strongly recommended that all candidates should acquire some knowledge of the French language before joining the Academy. All candidates will be examined by the proper masters on joining and, if found deficient in these preparatory parts of learning, will be sent back to their parents and *not admitted*.

Once admitted, the cadet was faced with the following curriculum:

Fortification (including the attack and defence of fortified places, the art of mining, the elements of field fortification, how to trace on the ground with and without mathematical instruments, the theory and practice of levelling, and how to estimate the works of a fortification); *Artillery* (including the general construction of brass and iron guns and their carriages, how to find the weights of guns, mortars and howitzers, how to find the quantity of powder a chamber contains, how to ascertain the number of horses necessary to draw the different natures of ordnance and the number of men required to construct a battery at night); *Mathematics* (including arithmetic, logarithms, geometry, algebra, trigonometry, mensuration, mechanics, fluxions, hydraulics and hydrostatics); *Drawing* (including field sketching and [under Paul Sandby R.A.] aerial perspective) and *French* . . . The Gentleman Cadets generally attend two and sometimes three courses of lectures in chemistry. They are also taught fencing and dancing; the exercise of small arms, and light field pieces.

At the end of the course there was a public examination to be passed before an officer could be commissioned, those who did best going to the Royal Engineers. The length of time a cadet took before passing out depended on the cadet himself and the number of commissions available. In peacetime cadets spent about 18 months or two years at Woolwich but, as soon as war broke out, the course was shortened. Of those who commanded Wellington's artillery, only one, Alexander Dickson, took a normal time over his course. William Robe spent only six months at the Academy, Hoylett Framingham only eight. It was four and a half years before William Borthwick passed his examinations and Edward Howarth took three and a half years. George Bulteel Fisher did not attend Woolwich at all. (Six of the battery commanders who served in the Peninsula did not go to Woolwich, but came from the Royal Irish Artillery, which was incorporated into the Royal Artillery as 7th battalion in 1801.)

Howarth was commissioned in 1771. Robe, Framingham, Fisher and Borthwick all became second lieutenants during the American War of Independence. By the time of the Peninsular War they were all, by contemporary standards, old men for active service. This was because there was no purchase in either the Engineers and Artillery. Merit was recognised only late and sparingly. Seniority dominated every officer's career and that seniority was decided by the date and order in which he passed out of Woolwich.

While the Ordnance system of promotion was equitable, it meant that officers advanced in rank even more slowly than did infantry officers who relied equally on seniority. One example will make this clear. Thomas Downman, a Horse Artillery officer of unquestioned merit, was commissioned as a second lieutenant on 24 April 1793. Three weeks later Jacob Brunt, after twenty-three years in the ranks, became an ensign in the Fifty Fifth Foot. He had neither money nor influence. Both men became lieutenants in September 1793, but from that point the infantryman drew steadily ahead. He became a captain in November 1797. The gunner became a second captain (a rank which did not carry the possibility of brevet promotion) in the same month but was not a full captain until July 1802. Brunt's majority was dated May 1805, Downman's January 1810. On 13 June 1811 Brunt succeeded to a lieutenant-colonelcy, but Downman did not get than rank regimentally until 1825, though he got it by brevet in December 1812.

This rigid adherence to seniority meant that all senior Ordnance officers were too old for their jobs. The senior artillery staff officer, himself a major-general, remarked that an officer 'rises so dismally by gradation' and experiences 'the misery of never rising in the corps to rank while able to discharge the duties belonging to it'. It was a vicious circle. The senior officers could not go on active service and, since pensions were only given for disabling wounds, they could not afford to retire. The junior officers could only wait until the seniors died in their beds. In the Peninsular campaigns twenty-six artillery officers died but only one was a regimental major (who died as the result of an accident) and eight were captains. It made a poor contribution to promotion when compared to an infantry regiment. In the same period the Royal Fusiliers lost through death one lieutenant-colonel, three majors and thirteen captains.

The system bred discontent among the junior officers. Captain Hew Ross wrote in 1811 when he was thirty-two:

My despondence arises chiefly from the unmanly and miserable feelings of my own corps. There has ever been a prejudice in the heads of the regiment against the inferior officers obtaining brevet. Our senior officers, having grown

Musket (*India Pattern*) (Tower of London, Crown Copyright)

grey in the subaltern ranks, cannot endure the thought of their followers being more fortunate . . . After seventeen years in the service, I find myself seventy steps from a majority.

By what Wellington described as 'some damned Ordnance trick', second captains, who for all other purposes ranked as captains in the army, were denied brevet promotion. As Second Captain Robert Cairnes wrote early in 1813,

> I should like to get a brevet majority before the peace had not Lord Mulgrave [Master General of the Ordnance] slammed the door to promotion in the faces of us poor second captains. Six of us are now commanding troops or [batteries] . . . Captains of the line (who were not in the army when some of us were captains) get the brevet . . . Is it feared that we shall come too soon to command? Look at our list of majors or even captains, and see how many men have left to them constitution and *energy* for a command.

Cairnes saw his wish fulfilled. In 1813 the second captains in Spain presented, with Wellington's warm support, a memorial to the Prince Regent for the redress of their grievance. The Master General was overruled and Cairnes and six other second captains of artillery became brevet majors before the end of the war.

Promotion in the artillery would have been even slower had it not been for the threefold expansion in the regiment. In 1791 there had been only 274 officers. By 1814 there were 727. Woolwich was hard put to it to keep pace with the call for officers, the more so since thirty-five died in the West Indies between 1793 and 1801. Nevertheless, the Royal Artillery remained a close-knit body with great, and justifiable, professional pride. It was a family affair. A high proportion of the officers were the sons of gunner officers, and they tended to marry the sisters of gunner officers. Although the Royal Regiment was scattered all over the world, it was highly centralised at Woolwich. There was the Academy and there was the artillery depot, presided over by Major-General Macleod, Deputy Adjutant General, Royal Artillery, who controlled all the artillery's activities with a staff of 'one assistant and five clerks, of whom four are merely sergeants'. Around the depot was a swarm of artillery wives whose husbands were overseas. Mrs Alexander

Baker Rifle (Tower of London, Crown Copyright)

Dickson, something of an outsider as Minorcan by birth, wrote: 'It is not the chiefs of artillery that are so arbitrary, but it is the council of a few married captains. They pass sentence of death upon every body's conduct.'

As a friendly infantryman said, 'with so little scope for distinction, it is surprising that your branch of the service should prosper as it does, and maintain the respectability that characterizes it.'

The troops and batteries never let the army down, but the senior officers were a different matter. Wellington did not have a satisfactory commander of his artillery until in 1813 he ruthlessly gave the command to Alexander Dickson on the strength of his Portuguese rank, although there were seven of his regimental seniors in the army. With the possible exception of William Robe, all Dickson's predecessors lacked energy and decision. Howarth, for example, was described by his own brigade major as 'excessively irritable and dissatisfied . . . He had neither confidence in himself or anyone else'. Wellington's opinion was, 'I think I will be lucky if he does not get me into a scrape'. William Borthwick was bluntly told by Wellington 'that he wanted an active officer to fill so important a situation as chief of artillery and recommended him to go home'.

A legend has grown up that relations were bad between Wellington and his gunners. There is very little contemporary evidence that this was so, although the old gentlemen at Woolwich disliked the general both for his cavalier treatment of their colleagues and for the tight tactical control he kept over his guns. Leaving aside the unfortunate episode of Norman Ramsay in 1813 (see below), there seem only to be two adverse references to Wellington in all the diaries and letters from gunner officers that have survived. The first is from Downman, notoriously an ill-tempered man, who accused Wellington in July 1811 of having no feelings, and that 'Ambition is his passion and carries him away'; and the second from Cairnes, who also accused Wellington of lack of feelings, but only after the general had taken away his carefully tended troop horses to draw the pontoon train — an occurrence that might well cause an outburst of ill temper. Most gunner officers joined in the general admiration for their commander, which grew steadily as the war progressed. Lieutenant Swabey, RHA, for example, remarked in May 1813, that 'Lord Wellington and his staff suddenly appeared amongst us and the influence of his presence seemed immediately to give life to every individual.'

The Ramsay incident did cause a momentary rift between Wellington and the artillery. The evidence is confusing but it seems clear that, in the aftermath of Vitoria, Wellington gave Ramsay definite orders to stay where he was with his troop until he personally gave him further orders. Ramsay, in good faith, obeyed an order given him by a staff officer and was not to be found when Wellington arrived to give him his instructions. Ramsay was ordered into arrest and not released for three weeks. Wellington was very angry, since the army's advance was delayed 24 hours by this incident. He was determined to make an example of Ramsay, though he had 'been heard so often to speak in terms of the highest applause of Ramsay'. In practical terms the incident was unimportant, the only result being that Ramsay's brevet majority was delayed for five months, but it added strength to the ill-feeling against Wellington at Woolwich.

The Royal Engineers were a very small corps. In 1792 there had been only seventy-three of them (at a total cost of £16,674 8s 4d). By 1813 their numbers had risen to 262 (costing £50,580 17s 11d). Like the artillery, they suffered from having too many inactive senior officers. In 1809 their youngest lieutenant-colonel was the same age as Wellington. They also suffered from a tendency to pedantry, induced by their Woolwich training. They regarded their principal task as the organisation of sieges, a slow methodical operation demanding both skill and judgement. An infantry officer might refer jokingly to 'the inherent pomp and acquired gravity of a Royal Engineer', but planning a siege was a serious business. A wrong decision might cost the lives of hundreds, if not thousands, of infantrymen — and of the handful of engineers who always accompanied the assault. Casualties among engineers were terribly high: 102 engineer officers served in the Peninsula and twenty-five of them died, twenty-four of them in action and one from exhaustion. Eighteen engineers were present at the siege of San Sebastian, and eleven of them were casualties. As Wellington remarked, 'We have had such an expenditure of engineers that I can hardly wish for any body, lest the same fate befall him as has befallen so many.'

Another function of the Royal Engineers was the supply of pontoons for field bridging. The pontoons in use had not been changed in design since the days of Marlborough. They were made of tin (which was rapidly destroyed by sea water), strengthened by wooden ribs and weighed 2 tons each. Moving them was a constant problem, the more so since the Engineers had no transport of their own and were dependent on the artillery. The transport return for the Royal Engineers in April 1811, read, 'Horses, Nil. Mules, 6. Carts, Nil.' Before the campaign of 1813, which entailed moving the pontoons from the Portuguese frontier to the Pyrenees and beyond, Augustus Frazer of the Horse Artillery had to consult the Chief Engineer, Sir Richard Fletcher. 'We have been putting our wits together to make something of the pontoons, which travel badly, break down, and in short do all that is not wished. Already have horses and bullocks been tried in the draft, without finding that either do well.' Some success was obtained by using smaller wheels at the front, but it cost the lives of 500 oxen to get the pontoon train to St Jean de Luz. When five pontoons were needed to form a flying bridge on the Adour in February 1814, thirty horses were harnessed to each, but this was not enough to move them through the

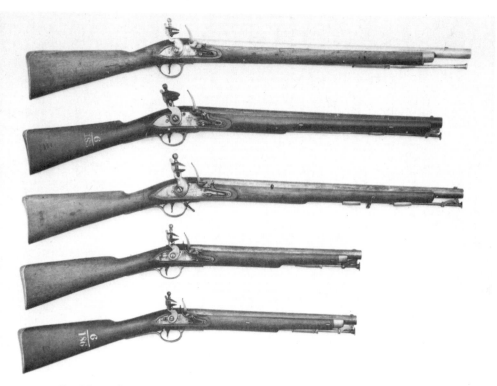

Carbines: (top to bottom) (Tower of London, Crown Copyright)
1   Pattern 1796 Cavalry Carbine   2   Musket-bore Carbine c 1830
3 Possibly private-issue Carbine c 1813   4 Paget Carbine   5 Paget Carbine

wilderness of sand on the river bank. For the last half mile each pontoon was carried on the shoulders of twenty-six Guardsmen.

Pontoons were therefore used only when there was no alternative. The bridge across the Adour was constructed of thirty-four fishing boats (*chasse-marées*) supporting a roadway constructed of five 13in cables covered with planks. On the Leis, a tributary of the Adour, the problem was to fill in two arches that had been blown out of the bridge by the retreating French. 'About twenty five elm trees, about twenty five feet long, and bundles of fascines, about twelve feet long, placed crosswise, and then covered with dirt, in two days' time made us a famous bridge.'

Anomalies were the hallmark of the organisation of the Royal Engineers, and they started at the top. Their professional head was the Inspector General of Fortifications, but no such post appeared in the estimates. His pay was found from the item that provided forage for the horses of the Ordnance department and, under this heading, he drew £4,638 a year in pay and allowances. There were no majors in the corps, but nor were there any personnel except officers. There was, however, a body called the Royal Military Artificers, comprising twelve companies each commanded by a sub-lieutenant (always a superannuated NCO), who was assisted by a sergeant-major seconded from the artillery. The normal tasks of the Artificers were those of skilled handymen in fortified places, and they included such tradesmen as carpenters, masons and plumbers. Eight companies were stationed in the United Kingdom, two in Gibraltar, one in Nova Scotia and one in the West Indies, and the companies had been in these stations since 1783. An Engineer officer wrote:

> They had attained what may for military men be styled a state of vegetation; so that they were [in 1811] a vast number of men who had actually grown grey in the corps, who had never entered a transport, nor made a single day's march from the headquarters of their company. Everywhere they intermixed with civilians; they married in a proportion unknown in any other corps; so much so that the number of women and children belonging to one company was often equal to that of a battalion of the line.

Another sapper officer described them as 'a set of undisciplined vagabonds'.

It was not to be expected that such a sedentary corps would be able to provide many men for active operations. In November 1809 their strength in the Peninsula was two sergeants and twenty-three rank and file, of whom four were sick and two missing. Their first reinforcements were twenty-five men who had never 'seen a sap, battery or trench constructed' when they landed at Lisbon in March 1811. Only eighteen could be mustered for the siege of Ciudad Rodrigo ten months later.

Further reinforcements arrived in time to allow 115 artificers to assist at the siege of Badajoz in April 1812, but it was still necessary to call on the infantry for the loan of miners. The carnage at Badajoz at last ensured a reform of the system. Wellington wrote to London:

> The capture of Badajoz affords as strong an instance of the gallantry of the troops as has ever been displayed. But I greatly hope that I shall never again be the instrument of putting them to such a test as they were put to last night. I assure your lordship that it is quite impossible to carry fortified places by *vive force* without incurring grave loss and being exposed to the chance of failure unless the army should be provided with a sufficient trained corps of sappers and miners.

The horrifying list of casualties that accompanied this letter arrived on 23 April, and on the same day a warrant was issued for the formation 'of an establishment for instructing the Military Artificers in military field works'. The Corps' name was changed to Royal Sappers and Miners, the establishment was raised to 2,800 rank and file and, most importantly, Engineer officers were appointed to command the companies. The equivalent of four companies served under Wellington for the siege of San Sebastian in the summer of 1813.

The reason for the anomalous composition of the engineering corps was that Engineers were still regarded as specialists only to be called in on special occasions, in the way in which one might call in a medical specialist. This mystique, which Engineers did little to dispel, was underlined by the high pay drawn by Engineers. While a captain drew 10s6d a day in the infantry, 11s0d in the field artillery, 14s7d in the cavalry and 15s11d in the horse artillery, a captain of the Royal Engineers received 16s7½d when serving at home and 22s2d when abroad, Engineers being

Heavy Cavalry Sword, 1796 (Tower of London, Crown Copyright)

the only officers to have an increment for overseas service.

The artillery had their own anomalies. In the horse branch the drivers belonged to the Royal Artillery. In the field gunners the drivers belonged to the Corps of Royal Artillery Drivers, which consisted of eleven troops each commanded by a captain commissary. Each troop was divided into five sections under a lieutenant commissary, and consisted, apart from ninety drivers, of craftsmen — farriers, smiths, harness-makers, wheelers and cartwrights. Since the number of ninety drivers bore no relation to the number required by an artillery unit, the drivers always had to be split up, never served under their own officers (who were responsible for their welfare and administration) and were usually shamefully neglected. Their discipline was almost always poor, and the corps was not unfairly described by a gunner officer as 'that nest of infamy'.

All the projectiles fired by the artillery of Wellington's army were, by twentieth-century standards, very small. The largest missile fired by any British gun weighed only 24lb, 1lb less than the normal shell fired by British field artillery in World War II. Nor were these projectiles very lethal. Most of them were round shot — solid balls of iron that could harm only those who stood in the direct line of flight. If a man was only 6in from its line, he was safe. Round shot could inflict heavy casualties on men in column. Outside Salamanca in 1813 'sixteen men were killed by one six pounder shot; they fell in a line perpendicular to our position, each man lying partly over another'. The effective range of Wellington's field guns was only 1,200 to 1,400yd, but effective range was taken to mean the distance to the point at which the round pitched. If the ground was dry, it would bounce and roll for anything up to two miles further, looking deceptively harmless.

More lethal than round shot but with a much shorter range was case shot, also known as cannister. This, a development of grapeshot, consisted of a cylindrical tin case, 'in diameter a little less than the gun or howitzer. It is filled with iron balls to make up the weight of the shot'. Cannister came in two sizes: 'light cannister' contained, for the six-pounder, twelve balls, each weighing 8½oz; and 'round seven' contained thirty-four 3½oz balls. According to the textbooks, 'little effect is to be expected from firing them beyond 300 yards [because of] the great divergence of the balls', but, after the battle of Salamanca, Captain Dynely, whose light

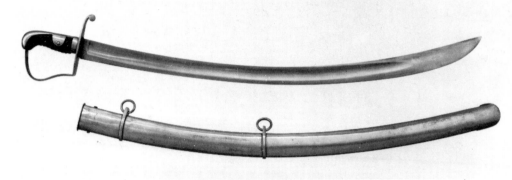

British Light Dragoon Trooper's Sword c 1800
(Tower of London, Crown Copyright)

six-pounders were firing from the lesser Arapile, wrote that 'never did artillery make better practice than our six guns on that day. We fired 492 rounds, very few of which did not go into the heart of their columns. It was not any joke for them whenever we played on them for any considerable time with "round seven" and cannister.' The range was about 800yd.

Less effective was common shell, which consisted of an iron sphere filled with explosive that was detonated by a fuse cut to length and lit before the piece was fired. The range was the same as that for round shot, but the fuses were seldom accurate, and were frequently blown out when the shell was fired. Even if they kept burning, it was possible for a brave man to kick out the fuse as it lay on the ground. At Ciudad Rodrigo, George Napier

> . . . was standing with some men who were digging a trench when a thirteen inch shell from the town fell in the midst of us. I called to the men to lie down flat [but] one of them, an Irishman and an old marine, a most worthless drunken dog, ran up to the shell, the fuze of which was still burning, and striking it a blow with his spade, knocked it out. Taking the immense shell in his hands he came and presented it to me, saying, 'There she is for you now, your honour!' He told me he had often done the same thing in Egypt where he had served under Abercromby. I never saw a cooler thing in my life and of course was obliged to give him a dollar and leave to get drunk if he got safe home to his cantonments.

Common shell was never fired from field guns, as experience had shown that it was liable to burst as soon as it left the barrel. Even with howitzers it was seldom satisfactory. After the siege of San Sebastian, Colonel Frazer wrote: 'They sent us wretched shells. Nearly half burst on leaving the howitzers.'

These three types of ammunition—round shot, cannister and common shell—were used in all European armies. The British had a secret weapon, however, in spherical case shot, better known as shrapnel shell after its inventor, Colonel Henry Shrapnell. He had combined the best points of cannister and common shell, so that the iron sphere was filled with small balls, and the explosive charge was detonated by lighting one of the pre-set fuses designed to burst at different ranges. This enabled guns to airburst shells over an enemy sheltering behind a crest, a position in which he would be safe from the other types of missile except the erratic and unobservable common shell.

Wellington had some early doubts about shrapnel, but experience taught him that it was effective, provided the shells were filled with balls not smaller than musket balls. By summer 1812 he was urging the gunners to take 'as much spherical case as you can carry'. For the campaign of 1813 the proportions of ammunition carried were laid down as follows:

For every 100 rounds, Roundshot	60
Spherical Case	30
Common case	10

Field howitzers, which could not fire round shot, carried half their ammunition in shrapnel.

The artillery pieces can be divided into two categories: field guns and howitzers, and siege guns and howitzers. Field pieces were made of brass. Brass guns were lighter than iron, but they had the disadvantage that after prolonged firing the metal overheated, causing muzzle droop; but field guns seldom fired sufficiently hard for this to be of importance. The field guns most used by Wellington's gunners were the light six-pounder and the light nine-pounder. Both were mounted on a block (or T-shaped) carriage, which had a central trail. The six-pounder had a 5ft barrel, an effective range of 1,200yd with a charge of 1½lb of powder and optimum elevation of 4°. The nine-pounders used twice as much powder to achieve a range of 1,400yd. They had 6ft barrels. Some use was also made of the heavy six-pounder, which also had an effective range of 1,400yd; and the light three-pounder (range 1,200yd) was used in 1808-9, and came into its own as a pack gun in the Pyrenean fighting.

The state of the roads in Portugal and Spain made the movement of guns difficult. The light six-pounder and its limber weighed 27½cwt, and the light nine-pounder 38cwt. These weights made heavy demands on draught horses particularly when the roads were wet. Before the battle of the Nive fires had to be lit along the roads before they were dry enough to move the guns. Nevertheless, there was a steady increase in the weight of the British guns. In May 1809 the British and German field artillery consisted of three batteries of three-pounders and three of light six-pounders. For the Vitoria campaign they had four troops of light six-pounders, two batteries of heavy six-pounders and seven batteries or troops of nine-pounders.

In every troop and battery there were five guns and one howitzer. The latter was the light 5½in model with a barrel of 27in. Complete with limber it weighed 26¾cwt, and its range, at the optimum elevation of 12°, was 1,350yd. Its charge was 1lb of powder.

Firing these pieces required a high standard of drill and physical fitness, especially as the line of fire could only be adjusted by moving the trail bodily sideways with handspikes. Elevation was altered by a screw under the rear end of the barrel. A well trained crew could get off eight rounds a minute but these could not be aimed as, each time the gun was fired, the target was obscured by a billowing cloud of smoke. The drill book laid down that the maximum effective rate was three rounds a minute of cannister or two of roundshot.

British siege guns were either eighteen- or twenty four-pounders. They were made of iron, the softness of the metal giving 'much security against bursting'. Unfortunately the vent holes in the iron guns tended to expand allowing the strength of the charge to blow out upwards. In the middle of the siege of Badajoz all the vents had to be blocked with molten copper and rebored.

There were four types of twenty four-pounders, the largest of which had 9ft barrels. Their maximum effective range was 2,400yd, which was obtained by using a 6lb charge of powder at an elevation of 10°. The eighteen-pounder, with an even longer barrel, had a range of 2,300yd, but, with its limber, weighed only 65½cwt compared to the larger gun's more than 4 tons. Both were fired from double bracket carriages with twin trails, but the twenty four-pounder had to be transported on a block carriage and laboriously transferred to a firing carriage before it could be used. Wellington took some eighteen-pounders with the army in case any small fortified posts had to be reduced, but their movement was always a trying business. It required more than 160 oxen to move them 'and their appurtenances' on the Vitoria campaign.

Firing siege guns was, of course, a much slower business than with field guns. The recoil would make the carriage run back as much as 8ft and it then had to be hauled back into place. The loading and laying drill took two minutes for each round but, with a great loss of accuracy, ten rounds could be fired in eight minutes in an emergency.

One brass piece was used in sieges. This was the 8in howitzer, which could throw a 41lb shell to a distance of 1,700yd. Wellington disapproved of the use of howitzers in sieges 'principally from entertaining an opinion that the fire of mortars and howitzers has an effect only upon the inhabitants of a town alone, and that a French garrison, in a Spanish or Portuguese town, would be but little likely to attend to the wishes or feelings of the inhabitants.' Thomas Graham, however, used 13,800 howitzer shells, 10,000 of the 8in type, when he took San Sebastian.

Battering a fortress called for a very high standard of accuracy and consistency from the gunners, almost all of whom were field gunners detached for the occasion. To bring a wall down, so that a breach would be formed, it was essential to hit the same stretch of wall repeatedly before it would topple forward into the ditch. In the 1812 siege of Badajoz 35,346 rounds were fired, of which 31,861 were round-shot for the twenty-four- and eighteen-pounders; and 2,523 barrels of powder, each containing 90lb, were used. At San Sebastian 70,831 rounds were fired.

Although the French, with the range of guns designed by General Jean-Baptiste Gribeauval, started the long wars with a great advantage in artillery, the British steadily overtook them. Their gunpowder was more efficient and their fuses more accurate. The shrapnel shell remained a British secret until a dozen years after Waterloo. The design of British guns also excelled that of the French before the end of the war and Marshal Marmont, himself an artilleryman of great distinction, considered the British equipment 'in every respect very far superior to anything he had ever seen'.

The British also experimented with rockets and, although Napoleon offered a reward to anyone who could copy the British model, the idea was not pursued in France. The native armies in India had used rockets for decades, and William Congreve decided to develop the military rocket so as to 'provide the facility of firing a great number of rounds in a short time or even instantaneously, with small means.' Congreve's rockets could be fired either from a trough (for small 6lb rockets) or from a light frame (for a rocket of up to 42lb). Troughs, frames and the rockets themselves, which had their propellant charge built into them, were easy to transport: '100 men can bring into action, in any situation where musketry can be used, nearly 300 12lb rounds, with ranges double of those of light field ordnance.' The range of a 12lb rocket was calculated as 2,500yd.

Such a weapon might have revolutionised warfare, but Congreve's rockets were most erratic in their performance and were as likely to go backwards as forwards. Wellington had experimented with rockets borrowed from the Royal Navy in 1810, remarking that 'It is but fair to give everything a trial.' The trial was a failure but three years later he was offered a Royal Artillery rocket troop and accepted it. 'The only reason why I wished to have it was to get the horses . . . I do not wish to set fire to any town, and I do not know any other use for rockets.' A trial firing was arranged in the south of France and an observer remarked: 'I think they would have hit Bayonne, for instance, somewhere or other, but the part of the town you could not very well choose.'

In fact the rocket troop (whose sister unit had already much impressed the eastern European sovereigns at the battle of Leipzig), did do some useful service at the crossing of the Adour. They might have done better if the Board of Ordnance which did, as Wellington hoped, send horses out with the troop, had not omitted to send out any trained rocketeers. Colonel Frazer, who was put in charge, wrote: 'I had to manage the medley called the rocket troop, composed of men hastily scraped together, utterly ignorant of the arm they are to use, the rockets equipped in five varieties of manner and liable to as many mistakes.'

8

Transport and Supply

Each soldier was entitled to a daily ration of 1lb of meat, 1lb of biscuit (or 1½lb of bread) and a quart of beer (or a pint of wine or 1/3 pint of spirits).

Each horse was entitled to 10lb of oats or barley or maize and 10lb of hay or straw daily. Each mule was entitled to 5lb of oats, barley or maize and 10lb of straw. At the start of the 1813 campaign Wellington's army had a marching strength of 81,276 all ranks, British and Portuguese. In the cavalry there were 7,600 troop horses, and the 350 cavalry officers had an average of more than two horses each. The British and German artillery had more than 500 horses to draw their guns and 2,184 for their ammunition waggons. The three Portuguese batteries required 700 mules. In the 109 infantry battalions there were 1,500 horses and 1,400 mules receiving forage from public funds.

The staff had a vast number of horses and mules. When Wellington's headquarters, together with those of Beresford and the northern Spanish armies, were stationed near Ciudad Rodrigo in May 1813, they drew forage for 1,500 animals daily. The Commander of the Forces was entitled to forage for 100 beasts, the Commissary General for forty. Even a Hospital Mate drew forage for two animals. The animal ration strength for the staff of the Light Division and its two brigade staffs was 203. There cannot have been less than 3,500 horses and mules attached to the headquarters of the divisions and brigades of the army. In addition there were the animals of such smaller corps as the Royal Engineers, the Corps of Guides and the Mounted Staff Corps. In the fighting echelons of the army there were some 20,000 animals drawing official rations, and a vast herd of private riding horses and baggage mules. In support there were more than 12,000 commissariat mules, whose task was to bring forward the 100,000lb of biscuit and 200,000lb of forage corn required daily. Accompanying the army was a herd of slaughter cattle large enought to provide 300 beasts a day for the meat ration. They were entitled to no rations and had to subsist by casual grazing at the road side.

This vast supply operation was entrusted to a small body of officers from the Commissariat Department. Their first responsibility was to the Treasury, which held them, or, in the case of their death, their heirs, accountable for all public monies that passed through their hands. Since the peace establishment of commissaries was minute, most of the officers sent on active service were bound to be untrained in their duties and their task was made no easier by the necessity of finding their way through the mass of petty regulations designed to prevent fraud in the sedentary conditions of a peacetime garrison. Wellington's comment was that 'the great business of the Commander-in-Chief is to discover a mode of carrying on the business of this important department as much in conformity with the instructions of the Commissary General as is possible.'

Horse Artillery coming into action, by Denis Dighton (HM)

Although Britain had been at war, almost continuously, for fifteen years when Wellington first landed in Portugal in 1808, few military operations had been carried on out of reach of the sea and of ships carrying provisions. The whole technique of supplying armies far from the coast had to be learned by experience. One of Wellington's first complaints was: 'I have had great difficulty in organising my commissariat for the march, and that department is very incompetent . . . The existence of the army depends upon it, and yet the people who manage it are incapable of managing anything outside a counting house.'

A proportion of commissaries would not have lasted long in any reputable counting house. The General Orders are punctuated by the record of the dismissal of commissaries for peculation but scrupulous honesty could hardly be expected. Until 1810 assistant commissaries, who handled large sums of public money, were paid only 5s a day when abroad although their pay was 15s in Britain. Their commissioning was a very minor part of the Treasury's patronage and successive First Lords and Chancellors had been glad to receive nominations from political supporters who had importunate dependants.

In 1810 entry into the service was first regulated by the Commissary-in-Chief, Colonel James Willoughby Gordon, who was later to be, for a short and unhappy period, Wellington's Quartermaster General. Henceforward new entrants must be at least sixteen and do a year's probation as a commissariat clerk. As such they would be paid 7s6d a day overseas while the lowest commissioned rank, deputy assistant commissary, would get 9s6d. Two years later an entrance examination in English and arithmetic was instituted by Spencer Perceval, the Prime Minister. One of the first candidates was found to have been cashiered from the army and another, sponsored by the Treasurer to the Navy, wrote that he was 'lernging a letel French [sic]'.

On active operations the life of a commissary was no sinecure. The Assistant Commissary General for the Third Division, who was paid 14s3d a day, had to provide each day for the division, '10,500 lbs of bread (or 7,000 lbs of biscuit), 7,000 lbs of meat; 7,000 pints of wine (or 2,333 $\frac{1}{3}$ pints of spirits)'. When on the march, he had to report to General Picton, no easy taskmaster, at three o'clock every morning. Then he would ride with the division on its march, searching to left and right of its route for possible sources of supply. At the same time he had to keep a close eye on a herd of slaughter cattle up to 500 strong, with their Portuguese herdsmen, and on the 600 divisional commissariat mules. The division would march about 15 miles, frequently in choking dust, but the commissary probably rode twice as far, moving from flank to flank. Then, when

> . . . the troops were allowed to bivouac and the officers and men were able to rest, sleep or enjoy some leisure, a commissary's hardest work began. It was then that he had to mount a fresh horse, scour the country in order to discover some concealed hoard of grain, accompany foraging parties, and proceed to organise the baking of bread and the slaughtering of cattle, and to find his way to headquarters to boot. Finally when he returned, wet to the skin and thoroughly exhausted, to his bivouac hut, he had to take up his pen to write, prepare statements, make out orders for tomorrow and, at the end of it all, snatch perhaps only two or three hours rest on a hard bed before jumping into the saddle again at dawn . . .
>
> Even after the wheat was found, a great deal remained to be done; for instance, the banks of rivers to be explored in seeking mills, mules appointed to work between these and the division, a spot determined on for a store to receive the flour when ground; and lastly the municipal authorities put into requisition, and women appointed to bake the flour into bread. Since it frequently happened that arriving by a route circuitously swerving from the line of march, I had no means of removing the wheat collected on the way till, arrived at the division, different parties of mules were accordingly thence dispatched in

Royal Artillery, by Denis Dighton (HM)

requisite numbers, and thus set to work to travel to and fro in various directions. A chapel or other large building on these occasions was now appropriated as a bread store, and a functionary employed, pen or pencil in hand, to deliver to the various women appointed by the *alcade* to bake the flour each in the oven of her own dwelling, their various proportions. I generally found a dull heavy man best answer the purpose of a vocation where strict attention was required hour after hour among these lively Spanish females, and there such an individual would patiently exert his utmost mental powers in the exercise of suitable accuracy to note in a small narrow cash book each and every singular delivery; that is to say many pounds to Maria, and Josepha, and Joaquina, and so forth; and then again, with a cough and a *per contra*, he would allow the same fair individuals credit for the bread returned. So that the division no sooner found its resting place for the day, than if the mills and mules worked well, appearances of business were speedily rife in the village. Some women would bring bags, some carried flour away in their aprons; at any rate, when sufficient time had elapsed, they returned laden with bread till the heap of flour in one corner of the building becoming exhausted, the corresponding mountain of bread in its other corner arrived at proper dimensions; and notice being then given to the sergeants of regiments that the full complement was ready, they attended for their daily supplies, and fetched it away.

A contrast is often pointed between the way in which the French army lived off the country while the British paid for what they took. This is true but from the viewpoint of the small producer it was a distinction without a difference. In peacetime neither Spain nor Portugal had been able to live at more than subsistence level on the produce of their own agriculture, and Portugal imported much of the food for the great cities of Lisbon and Oporto. The presence of two large and voracious foreign armies, and the dislocation of agriculture due to war and conscription, meant that there was not enough food to go round. While near the coast, the British imported much food—meat from the Barbary Coast, corn from America, hay from Ireland—but once the army was on the move and out of touch with its depots, it ate up the subsistence of the countryside around it as much as the French did. As a commissariat officer remarked:

True nothing was ever taken [by the British] except in exchange for cash and receipt notes payable by the Commissary General; but as the Spanish and Portuguese ingenuously declared, in the event of a total lack of supplies, and in the face of the quantities absorbed by the armies, they could not eat our money or our receipt notes, neither could they purchase anything with them for miles around. How were they to live?

All too often receipt notes or commissary bills had to be used instead of coin, and eventually they were all honoured; but to a smallholder on the Spanish border payment by receipt might well mean that he would have to go to Lisbon if he wanted cash quickly. Even when he reached the capital, he would probably have to wait weeks before coin was available to pay him. Usually he sold his receipts, at a considerable discount, to a dealer, one of the class Wellington described as 'our worst enemies'. 'I am certain', he wrote, 'that if our debts and the Commissariat bills had never been purchased by the *sharks* in Lisbon, our finances would be in a very much better state; those who have really supplied us with something for our money would have received more for their commodities than they have received.'

The problem was that it was impossible to obtain enough coin. Britain was the richest country in the world, but her stocks of gold were not inexhaustible. Since 1793 she had been pouring bullion into Europe to finance Pitt's grandiose coalitions and to pay for her own multifarious, if ineffective, military operations all over the world. Napoleon's Berlin Decrees and the mounting tension with the United States, culminating in the war of 1812, curbed her ability to earn sufficient to pay for the war. The Bank of England had suspended cash payments in 1797, but the example of the French *assignats* was a terrible warning of the perils of a paper currency. David Ricardo and the other fashionable economists of the day demanded an immediate return to a system based squarely on gold. In 1810 a committee of the House of Commons dominated by William Huskisson resolved that all banknotes should be withdrawn within two years. Spencer Perceval, who realised that such a step would mean the abandonment. of all Britain's overseas military operations, persuaded the House to reject the committee's report by a decisive majority. His position had been made no easier by disastrous harvests in 1808 and 1809; famine in England had only been averted by the import, under licence, of 1,500,000 quarters of wheat from, of all places, France. Naturally it had to be paid for in gold.

The Treasury employed agents, some of them of dubious honesty, to scour the world for Spanish and Portuguese dollars. A scheme was financed to sell mercury in Mexico in exchange for gold. There was found to be a glut of mercury there. In 1809 Spanish dollars to the value of £115,000 were bought in China, but when they reached Europe, they were found to be so defaced by Chinese hieroglyphs that they had to be reminted.

Perceval's efforts to find coin with which to finance Wellington's campaigns do him the greatest credit. Only two avenues did he leave unexplored. One was to put the London bullion market under government control, a step no government could believe itself justified in taking, but which allowed speculators in London to buy gold and ship it out to profitable markets overseas. The other is less explicable. He did not attempt to procure gold from Britain's Indian possessions. It was not until five months after his death that his successor wrote to Wellington to say that he had taken the 'most effectual measures in my power for obtaining a supply of specie from the East Indies, from which we have hitherto literally drawn nothing in all our distresses'. It was a supply of gold pagodas from India, reminted in London into guineas, which made the campaigns of 1813 and 1814 possible.

Matters were made no easier by the estimates submitted by Wellington's Commissary General, John Murray. In September 1809 he calculated the army's expenses at £235,000 a month. By mid-May 1810 the figure was £300,000, at the end of May £376,120, and on 6 June £421,565 5s 2d.

Part of the steep increase was due to inflation in Portugal. The presence of the army caused all prices to rise and sterling fell steadily against the Portuguese dollar. In peacetime a dollar was 4s, but by September 1809 it cost 5s2d in Lisbon. In

Battle of Rolica, by W. Heath (NAM)

March 1812 the Acting Commissary General was sharply reprimanded by the Treasury for buying 400,000 dollars in Gibraltar at 5s8d each, although the army was 5,000,000 dollars in debt and the troops two months in arrears of pay. By February 1814 'dollars cannot be had under 7/-'. Not only the farmers suffered from the shortage of coin, but the troops almost always were months in arrears. In December 1813 the army was 'Only paid up to May and the staff to April'. Even when they did get paid, they lost more than a quarter of the value when they changed it into local currency.

One currency problem Wellington did solve. When the army crossed the Pyrenees, it was vitally important that it should pay its way if it was not to raise in southern France the kind of resistance the French had raised in Spain. No French currency was avilable and the peasants would not accept Spanish coin. By means of a confidential circular to commanding officers, Wellington collected forty experienced forgers from the ranks, and working under strict supervision, they converted Spanish coin into French so skilfully that they could only be identified by a secret mark made on each.

Collecting the food for the troops was only half the Commissariat's problem. Transporting it was quite as difficult. Neither Spain nor Portugal were remarkable for the quality of their roads, and many important operations took place away from such passable roads as did exist. The commerce of both countries had, in peacetime, been largely mule-borne, and Wellington was fortunate that large numbers of muleteers, thrown out of work by the dislocation of trade that followed the French occupation, took service with the British, bringing their animals. Each muleteer was entitled to a dollar a day for himself and a dollar for each of his mules, and man and beast also received rations. Their pay, like that of the troops, was usually months in arrears. In December 1813 Wellington reported that 'Some of them are 26 months in arrears; and only yesterday I was obliged to give them bills upon the Treasury for a part of their demands, or lose their services; which bills they will, I know, sell at a depreciated rate of exchange to the *sharks* who are waiting in this town [St Jean de Luz] to take advantage of the public distress.'

The loyalty of the Spanish muleteers was one of the major factors in the allied success, but even they were not perfect. 'They do not choose to attend to the Portuguese troops. To oblige Mr Kennedy [the Commissary General] they would probably once or twice carry provisions to a Portuguese regiment, but they would prefer to quit us and attend the French to being obliged to perform this duty constantly.'

Fortunately the Peninsula had a particularly fine strain of mules. An assistant commissary wrote:

I have never seen such fine and powerful beasts. When they are on the road they are decked with numbers of bells which tinkle melodiously in the distance. If they have not got these bells, the leading mule at the head of the column has a bell, or rather a cylinder, slung round his neck, the constant clanging of which makes the rest follow. Their endurance, strength, unexacting wants and gentle pace, and the fine manner and certainty with which they climb up and down the impracticable mountain roads, in which the country abounds, are incredible. I have often travelled as many as forty five miles with them in one day, and they carry the largest loads day after day on long marches, and patiently and unwearyingly subsist on the most exiguous supplies of food and water. The muleteers form a large and hardy class of men. They seldom change their clothes or sleep in shelter throughout the year; they are constantly on the road and are very merry and constantly singing . . . They wear large black felt hats, with tassels, short jackets, a mantle, a blanket with a hole in the middle for their heads, blue plush breeches, and spats or sandals.

All the forward transport of the army (except the artillery) was done with mules. In an infantry battalion the ten company commanders, the paymaster and the surgeon all had to provide themselves with a mule (for which they received an allowance from the Treasury) for 'the carriage of the camp kettles of their companies, of their books, and of the medicine chest respectively'. In addition, the Commissariat provided each battalion with one mule to carry entrenching tools.

At brigade and divisional level there was a vast number of mules. The force of even infantry divisions and eleven regiments of cavalry that set out on the Salamanca campaign totalled 47,470 men. Its forward supply required 6,917 commissariat mules. The First Division, 7,500 men, with its battery of artillery, had 700 mules attached to it. The 4,000 men of the Light Division and their battery needed 514. Cavalry, with their vast demands for forage, needed more mules for a brigade than did a division of infantry: on the Salamanca campaign, for instance, the heavy cavalry brigade set out with 1,290 men and 1,350 horses, and their allocation of commissariat mules was 790.

Each commissariat mule carried a load of 200lb, in addition to its own rations of 30lb of fodder, which allowed it to make a three-day journey from the depot and return without eating into its 'payload'. 'Upon this calculation a mule should carry biscuit for six days for 33 men; rum for 6 days for a hundred; rice for six days for 20 men; corn for 6 days for 3 horses and 20lbs over'. This, according to one of Wellington's memoranda in November 1811, meant that the Light Division, then having a strength of 4,736, including muleteers, and assuming that it was stationed 12 leagues from the nearest depot, would require the following:

Mules to supply them with bread	144
.... with spirits	48
.... with rice &c.	24
	216
and they have 398 horses [incl bn mules] whose corn would require	116
To this add one spare for every six	55
	387

By the same calculation the division's Horse Artillery troop, with 243 men (including muleteers) and 206 horses, would need 205 mules.

Supplying the depots from the nearest navigable water was the work of a vast train of country carts each capable of carrying 1,000lb but limited by Standing Orders to 600lb. Each cart was drawn by two bullocks and:

consisted of rough planks nailed to a massive pole or shaft. At right angles to the shaft, and under the planks, two blocks of semi-rounded wood were fixed, having a hole in the centre, and through these holes the axle was fitted. It was a live axle fixed firmly to the wheels. As these axles were never greased they make such a terrible squeaking and creaking that the scratching of a knife on a pewter plate is like the sweet sound of a flute beside them . . . The draught bullocks are very large animals in this part of the world; they are also docile and fine to look upon. They are harnessed by means of a wooden yoke, which is fastened behind their horns and attached to the axle by leather straps. Moreover they are shod with a kind of iron shoe, and in this way manage to drag a load of half a ton up hill and down dale along the roughest mountain roads with the greatest ease.

Moving heavy artillery was the most testing of all transport operations. Before the siege of Ciudad Rodrigo, thirty-four twenty-four-pounders, four eighteen pounders, sixteen 5½in howitzers, eight 10in mortars and two 8in howitzers were collected at Almeida, together with 800 rounds for every gun and 400 for every mortar and howitzer. They were brought by water as far as Lamego, the highest

Battle of Busaco, by St Clair (NAM)

point to which the Douro was navigable. There 1,100 bullocks were collected. To move a twenty-four-pounder on a block carriage in fine weather over good roads needed five pairs of bullocks; in wet weather or on bad roads seven or eight pairs were required. Apart from the guns, 170 pairs of oxen were needed to move the ammunition and siege stores, and 538 mules to carry the 600 barrels of powder.

Such an operation could only be undertaken when the army was stationary and close to its depots, which must be well stocked, since the bullocks that took the stores to them had to be diverted to move the artillery. There was a great difference between the methods used to victual the army when it was stationary and when active operations were going forward. When the troops were static on the Portuguese frontier, the commissariat officers had a comparatively easy time. There was little foraging to be done, since most of the food was imported through Lisbon or raised in Portugal by contract, largely through a British-educated Portuguese merchant, Henrique Teixara de Sampaio. One observer thought Sampaio 'a sly, money-making man' and there is little doubt that he made a large unofficial fortune by discounting bills and speculating in corn. Nevertheless, his contribution to the allied victory was immense. He was a merchant on the largest scale, with commercial contacts all round the Mediterranean and in North and South America. He was also rich enough to be able to wait until the British Treasury could find the money to pay him. Thanks to his work, and to contributions from smaller contractors, the thirty-seven military depots in Portugal, from Barca de Alva in the north to Estremoz in the south, were kept replenished, so that the British army on the frontiers of Portugal, and for some distance into Spain, could manage to subsist.

When the army made its great movements, the situation changed. It was impossible to make large dumps of stores deep in French-occupied territory. Once the troops were more than 50 miles from their depots, they became dependent on local purchase, except for the slaughter cattle that marched with the columns. Even slaughter cattle became short as the war dragged on. In April 1813 Commissary General Kennedy reported to Wellington that

> . . . we had eaten nearly all the oxen in the Country, that the cultivation of the country could not go on for want of them, and that he scarcely knew where to turn for want of them, as there was this year no reserve store near Lisbon. Lord Wellington said, 'Well, then, we must now set about eating all the sheep, and when they are gone I suppose we must go.' And General Murray [Quartermaster General] added, 'Historians will say that the British army came and carried on the war in Portugal until they had eaten all the beef and mutton in the country, and were then compelled to withdraw.

Two months after that conversation the army marched out of Portugal for the last time. By the end of July they were stationed along the French frontier, having achieved a crushing victory at Vitoria and an administrative feat of unrivalled brilliance in moving an army of 106,000 men, British, Portuguese and Spanish, in a triumphant sweep across Spain from west to east without serious shortage of supplies. An infantry subaltern wrote:

> Owing to our rapid advance we have been most miserably supplied this last ten days, as our stores have not been able to keep up with us. Sometimes our men get two ounces of flour served out to them, other times ¼ pound of bread, other times raw wheat & sometimes nothing at all. Meat we have always got a tolerable supply of as we drive a good herd of oxen with us. Officers are equally bad off with the men.

On the same day a captain of Horse Artillery was writing, 'It cannot be supposed that the march of such an army could be accomplished without some privations; but they have been trifling, and have in no way injured the health, order or equipment of the army.'

The meat ration never failed. In November 1813 the Acting Commissary General said 'that 300 bullocks were killed daily, and the Commissariat department had at present about six weeks consumption at this rate. He added that the government intended in future to send out 100 oxen monthly from Ireland.' What the meat tasted like after its long march is another question. Moreover the wastage was enormous. One commissariat officer wrote from the French frontier that 'out of a consignment which I received the other day from Palencia, and which consisted, at the commencement of the march, of 500 head of cattle, only 180 reached me'. 'The Commissary General almost despairs of getting more up, although he has nade depots of bran and straw on the road to try and obviate the total want of food for the cattle].'

The worst of the Commissariat's problems should have been over when the army reached the French frontier. Wellington had arranged for his supply base to be moved from Lisbon to the northern Spanish ports. On 10 June he had sent orders for 'certain ships loaded with biscuit and flour, and certain others loaded with a heavy train of artillery and ammunition, and some musket ammunition', which were lying at Coruña, to move to Santander. If the naval commander 'should find Santander occupied by the enemy, I beg him to remain off the port until the operations of this army have obliged the enemy to abandon it'. Unfortunately the navy, torn between the demands of the American war and its own greed for prize money, failed to deliver the goods. Wellington had to complain:

> The ships which were ready in the Tagus on the 12th May had not sailed on the 19th June; and our magazines of provisions and military stores, which I expected to find at Santander, have not yet arrived. Of some kinds of ammunition we have none left; and I have been obliged to carry French ammunition of a smaller calibre than ours in our reserve. Surely the British navy cannot be so hard run as not to be able to keep up the communication with Lisbon for this army.

Meanwhile the commissaries had to do the best they could to find food for the army and its animals.

The British advance guard moving towards Pombal, 1811, by St Clair (NAM)

In 1809 the kindest thing Wellington could find to say about his supply officers was that 'The gentlemen of the Commissariat department are very new in their business, and I am not without grounds of complaint of their want of intelligence; but I believe they do their best.' At that time there were thirty-four commissioned officers on the Commissary General's staff. Commissariat clerks were being hired on the beach from among such of the troops as were able to read and write. Before the end of the war the staff included eighty-seven commissioned officers, 255 clerks and a multitude of Spanish and Portuguese assistants ranging from storekeepers and interpreters to bakers and herdsmen. Thanks to the efforts of Spencer Perceval and Willoughby Gordon, to the assiduity and intelligence of Commissary General Kennedy and the unremitting attention to detail of Wellington himself, the Commissariat had become a fully efficient body, capable of doing its all but impossible job of supplying the army in all sorts of conditions. Wellington himself, after the war, wrote: 'Much of the success of this army has been owing to its being well supplied with provisions.'

9

Making up the Numbers

On 29 April 1813 Wellington had under his direct command 75,152 rank and file in the infantry and cavalry. Of these 26,351 were Portuguese, 4,871 were German and 768 French. Thus, of the army that won the decisive victory at Vitoria, less than three men in five were natives of the British Isles.

It had been British policy since Marlborough's day to compensate for the smallness of her army by hiring foreigners, usually Brunswickers and Hessians, to make up the numbers to a point where she could compete with continental nations. Napoleon's hegemony over Europe put a stop to the business of renting battalions and brigades from German princelings, but it did not wholly stop recruiting on the continent, and it provided a stream of refugees, both officers and soldiers, who were in no sense hirelings. By 1813 one man in eight of the regular army was a foreigner.

For the most part these refugee troops went into special foreign regiments. Parliament had been sensitive about foreign troops in Britain since the days of William III and his Dutch Guards. A report made to Parliament in 1812 said that in the regiments of the line there were only thirty-one foreign officers and 393 other ranks, 'the latter being, for the most part, men of colour belonging to bands'. Most of the foreign officers were German or French but at least one was a United States citizen (as distinct from the considerable number of officers from loyalist families), and the Forty Eighth Foot had a lieutenant who was 'a native of Portugal'.

The only legal way for a foreigner to enlist in a line regiment was to join the Sixtieth (Royal American) Foot. In 1756 Parliament had authorised the creation of a regiment of up to four battalions, for service in America only, in which both officers and other ranks could be Protestant foreigners. In 1797 an amending act permitted the creation of further battalions of the Sixtieth, although the restriction of service to America (taken to mean anywhere on the far side of the Atlantic) remained, only to be frequently ignored.

The first of the new battalions to be formed, the fifth, came into existence in December 1797 on the Isle of Wight. The basis of the unit was a draft of 300 men from a German regiment in the British service, Hompesch's *Chasseurs*, together with four lieutenants and sixty men (with six wives and three children) who had enlisted from the Dutch service when Holland was overrun in 1796. The Dutch element was increased when 600 men from Löwenstein's *Jägers*, formerly part of the garrison of the Dutch West Indies, were drafted into the battalion in 1799.

The fifth battalion of the Sixtieth was, at the time of its formation, unique in the British line because it was armed with rifles and dressed in green jackets. The regimental traditions, based on the need to outfight the Indians in the forests of North America, had always stressed the need for 'cultivating the intelligence of every individual members of the corps', and this tenet was strengthened by the fifth battalion's first commanding officer, Francis, Baron Rottenburg, whose teachings and writing formed the basis of all subsequent British training of light troops.

The battalion was an admirable unit and served in the Peninsula for longer than any other. Its problem was keeping up its strength. At the moment that it landed at Mondego Bay in 1808 to cover the disembarkation of the rest of the army, a party under Lieutenant Heinrich Hoffmann was recruiting for them in French-occupied Germany. Most of the recruits had to come from deserters and prisoners-of-war from the French armies in Spain. The selection of such volunteers always presented difficulties, as it was hard to know which of them might not take the first opportunity to desert back to the enemy. No native-born Frenchmen were accepted, but 'Austro-Hungarians, together with all Germans north of the Rhine, particularly Hessians, are those upon which we can place the most dependence'. Such people were in plentiful supply, and in 1813 a depressingly named unit, 'the battalion of German Deserters', which formed part of the garrison of Cadiz, became the eighth battalion of the Sixtieth.

Until October 1811 Wellington had another British regiment which, apparently illegally, consisted largely of Germans. This was the Ninety Seventh, known until 1809 as the Queen's Germans, which had been raised in 1798 from Tyroleans (known as Swiss) in the Spanish service who formed part of the garrison of Minorca when it was captured by Sir Charles Stuart. They had originally served in the Austrian army but were captured in Italy by the French, who sold them for two dollars a head to the Spaniards. When they became a British regiment, an attempt was made to hire Austrian officers to train them, but this came to nothing. They distinguished themselves at the battle of Alexandria in 1801, and earned the title of Queen's German Infantry. They were taken into the line in 1805 as the Ninety Seventh (Queen's Germans), but the ranks became increasingly filled with British recruits, and the title was amended in 'Queen's Own' in 1809, although even at the end of the war six of their eleven captains were foreigners. The regiment fought well at Vimeiro, Douro and Talavera but, like other single battalion regiments, its strength fell steadily. By the summer of 1811 there were only 250 men in the ranks, and it was sent home to recruit with Wellington's assurance that its conduct had been 'particularly distinguished'.

The raising of specifically foreign regiments had been legalised in 1794, with the proviso that such units should not come nearer to England than the Isle of Wight. Many of them had romantic and improbable names, such as the Duke of York's Greek Light Infantry, the Royal Corsican Rangers and the Calabrian Free Corps, but only two of them served under Wellington's direct command. One of these two was the *Chasseurs Britanniques*, raised in 1801 from the remains of a French *emigré* army. The number of reliable French recruits was very small, however, and its strength had to be kept up with Italians, Croats and Poles from the prison camps. They reached Lisbon in February 1811 and struck Major Dickson of the Artillery as 'a fine body of men'. They fought well at Fuentes de Onoro, but desertion was always a problem, especially when the army came to the French frontier in 1813. At the battle of San Marcial several of them, still in their scarlet coats with light blue facings, fought on the French side, so confusing the Judge

Advocate General that he was taken prisoner. Almost all their officers were French, and they did a remarkable job in keeping the regiment together.

Wellington's other foreign regiment was the Duke of Brunswick Oels' Corps of *Jägers*, a twelve-company battalion formed from the survivors of a Brunswick corps raised to fight beside the Austrians in the war of 1809. After Wagram they fought their way through to the north coast of Germany and were evacuated by the Royal Navy.

Originally excellent fighting material, they were much diluted from the prison camps. They reached Lisbon in November 1810 and, according to a surgeon, 'Their appearance excited general astonishment. Anything so fierce I never before saw; their dress is black, and in their caps they wear a Death's Head.' They started to desert as soon as they joined the army on the Spanish frontier. On 17 January 1811 Wellington reported, 'fourteen deserted to go to the enemy; eleven were caught, one was shot while making the attempt, and only two got off. These were men who had only joined the army two days before. I find they were prisoners [of war] two days before.'

Although there was some good material in the ranks, the Brunswickers were something of a liability. Wellington commented:

The men are either very old or very young; and they are very sickly. They are very irregular in their discipline and habits. The officers are Germans who have no experience of service, (the lieutenant-colonel, who is dead, may have

Beresford unhorsing a lancer at Albuera, by W. Heath (NAM)

had), but who have all the vanity of a great deal. I am not very fastidious about troops; I have them of all sorts, sizes and nations: but Germans in our army pass for Englishmen: and it is really not creditable to be a soldier of the same nation with one of these people.

Wellington's largest body of Germans came from the King's German Legion. This was on a different footing from the other corps, since it was built on the foundations of the Hanoverian army, which, like the British, owed allegiance to George III in his capacity as Duke of Brunswick-Lüneburg. In recognition of this the KGL were allowed to serve in Britain; whereas all the other foreign corps had their depots on the Isle of Wight, the Hanoverians had theirs at Lymington and Bexhill.

The Legion had its origins in two battalions of light infantry, the King's German Regiment, whose formation was authorised in 1803 soon after the French overran Hanover. This small body was soon expanded and eventually it comprised five regiments of cavalry (three of hussars and two of dragoons), two battalions of light infantry, eight battalions of line infantry, two troops of horse and four batteries of field artillery, and a handful of engineer officers. The men were enlisted on the same terms as British soldiers, being entitled to a bounty on joining and a pension if disabled by wounds, but they had one significant advantage over the British. Although there was no restriction on the places where the rank and file could serve, 'the officers cannot be employed out of Europe'. Since it would be absurd to send units without their officers, the Hanoverians in the ranks were safe from service in the West Indies.

Although the basis of the Legion was Hanoverian and, until July 1806, the officers took their seniority from their standing in the Hanoverian army, 'All foreigners, but preferably gallant Germans, are invited to take service'. In practice the Legion was forbidden to enlist 'natives of France, Italy and Spain . . . and no British subject may be accepted', though there were a handful of British officers in the junior ranks. They could, however, take 'men of other European states, also Polish, Hungarians, Danes, Russians and Germans, who reside in this country . . . [and] Dutch nationals from the prison ships'.

The regiments, battalions and batteries of the Legion were excellent troops, counting for all purposes as British, especially after 1808, when they adopted the British drill and field exercises which, until then, they had only used for parades and guard mounting. The First Hussars of the Legion were acknowledged as being the best cavalry regiment on either side in the Peninsula, and the two dragoon regiments achieved the most notable feat of cavalry action during the war when they broke two French squares at Garcia Hernandez. The first, second and fifth line battalions fought throughout the war under Wellington, the other battalions being with him either part of the time or on the east coast. The best of the infantry, however, were the two light battalions, which saw their first action at Albuera and were later awarded the unique battle honour for Venta del Poza in October 1812. The German artillery also gave a good account of itself, perhaps in part because, being denied admission to the Royal Military Academy, the officers set up their own artillery school.

Battle of Salamanca, by J. A. Atkinson (engraved Lewis) (NAM)

The Legion had some of the recruiting problems of the other foreign corps, but it always got the first choice, after the Sixtieth, from the prison camps, and obtained some valuable men from the French Hanoverian Legion, a conscript body. Desertion was always on a modest scale and the Legion fully earned Wellington's tribute: 'It is impossible to have better soldiers than the real Hanoverians.'

The regeneration of the Portuguese army from the slough into which it had sunk by 1808 was a very remarkable feat. It had been drifting steadily downhill since 1763, when Count Wilhelm of Schaumberg-Lippe-Bückeburg had injected some semblance of life into a body that was little better than moribund. Decades of subsequent Portuguese neglect were consummated by deliberate French destruction. In 1807-8 Junot sent off the more effective parts of the army to serve in eastern Europe and disbanded the rest.

Wellington advocated raising a Portuguese army to fight beside the British on the day he first landed in Portugal: 'My opinion is that Great Britain ought to raise and pay an army in Portugal consisting of 30,000 Portuguese troops. But if you should adopt this plan, you must send everything from England—arms, ammunition, clothing, and accoutrements, ordnance, flour, oats, &c.'

This was written before he caught his first sight of such Portuguese troops as then existed. As one of his officers remarked, they were 'a miserable, undisciplined rabble', but, as it happened, no steps were taken to implement Wellington's

Battle of the Pyrenees, by W. Heath (NAM)

suggestion until Sir John Moore's expedition had ended in apparent failure at Coruña. Soon afterwards the Portuguese Regency asked to have a British general as commander-in-chief. They wanted Wellington for this post, but he was already destined for higher things, and it was agreed that he should be appointed Marshal General of Portugal and given the joint command of the British and Portuguese armies. Another officer had to be found for the immediate Portuguese command.

It was not an easy post to fill, and few of those who had seen the Portuguese troops in the Vimeiro campaign had much ambition to fill it. The man appointed had to be a good trainer of troops and a man of iron determination; junior to Wellington, who was almost the junior lieutenant-general in the army, and personally acceptable to him; and also be able to speak Portuguese, an acquirement never widespread among British generals.

The man chosen was William Carr Beresford, forty-one years old and the natural son of the first Marquess of Waterford. There was no doubt about his abilities as a trainer of troops. The Eighty Eighth Foot, the Connaught Rangers, of which he had been successively lieutenant-colonel and colonel, was one of the most efficient and strictly disciplined regiments in the army. He was also very much junior to Wellington, being the 104th major-general on the Army List, though this turned out to be something of a disadvantage, as his Portuguese rank of marshal put him above many of his British seniors, who were disposed to resent the fact. On the other hand, he was well able to work with Wellington, who said in 1810: 'It is impossible for two people to understand each other better than Beresford and I do.'

His knowledge of Portuguese was assumed from the fact that he had spent a year as governor of Madeira. He said, in fact, 'I was not very much master of the language'.

Beresford neither wanted the command nor did he see much prospect of being able to exercise it successfully. 'The choice was not left to me, and the first thing I was told was that it was not optional. From the probable state of affairs in the quarter I am bound to, it is not impossible that I shall have my voyage for my pains, and return immediately.'

Beresford's reputation has suffered from the malignant hostility of William Napier, but, apart from Wellington himself, no single man contributed more to the French defeat in the Peninsula. He was not a conciliatory man, and he drove others as hard as he drove himself. His senior ADC wrote: 'There exists not a more honourable, firm man or a more zealous patriot. His failings are mere foibles of a temperament naturally warm and hasty, and great zeal to have everything right, without much patience. Those who accuse him of severity are either those who have felt it because they deserved it, their friends, or people wilfully ignorant of the state in which he found this army.' Another officer who served under him wrote:

He is a very brave officer and with a greater share of talent than our generals probably average, and the spirit with which he embarked, and the firmness which he displayed in this nation's service cannot be too highly commended. Faults, grievous faults, it cannot be denied that he possesses, of which ungovernable temper and obstinacy are the most prominent. These are two traits which would even lead one to doubt the goodness of his heart, which on the other hand is manifested by many examples of his private kindness and unsolicited benevolence.

It needed a man of Beresford's determination to make an army out of the Portuguese rabble. On arrival in Portugal he confessed: 'The confusion and chaos in which I found everything is not to be described, nor could I have believed that human ingenuity could so perfectly have confounded everything.' When he wrote those words the only force opposing Soult's army at Oporto was described by their British commander in these unflattering terms:

The troops here consist of nearly 2,000 of the Coimbra militia and 200 students, the former in the worst possible state and never having fired a blank cartridge, but I have not 400 firelocks in what may be termed a state for service and at least 600 men included in the above number must march with pikes . . . The officers are totally incompetent to drill them to keep them in order and the consequence is that they are constantly engaged in irregularities of every kind, nor can I in the least reckon upon their exertions in the moment of action.

The Portuguese officers were the root of the problem. 'The men', wrote Beresford's ADC, 'are well enough, very obedient, willing and patient, but naturally dirty and careless of their persons, dreadfully sickly, and they have a natural softness, or want of fortitude, which makes them yield immediately,

Artillery on the march, by J. A. Atkinson (NAM)

without exertion, to sickness or fatigue. The officers, for the most part, are detestable, mean, ignorant and self-sufficient'. This was scarcely surprising, since the system by which the officers were appointed had all the worst features of the British system before the Duke of York's reforms but with some additional depravities of local derivation. Subalterns were appointed not by the Crown but by the captains of companies, who sometimes made ensigns out of their own servants and were waited upon by them at table. Promotion was exceedingly slow. In one battalion of the Fourteenth Line Regiment, 'the senior captain has served for 37 years, the first lieutenant 25, and the ensign 16'. In one of the cavalry regiments 'the three eldest cornets make up near 180 years age'.

It was not surprising that the better type of Portuguese was reluctant to join the army. As Major Le Mesurier wrote of the Fourteenth Line, 'The officers are very different from those I have been accustomed to recognise under that name: in opinions, manners and appearance the generality of our sergeants have the advantage of about two thirds, and are on a level as to birth and education.' In every battalion one subaltern's vacancy was filled by its patron saint and the money given to the church. Not that the pay was great. As Le Mesurier said, 'The pay of a lieutenant is 12 dollars a month, that of a captain about 22, and even this they are obliged to receive in paper money which loses 30%! This brings the daily pay of a lieutenant to 1/6d, that of a captain to something less than 3/0d per day! I receive the pay of a British major which is literally more than double that of my [Portuguese] colonel.'

To help him in his task of reconstruction, Beresford was allowed to have the services of a number of British officers. These came in two categories. Four majors and twenty captains were given one step in rank and held against a special establishment 'for a particular service in Portugal'. They then received an additional step in Portuguese rank, so that Havilland Le Mesurier, who had been a captain in the Twenty First Foot, found himself overnight an extra-regimental major in the British army and a lieutenant-colonel in the Portuguese. A much larger number of officers, up to 200 at a time, served in the Portuguese army at one rank higher than that they held in the British. They retained their British regimental rank while they were with the Portuguese. Both categories were entitled to pay for both their British and their Portuguese rank, but some declined to draw their Portuguese pay 'as I cannot see any credit in serving them for the pittance of pay, particularly when I know they are so poor they cannot pay their own officers'. Some British officers, however, demanded even more from their government.

Between 1809 and 1814 about 350 British officers served with the Portuguese, apart from a number of doctors. Forty were killed in action, thirteen died from other causes and two were cashiered for misconduct.

A small number of other ranks were also attached in March 1809 to help with drilling the Portuguese, most of them from the Buffs and Ninety First. The corporals and privates were soon dispensed with, because 'they have now been absent from their regiments three months [and] that time was full long enough to drill anything on which they could have been employed'. The sergeants stayed on and were joined by others, and many of them were commissioned as ensigns in the Portuguese army. Twenty-three of them were later given British commissions.

Beresford and his team set to work with skill and determination. The British drill books were translated—Dundas for the line regiments, Jarry and Rottenburg for the light troops. The troops were taught to drill to English words of command and to respond to British drum and bugle calls. Pay and rations were increased for all ranks. Every battalion and regiment was given either a British lieutenant-colonel or a British major, and at least two of their companies were commanded by British lieutenants with Portuguese ranks as captains. The Portuguese officers were forced to do their duty, and some were pensioned. In the Nineteenth Line, for example, two field officers and five captains were 'superannuated'. Richard Bourke reported that in the Fourth Line, 'The senior major at present with it is of little service in the field duties from want of practice in his younger days and his unwieldly bulk at the present.' The major was pensioned. Others, not so old but even less efficient, were unceremoniously removed. These were those

> . . . who from various motives thwarted the measures, the old men who would not submit to the new measures which gave them double trouble, officers whose principal subsistence was by defrauding the soldier which they could no longer do with impunity. Such as these raised constant intrigue and cabal in the regiments, but time and a firm military government rooted them out, and the increase in pay from England has made it so much more worth the while of officers that they are replaced by others that are both respectable, active and obedient.

Naturally there was much resentment among the Portuguese officers who found themselves superseded by foreigners of half their age. The head of the artillery, Brigadier José Antonio de Roza, during the first three months of Beresford's command, 'never has answered a single letter of application that has been made to him by the British officers, from the jealously that the old officers have evinced with respect to us'. Later, when he realised that the British did not intend to displace him, de Roza cooperated happily and effectively.

Nor were the ruffled feelings all on one side. Major-General Christopher Tilson sought to 'be allowed to return to England, if it is intended to employ his services again in cooperation with the Portuguese troops.' Two of Beresford's British lieutenant-colonels returned to England without the formality of asking for leave.

The worst of Beresford's handicaps was the attitude of the Portuguese government. Despite the fact that this makeshift body was kept going by a British subsidy from Britain which, by 1811, amounted to £2,000,000 a year, their cooperation and zeal varied in direct proportion to the danger to Lisbon. In particular they could never be cajoled into establishing a workable supply system, knowing that, if ever the situation became desperate, Wellington would feed the Portuguese soldiers from British sources rather than see them become ineffective from starvation.

In the early days Beresford was also hampered by a disagreement with Wellington who believed that the British officers should be used as advisers to the Portuguese rather than serving in the regiments. Nor did he believe that British officers would serve with the Portuguese without the bribe of a step in British rank.

Wellington was wrong on both counts. There was never a shortage of good officers prepared to serve under Beresford and, since the Portuguese army had to be prepared for the field in a short time, it was essential to have British officers in the regiments. Beresford explained that:

If we had regard only to the discipline (field) of these troops and [if] we had sufficient leisure to proceed regularly on that; that is, if we could remain undisturbed twelve or eighteen months, then a general superintendence might suffice; but, unfortunately, we have more to do than make good; we have had, and yet have, to correct bad habits of every description; and nothing but British officers being incorporated in their regiments would enable me to get the better of it.

Wellington was not long in realising that Beresford was right, and gave him his fullest support.

At full strength the Portuguese regular army consisted of twenty-four regiments of infantry of the line, each comprising two battalions of 700 rank and file each. There were also eight, later twelve, battalions of *cacadores* (light infantry), a proportion of whom were armed with rifles. There were twelve regiments of dragoons and four regiments of artillery. Every infantry unit was in battle at one time or another and, when Wellington invaded France in 1813, he was accompanied by all the infantry except three line battalions and one battalion of *caçadores*, which were left in garrison in Portugal.

The cavalry was never reliable. On occasions units met the French on equal terms; on others they showed themselves 'worse than useless'. The artillery, by contrast, was excellent, particularly at El Bodon in September 1811 when the gunners fought their guns until they were cut down by French horsemen.

Wellington started with a poor opinion of the Portuguese army. In May 1809 he wrote to Beresford: 'Your troops made but a bad figure this morning at the review. The battalions very weak, the body of men very bad; and the officers worse than anything I have ever seen.' By the end of the year he was prepared to recommend that, if it became necessary for the British to evacuate Portugal, 'Government ought to endeavour to bring off as large a proportion of the Portuguese army as possible, which is becoming so good as to be worth the expense of removing them.'

The first real test came at Busaco in September 1810 when, for the first time, Beresford's men were committed to a major action. A sapper officer wrote: 'The Portuguese astonished us by their coolness and bravery, more particularly the *caçadores*.' Three years later, after Vitoria, General Picton, a harsh judge of troops, wrote: 'There was no difference between the British and the Portuguese, they were equal in their exertions and deserving of an equal portion of the laurel.' At the same time Wellington made the characteristic comment that 'I believe we owe their merits more to the care we have taken of their pockets and bellies than to the instruction we have given them.' He added that 'no troops could behave better; that they never now had a notion of turning; and that nothing could equal their forwardness and ready willing tempers.'

The French could never have been driven out of the Peninsula unless an efficient Portuguese army had been fashioned to fight alongside the British. That army could not have been created without the guidance, skill and determination of Beresford. Wellington paid many compliments to the Portuguese army and its commander but the highest came after the Peninsula had been cleared of the French. Before he left Vienna to take up the command in the Netherlands during the Hundred Days, he wrote to Beresford and asked him to come to Belgium and bring 12,000 or 14,000 Portuguese soldiers to take part in the final campaign against Napoleon.

10

Medical and Spiritual Comfort

The organisation of the army's medical services was quite as complex as that which controlled the army as a whole. On the one hand was the Medical Board consisting of the Physician General, the Surgeon General and the Inspector General of Hospitals. These three dignitaries, who had large private practices, were not under military discipline and when, in 1809, the Physician General was asked to go to Walcheren to investigate the epidemic which was decimating the army there he declined on the ground that 'he was not acquainted with the diseases of soldiers in camp and quarters'. The Board was replaced and a Director General appointed. The Duke of York, who had no say in his appointment, described him as 'an old driveller'.

The function of the Board was the provision of medical officers. This they did with the greatest indolence. Wellington had constantly to complain 'how much we are in want of medical assistance. This arises chiefly from the practice of waiting till the last moment to send out the officers required from the Medical Board. The returns go to them regularly, but for what purpose it is difficult to say.'

Medical supply was not subject to the Board but came under two separate functionaries — the Purveyor General, who provided all non-medical supplies for hospitals, and the Apothecary General, who supplied all drugs, dressings and, for hospitals, surgical instruments. The latter office had been made hereditary in 1747 by a warrant from King George II.

At the working level, medical officers fell into two categories — those who staffed hospitals and those attached to regiments. In the first category were Inspectors of Hospitals, Deputy Inspectors, Physicians, Staff Surgeons, Purveyors and Apothecaries. Regimental medical officers, who had to provide their own surgical instruments, were either Surgeons (ranking as captains) or Assistant Surgeons (ranking as lieutenants). Each battalion had one surgeon and two assistant surgeons.

Before the war regimental medical appointments had been in the colonel's gift and frequently went by purchase. The war brought a shortage of surgeons and wrote Dr McGrigor, 'it was found absolutely necessary to advertise for them . . . offering commissions to such as could pass some kind of an examination. It was the occasion of many uneducated and unqualified persons being introduced into the service . . . Not a few apothecaries and even druggists apprentices found their way into the service in this manner.' In 1811 Walter Henry found himself gazetted an assistant surgeon after a training which, in his own words, consisted of passing 'a winter in Dublin [and] a year in London, where I became the pupil of Sir Everard Home. I cannot say that I derived much instruction from the lessons of a man so distinguished or much improvement from witnessing his practice.'

In the earlier days of the Peninsular War the hospitals were far from satisfactory. Lieutenant Hall, who was at the hospital station of Celorico in the winter of 1811, wrote: 'Two patients occupied each bed, and when one died, another was brought in to fill his place and share, in mind as well as body, the infection of his disease. Another evil, even more fatal, arose from the ignorance of the medical staff. There were doubtless at the head of the department men both skilled and conscientious, but amid such pressure of duty, they could do little more than give a very general inspection to the several hospitals, while the detail of management fell upon the Hospital Mates, many of whom were grossly inattentive and ignorant of the first rudiments of their profession.' Sergeant Cooper left an account of the hospitals he was in at various times:

> The hospital at Olivenza was a long low room, with another at right angles to it; the ventilation bad, many deaths daily.
>
> The hospital at Vila Vicosa was in a convent; about 150 patients in four corridors; next to no ventilation; small windows; great tubs or barrels for all purposes; the stench horrible; logs of burning fir at the four corners of the building to drive away the infection; smoke blinding.
>
> The hospital at Elvas, a long bomb-proof room; no ventilation, except by the door and chimney; twenty patients of whom eighteen died.
>
> The hospital at Celorico — two small rooms, crowded with sick; no ventilation; no chamber utensil; the patients nearly all delirious.

In these conditions the surgeons preferred not to operate if it could be avoided since gangrene was all but inevitable. In 1810 Harry Smith of the Rifles who, for five months, had been doing duty with a musket ball embedded in the Achilles tendon was sent before a medical board near Lisbon. Two of the three doctors advised 'me to remain with a stiff leg of my own as better than a wooden one, for the wounds in Lisbon had sloughed so of late and they were dubious of the result'. The third doctor thought the risk worth while and Smith agreed with him. 'Very well', said the surgeon, 'if you are desirous we will do it directly.' 'It was,' said Smith, five minutes, most painful indeed, before it was extracted. The ball was jagged and the tendonous fibres had grown into it. It was half dissected and half torn out, with the most excruciating torture for a moment, the forceps breaking which had hold of the ball . . . My leg was aching and smoking from a wound four or five inches long.'

When Marshal Beresford was wounded at Salamanca, his surgeon remembered how he found him:

> lying on his back dressed in a blue frock coat with a white waistcoat. Just below the left breast was a star of blood, bright and defined as a star of knighthood. It was about the size of that chivalrous decoration, and occupied the exact spot where it is usually fixed. There was a small rent in its centre, black and round. The eyes were half closed; the countenance in perfect repose, perhaps a little paler than when I had last seen it. In an instant the marshal's dress was torn open, and my forefinger, that best of probes, was deep in his side. Not a muscle

moved, not a sound was uttered. I felt the rib, smooth and resisting below, while the track of the bullet led downward and backwards, round the cavity of his ample chest. I now spoke for the first time, and said, 'General, your wound is not mortal.' This observation of mine seemed to have been heard with perfect indifference; for without taking the slightest notice, he looked up and asked, 'How does the day go?' 'Well,' I replied, 'the enemy has begun to give way.' 'Hah!' rejoined the marshal, 'it has been a bloody day.' I proceeded to cut out the bullet. My knife was already buried deep in the flesh, its point grating against the lead, when the marshal, feeling I had ceased to cut, and calcu- lating, perhaps, that my steadiness as an operator might be influenced by the rank of my patient, again turned round and with as much *sangfroid* as if he had been merely a spectator, said in an encouraging tone, 'Cut boldly, doctor; I never fainted in my life:' almost at the same moment I placed the bullet in his hand.

Transporting the wounded was a difficult and agonising business. Captain Neil Douglas, who was shot in the shoulder at Busaco, was lucky enough to be taken aboard one of the army's few spring waggons. Even on that 'Of all I ever experienced, the jolting of that conveyance was the most painful. A thousand times I was inclined to come out, and lay down by the roadside but every now and then we came upon soft spots, which I always flattered myself would continue.' Less fortunate sick and wounded had to suffer long journeys lying on the rough planking of the unsprung commissariat waggons with their screaming axles. When Lieutenant George Simmons 'received a ball which broke two ribs near the backbone, went through my liver and lodged in my breast', the ball was extracted on the battlefield and he was then hoisted on to a horse. 'I had to ride twelve miles. The motion of the horse made the blood pump out, and the bones cut the flesh to a jelly.'

Medical science was in a primitive state and even the best of the doctors acknowledged that there was, in many cases, little that they could do. After working among the wounded at Vimeiro, Dr Adam Neale wrote that 'To several, a simple inspection of their wounds, with a few words of consolation, or perhaps a little opium, was all that could be recommended. Of these brave men the balls had pierced organs connected with life; and in such cases, prudence equally forbids the rash interposition of unavailing art, and the useless indulgence of delusive hope.'

For most diseases the treatment was frankly experimental. A regimental surgeon who suffered from 'Guadiana fever, a bad remittant and intermittant fever', probably malaria, described his treatment by a colleague who, 'from a desire to save the vital fluid and economize strength, would not bleed me as I wished; but when the determination to the head became urgent, he sheared and shaved my curly locks one hot afternoon and attached three dozen leeches to my poor caput. A few hours afterwards, they carried me into the yard, placed me erect, and poured four or five and twenty buckets of cold well-water over me from a third storey window. After this terrible shower-bath, I was rubbed dry and put to bed. All was cold and numb above my shoulders—but there was a violent reaction during the night, and I became delirious next morning.' More agreeable and no less efficacious was the treatment given to Captain Schoedde of the Sixtieth. He recovered on a regimen prescribed by an old Portuguese army doctor of 'the best of living and at least two bottles of Madeira *per diem*.' Schoedde lived until the age of seventy five.

Bleeding was the great cure-all. One officer was saved from pneumonia by 'the surgeon taking in twenty four hours one hundred and sixty ounces of blood.' From Major Goldie, who was 'desperately wounded by a musket ball through the lungs' they took three hundred ounces of blood in two days and he lived for many years with the ball still in his chest.

Unusual cases had to be treated pragmatically. At Fuente Maestro a battalion of troops, tired from a long hot march, drank from an old fountain. 'Next morning about a hundred and fifty came to the various regimental hospitals, and at first their cases looked rather alarming, for they were all spitting blood. On examination it was found that they had fished up three or four hundred leeches from the old fountain. These blood suckers had attached themselves in the mouth, throat, nostrils, gullet and even the stomach . . . We had a very bloody day in the hospitals, although no lives were lost, except the leeches, and very hard it was to eject them. Some were noosed with a silk ligature by the tail and torn off, though many were cut in two, leaving the tail still sticking. Several were dislodged by a strong solution of salt, and tobacco was used to others. Powerful emetics were necessary to oust the knowing ones which had reached the citadel of the stomach.'

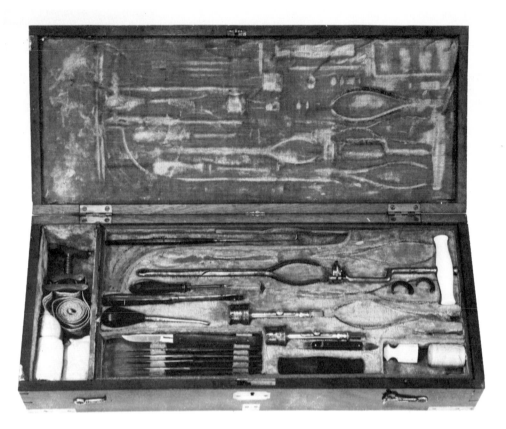

Instrument case of 21st Light Dragoons (R.A.M.C. Museum, Millbank)

A great change for the better came over the medical department in the Peninsula when it came, in 1812, to be led by James McGrigor, a great doctor and one of the few men in whom Wellington had absolute confidence. The kindliest of men, McGrigor was a terror to medical men who failed in conscientiousness and he turned a searching eye into every nook and cranny of the hospital stations. His greatest contribution to the health and comfort of the sick and wounded was when he persuaded Wellington to adopt portable hospitals to accompany the army on the march. These prefabricated wooden buildings, shipped out from England, greatly reduced the distance patients had to travel before receiving any but emergency treatment and allowed them to recover in more salubrious conditions that the convents and bomb-proofs described by Sergeant Cooper. This reform must have saved hundreds, if not thousands of lives, and had the additional advantage of making it possible to disperse the great concentration of convalescents and malingerers at Belem, on the outskirts of Lisbon.

When the French war broke out in 1793 there was a chaplain on the strength of every regiment. His pay was 6s8d a day, even less than an assistant surgeon. Being a chaplain did not entail attendance on the troops. The Rev Peter Vataas of the Fourteenth Light Dragoons had been on leave for 52 years when his post was abolished in 1796. The business of reading the weekly service to the soldiers was carried on by penurious curates who were glad to do the job for half a crown a week. When the army went to the Netherlands in 1793, only one chaplain, the Rev John Gamble, could be induced to accompany the troops. In 1795 none could be found to serve with Abercromby's force in the West Indies.

The Duke of York set about remedying this situation as soon as he became Commander-in-Chief. In 1796 he established the Army Chaplains' Department and made John Gamble Chaplain General at a salary of £1 a day, soon raised to £565 a year. Gamble was a man of many parts and also received £600 a year to advise the army on the establishment of telegraphy (semaphore).

A circular was sent to all chaplains offering them the choice of attending to their duties in person with pay of 10s a day or of retiring on a pension of 4s a day. All but two chaplains, those of the Life Guards, chose the pension. Few new chaplains came forward until regimental chaplains were abolished and, in 1808, the pay was raised to 16s a day, the same as a major of infantry. Even so no chaplains landed with Wellesley in Portugal in 1808 although two came ashore on the day after the battle of Vimeiro. Five marched with Moore to Coruña and it was one of them, the Rev H. J. Symons, chaplain to the Guards brigade, who read the 'few and short' prayers over Moore's grave. The ceremony was hasty because, in Symons's words, 'it was now daylight. The enemy immediately opened fire on the ships in the harbour, and the funeral service was, therefore, performed without delay as they were exposed to the fire of the guns.'

Throughout the Peninsular campaigns, chaplains were in short supply and those that did appear were not always of the best quality. A notable exception was John Owen until he went home to succeed Gamble as Chaplain General in 1810. When a guardsman warned him that, if he insisted on moving with the forward troops, he would certainly be killed, Owen replied, 'My primary duty is to those now departing this life.' On the other hand, there was Mr Heyward, the chaplain at

Cadiz, whose hypochondria was a joke throughout the army. Not that he was without his own sense of humour. When General Graham arrived late for morning service, he asked to have the sermon repeated. Heyward, unruffled, complied and, when asked if he had not thought the repetition a bore, replied, 'Indeed, sir, you quite mistake my thoughts; few divines have enjoyed like myself, the satisfaction of having their sermons encored.'

Unfortunately many of the chaplains resembled the one who preached to the Light Division in 1811.

He might have been a good man, but he was not prepossessing, either in his manners or his appearance. I remember, the first Sunday of his arrival, the troops were paraded for Divine Service, and had been some time waiting in square, when at last he rode into the centre of it, with his tall ungainly figure mounted on a starved, untrimmed, unfurnished horse, and followed by a Portuguese boy, with his canonicals and prayer books on the back of a mule with a hay bridle, and having by way of clothing about half a pair of straw breeches. This spiritual comforter was the least calculated of any that I ever saw to excite devotion in the minds of men who had seen nothing in the shape of a divine for a year or two.

Wellington was distressed by the shortage of clergymen, complaining that 'we do not get respectable men in the service. I have an excellent young man with the army, Mr Briscall, who is attached to headquarters, who has never been a moment absent from his duty; but I have never seen another who has not applied, and made a pitiable case for, leave of absence, immediately upon his arrival; and excepting Mr Denis at Lisbon, who was absent all last year, I believe Mr Briscall is the only chaplain doing duty.'

Samuel Briscall, the son of a Stockport surgeon, was a Fellow of Brasenose who became a chaplain to the forces in 1808. He landed in Portugal five days after Vimeiro completely unaccustomed to the military life. 'My second night, we had thunder and lightning with torrents of rain. I and my poor blanket were in a completely soaked condition, but I suffered nothing. In this state I have done nothing but read prayers to the wounded, for Sunday is as much a marching day as any other.' Even his arrival in Lisbon was not the end of Briscall's troubles. 'The odious custom in Lisbon of turning out into the street for a certain necessary purpose has been of serious consequence to me, for in my great bustle and confusion I made use of some paper in which I had wrapped a £20 note and the note is lost to me, I suppose for ever.' Despite this, 'I have had very good health, the scene is tolerably agreeable and I have the opportunity of seeing the country and gaining useful information at an expense which is perfectly covered by my salary . . . My employment', he wrote some months later, 'is as usual, duty to the troops, attendance on the sick and wounded and on criminals; two were executed yesterday and still hang by the roadside as a warning against plunder to the army as it passes by . . . We ought to be six chaplains in this part of the army, but most of these momentous duties fall to my share somehow.'

When Briscall fell sick and had to spend a year in England, Wellington again tried to persuade London to send out more 'respectable and efficient clergymen'.

It has come to my knowledge that methodism is spreading very fast in the army. There are two, if not three, methodist meetings in this town, of which one is in the Guards. The men meet in the evening and sing psalms: and I believe a sergeant now and then gives them a sermon . . . The meeting of soldiers in their cantonments is, in the abstract, perfectly innocent; and it is a better way of spending their time than many others to which they are addicted; but it may become otherwise; and yet until the abuse has made some progress, the commanding officer would have no knowledge of it, nor could he interfere. Even at last, interference must be guided by discretion, otherwise he may do more harm than good; and it can in no case be so effectual as that of a respectable clergyman.

Briscall returned to the army late in 1813 and conducted his first service in the village of Vera on the Bidassoa. Larpent wrote:

We were in the newly repaired public town room which had just been made water and wind-tight for a hospital. It was washed, Dr McGrigor told me, for those [wounded] soon expected. I believe he wished not a little that we had gone somewhere else to pray and not made dirt in his department. The service was short, plainly read, but tolerably well; the sermon homely and familiar, but good for the troops, I think but very fair and useful for anyone.

Wellington had a high opinion of Briscall and, on 19 January 1814, appointed him his domestic chaplain. He did not, however, believe in having too much of a good thing. According to a Guards officer, 'Lord Wellington was very regular in attending Divine Service but always limited the time of its duration, saying to the chaplain, "Briscall, say as much as you like in five and twenty minutes, I shall not stay longer."'

11

Headquarters

Before considering how Wellington and his generals exercised their commands, it is important to remember the limitations under which they and their staffs worked. One of the most serious handicaps was the absence of reliable maps. A start had been made with producing accurate maps of England, but it was a very small start. The Royal Engineers had begun with a survey at an inch to the mile of Sussex, but when it was complete, the government refused to find the funds to print it and it was published commercially in 1795. Before 1809 the maps of Kent and Essex had been published and the survey of Hampshire was almost complete. The rest of Britain was not accurately mapped.

Naturally the situation was worse for overseas operations. In 1808 the army landed in a part of Portugal of which they had no map. For the day on which Vimeiro was fought, Wellington had issued orders for an advance to Mafra. He later gave two reasons for this: 'By this movement the enemy's position at Torres Vedras would have been turned, and I should have brought the army into a country of which I had an excellent map and topographical accounts . . . and the battle, which it was evident would be fought in a few days, would have had for its field a country of which we had a knowledge.' Moore's campaign in the same year was largely dictated in its early stages by the absence of maps and the fact that no one in Portugal could give him accurate information of whether the Lisbon-Coimbra-Almeida road was passable for artillery.

The problem repeated itself when Wellington marched into Spain. Just before the Talavera campaign he wrote to the British Minister at Seville: 'I shall be very much obliged to you if you will send me any topographical or geographical information respecting Spain which can be produced. I particularly wish to have two copies of Lopez' map.' Lopez' map was the great standby of both sides. It was reasonably accurate for Spain, but its representation of Portugal drew largely on the cartographer's imagination, a fact that caused Massena untold trouble on his advance to Busaco. By 1810 a British map of the Peninsula on four large sheets had been published by William Faden, mapseller of Charing Cross. The scale was 14 miles to the inch and, although it was a great improvement on Lopez, General Graham remarked that it 'deserves to be burned by the public hangman'.

The whole business repeated itself when the army approached the French frontier. In August 1813 Wellington wrote to the Secretary for War,

I write to Mr Smith [probably his brother-in-law, Charles Culling Smith] by this occasion to beg him to buy me Cassini's map of France, and likewise a map which it is said he has published of the Pyrenees. As I understand these maps are very scarce, I shall be obliged to your lordship if you will assist him with the influence of government, as it is very desirable that I should have them. [One copy arrived from the Secretary of State's office a month later but it was] of a shape that I cannot conveniently carry, as we have no wheeled carriages with the army, except the artillery. I have therefore had cut out the sheets, of which I enclose the numbers, containing the country immediately upon my front, which I have had pasted upon linen by the Staff Corps, and made to fold up to the size enclosed. I shall be obliged if you will have the others done accordingly to the same size.

A second handicap was the difficulty of communication. Every order or letter had to be written in longhand with a quill, which had to be sharpened with a penknife at frequent intervals. Then, unless it was of minimal importance, it had to be copied laboriously by the Military Secretary or an ADC. Occasionally a pass-order, an order that was passed from one recipient to the next, was used, but normally as many copies had to be made as there were addressees. Once completed, an order could not travel faster than the pace of a horse. According to the Prussian General Müffling, Wellington's ADCs were 'mounted on the best horses of England's famous breeds and made it a point of honour, whenever the Duke added "*Quick*" to a message, to ride twelve miles in the hour or four miles in eighteen minutes.' Such speeds could only be maintained for short distances, and only urgent and important messages were entrusted to ADCs. Routine correspondence was carried by letter parties, by the Corps of Guides or by civilian mails.

Letter parties were detachments consisting of an NCO and half a dozen dragoons, who were stationed at intervals on the roads between the various large portions of the army. The distance between those parties was determined by the distance a horse could conveniently travel. Such a chain of parties was established almost permanently for a year after April 1811 when the main body of the army lay opposite Ciudad Rodrigo, with headquarters at Freneda, while Hill's corps watched Badajoz, with headquarters at Portalegre. The distance between the two command posts was about 120 miles and letters took about 48 hours to cover the distance. This military postal service had regular times of departure and arrival each day but, as Wellington remarked later in the war, 'I have never yet seem communications by letter parties upon which any reliance whatever could be placed'.

Letters to addressees off the regular routes were carried by members of the Corps of Guides, a locally raised corps consisting of Portuguese with a sprinkling of Italian deserters from Junot's army in 1808. By the time the army finally left Portugal in the spring of 1813 the corps consisted of two troops, each having a captain, six other officers, a sergeant-major, sixteen NCOs, seventy-five troopers, a trumpeter and three farriers.

Behind the lines all mail not important enough to be carried by an ADC was sent by the Portuguese civilian mail. The Portuguese Post Office was a lethargic body that had to be subsidised from British funds in order to provide a basic service up to the frontiers of the kingdom. Portuguese mail went at a mule's pace, about 50 miles a day. When Wellington was at Celorico, about 200 miles from the capital, he wrote that, 'the communication is so slow that a reference to me [from Lisbon] must take eight days'.

All these methods of transmission were subject to natural hazards. A bad storm could bring all movement to a halt, flooding gullies and washing away bridges. Horses and their riders were liable to fail. In May 1809 the lieutenant-colonel of the Fifty Third wrote: 'We did not march on the morning of the 12th till 8 o'clock, owing to the horse of the officer sent with the order having fallen lame.' This was a minor mishap compared to the chaos caused on the retreat to Coruña, when General Baird entrusted an order to a dragoon who got drunk and lost it. As a result General Fraser's division had 48 hours' unnecessary marching in appalling weather.

Communications with England were erratic. An average voyage to Lisbon from England was a fortnight but it could take eight weeks and one officer got from Plymouth to Freneda on the Spanish border of Portugal in seven and a half days. While this left Wellington free from detailed interference from London, he was dependent on the sea-voyage for all his munitions, much of his food and much of his information about the French. He could never tell when reinforcements would arrive. The Fifty First embarked at Spithead on 22 January 1811. They did not reach Lisbon until 9 March having 'been obliged to put back into Torbay six different times before we could weather Cape Finister [sic]'. Seven weeks cooped up in a transport was bad for the health of the troops and worse for the horses.

The difficulties with maps and communications were common to both the contending armies. The French found communications even more difficult than the British. Wellington's couriers could ride alone; their French opposite numbers had to be heavily escorted, owing to the activities of the guerillas. The British had a unique disadvantage — an almost total absence of trained staff officers. Apart from a handful of senior officers in London and the major garrisons overseas, there were, in the whole British army only ten full-time staff officers. These were the Permanent Assistants in the Quartermaster General's Department — three lieutenant-colonels and seven majors — none of whom served in the QMG's Department. In 1813 four of them were with Wellington, while the other six were engaged in doubtless vital tasks at Lichfield, Edinburgh, Plymouth, Colchester, Portsmouth and Brighton.

All other staff officers were 'effectives in regiments' and the rule was that the staff in any theatre had to be furnished from the units serving there. Despite occasional exceptions to this rule, it was a heavy drain on battalions which were usually short of officers in any case through casualties, sickness and postings. One AQMG was recalled to London in 1812 and Wellington had to make a special appeal to the Horse Guards, writing 'General Hill has informed me that he shall feel the greatest inconvenience from the want of the assistance of Colonel Jackson, and I certainly don't know where I shall find an officer qualified to replace him in that situation. It might not be difficult to find one to replace him as a mounted officer in the Coldstream Guards.' According to the Regulations 'No regiment of cavalry or battalion of infantry shall be required to furnish more than two captains and two subalterns for staff situations' but in November 1812 the single battalion Sixth West India Regiment had four captains and three subalterns on the staff and the First Guards, with three battalions, had nineteen officers (captains and below) in staff situations.

There had been a Staff College, properly called the Senior Department of the

Baggage on the march, by St Clair (NAM)

Royal Military College, in Britain since 1799. The syllabus embraced 'mathematics, fortification, castramentation, military topography, reconnoisance [sic] of ground, disposition and movement of troops under different circumstances of offensive and defensive warfare, French and German, &c., military surveying.' The department could accommodate thirty students, but it was rare for all the vacancies to be filled, perhaps because the student had to pay a fee of 20 (later 30) guineas in advance. He also had to provide his own subsistence during the course although forage was provided for his horse. Until 1806 the principal lectures were in French.

Of the eighty one officers who, at one time or another, served in the QMG's department in the Peninsula, only thirty-five had been to the College. One who served in the AG's department had also been there.

The military staff of any general's command consisted of two branches—those presided over by the Adjutant General and Quartermaster General. In addition, every general commanding an independent force or garrison had a Military Secretary, who was usually also his senior aide-de-camp.

According to the Regulations, the responsibilities of the AG were 'The arming and clothing of the troops, leave of absence, the discharging or transfering of soldiers, the appointment or removal of general officers to or from the staff, military regulations, the drafting, casting, &c. of horses in regiments of cavalry and all subjects connected with the discipline, equipment and efficiency of the army.'

136

The QMG was responsible for 'routes, camp equipage and other requisites for cantoning and encamping the troops, also all [matters] relating to quarters, marches, camps, plans and dispositions for defence; likewise embarking and general conveyance of troops.'

The most noticeable omission from these two definitions of function is that there is no provision for the duties of what would now be described as the 'general' or operations staff. Nor was the collection and analysis of intelligence allocated to either department, although the AG usually laid claim to it on the grounds that the guarding of prisoners of war came under his disciplinary duties.

In practice Wellington divided the operational functions between the two departments, but kept the control of them firmly in his own hands. The lion's share fell to the QMG, which was logical, since his department was responsible for all movements of troops, although by tradition the AG was the more important of the two officers. The main reason for favouring the QMG was, however, that George Murray, who, with one break of a year, was QMG from 1809 to 1814, was a more reliable staff officer than Charles Stewart, AG until 1812.

As a result the AG's office became very much a matter of routine. When Edward Pakenham took over the post, he referred to it as 'this insignificant clerking business', and slipped away to command troops whenever possible. Stewart, although ready to command cavalry at the slightest provocation, fought for the rights, as he understood them, of his office. When Dr McGrigor arrived at headquarters to take over the medical department, Stewart tried to pre-empt his right of access to Wellington. Seeing McGrigor approach the office door, he told him 'that it was unnecessary for me to come to Lord Wellington, that I might come his [AG's] office and he would transact my business for me with his lordship, whom it was unnecessary to trouble.' Fortunately, Wellington appeared at his door and told McGrigor to come in.

Stewart was a brave but vain man with a liking for intrigue. Castlereagh, who was his half-brother, had 'a real respect for his understanding and a high opinion of his good sense and discretion', but it is hard to believe that he was very intelligent. He was even prepared to argue the supposed rights of his department with Wellington himself. In Wellington's words,

It happened one day that some prisoners were taken, and my aide-de-camp, happening to be on the spot, examined them immediately and brought me the result. In consequence of this Stewart refused to execute the rest of his duty as to these prisoners, and declined to take any charge or care of them whatsoever; and he left them to escape or starve as far as his department was concerned. This was too much; so I sent for him into my room. We had a long wrangle, for I like to convince people rather than stand on mere authority; but I found him full of the pretensions of this department of his, although he and it and all of them were under my orders and at my disposition. It was in vain that I showed him than an accidental interference under emergent circumstances with what was ordinarily his duty could not be considered as an affront to him. At last I was obliged to say that, if he did not at once confess his error, and promise to obey my orders frankly and cordially, I

137

would dismiss him instanter, and send him back to England in arrest. After a good deal of persuasion, he burst out crying, begged my pardon, and hoped I would excuse his intemperance.

Stewart's 'pretentions' may have been the result of his conviction that he was a great commander *manqué*. His opposite number, George Murray, had no such illusions. 'He was,' said Wellington, 'an excellent subordinate officer, but not fit to be trusted with a great command. His defect was the not being able to form troops *upon the ground*. He could form them very well on paper, but he had not practice enough in the other way. He had served too much upon the staff, and he was conscious of it himself.' Murray's strategic judgement was suspect, but he was a superb staff officer and Wellington could rely on him to see that his plans were translated into flawless orders.

A graduate of the Staff College, Murray was a keen geographer and, after his appointment to serve under Wellington in 1809, his first care was to set in motion a systematic survey of Portugal. Every road, every bridge, every ford, every possible defensive position the army might need was reconnoitred and its particulars noted for future reference.

Murray sent out sketching officers throughout central Portugal. They worked behind, and in front of, the army's position, amassing the details needed to ensure the smoothest possible marches for the troops in any manoeuvre that might become necessary. Their instructions were

. . . to observe the general features of the country through which they pass, whether hilly, level, wooded, open or enclosed, the state and breadth of the roads, whether they are practicable for artillery, their bearings by compass, and the passes and positions in the route. Such parts of the country as may be sufficiently open and level to enable cavalry to act with advantage should be remarked. The rivers should be particularly attended to, their breadth and depth at the time of passing them, and (as far as can be ascertained by enquiry) their state at other seasons of the year should be noted. The bridges, whether of wood or stone, their length and breadth and whether capable of bearing artillery, or if they could easily be made so, should be mentioned. An opinion should be formed of the population of the towns and villages, their distance from each other, and their means of supplying cantonments, provisions, water and fuel. The situations favourable for encampments should be observed and whether water, fuel and materials for hutting are near them. The probability of obtaining mules or draft oxen and carts on the roads should be considered as intimately connected with the movements of troops in this country. In general, whatever can facilitate or retard the march of the army must be carefully attended to, and the whole digested into a written report, accompanied by such sketches as circumstances may admit of. [For such positions as might be of significance at some future date, the officer] will make a sketch of the ground upon a scale of 3 inches to the mile, accompanied by explanatory references.

By the end of 1810 headquarters had an accurate map of the whole of central Portugal at a scale of a ¼in to the mile. This gave Wellington an incomparable advantage over Massena, who had to rely on Lopez' maps, eked out by information from Portuguese traitors who were as ignorant of their country's topography as were their loyal compatriots.

In front of the 'sketching officers', in front of the cavalry patrols which probed towards the French lines, were the 'observing officers', who rode deep into enemy-held territory alone or with a handful of Spanish companions. Their task was to discover where the French troops were and what they were likely to do next. The most famous of these was Major Colquhoun Grant, the story of whose capture and escape reads like a thriller. Another was Lieutenant Andrew Leith Hay. Not content with penetrating into King Joseph's realm as far as Toledo in March 1813 and sending back valuable information, he set up his own news service to let the Spaniards know how the war was going. He wrote a proclamation, had it translated and printed.

Thousands of copies were put into immediate circulation. They were read with avidity; and to prevent the possibility of a doubt as to the author, I despatched copies in my own name to General Maransin, General Laval at Madrid, and to the headquarters of the [French] Army of the South. So important did General Maransin consider the removal of the impression produced by the circulation of this document that he published an answer to it . . . Having received the proclamation of General Maransin, and affixed a reply to several copies, dated from the heights [on the other side of the Tagus], I prevailed upon a Spaniard to place them on the gates of Toledo . . . This mode of life was extremely interesting. The constant sight of, and almost communication with, the enemy, produced excitement; while the fact of an officer, removed one hundred and fifty miles from the nearest troops of his country, being enabled to continue in safety close to the quarters of an enemy's army for months, proved the current of popular opinion to be decidedly in favour of the cause of which he was the partisan.

The support of the inhabitants was the key to the success of Wellington's intelligence system. No one could be braver than the 'observing officers', but they could have achieved little without the active and consistent support of the Portuguese and Spaniards. Throughout the occupied parts of the Peninsula, in every town and most villages, there were 'correspondents', men who reported every movement made by the French, counting the files as battalions or detachments marched through towns and identifying the regiments. These were the bravest and most valuable of all the patriotic Spaniards, who made it possible for Wellington to build up a detailed order of battle for the enemy's army and to anticipate their next move. Of all these 'correspondents' none was more distinguished than Dr Patrick Curtis, Rector of the Irish College at Salamanca. William Tomkinson, Sixteenth Light Dragoons, who occasionally acted as an 'observing officer', met him in 1812 and described him as

Troops bivouacked near Vila Velha, by St Clair (NAM)

. . . a superior, quiet sort of person; and, during the time the enemy occupied Salamanca, was on such terms with them as not to be suspected . . . The Spaniards are very good in obtaining and forwarding information — as in the instance of this priest — he ascertains all the detachments in the country, the strength of any large assemblage of troops, by either having persons to count them as they enter the towns, or from the returns made by the *alcades* for provisions. These when obtained are sent by foot-messengers, who can march ten leagues a day, and, if requisite, they can be forwarded from place to place by priests or *alcades* who can be trusted, finding messengers at every place. They go frequently night and day.

Wellington's other great source of intelligence was the rich harvest of enemy despatches brought in by the guerillas, who specialised in waylaying French couriers. On 14 December 1808 the whole course of the war had been changed when peasants murdered a French ADC and sold his despatches for 20 dollars to Moore's headquarters. From them Moore learned the whole disposition of the *Grande Armée*, and was able to lay his plans accordingly. That information was carried by a courier riding alone with his letters *en clair*. Later no despatch travelled with less guard than a squadron of dragoons and, increasingly, cipher was used.

The flow of captured letters never ceased, but the cipher presented great problems, particularly when the Great Paris Cipher was-used. This consisted of a long list of arbitrary numbers each referring to a place, a person, or military term (*armée, division, cavalerie* etc). There were also numbers for individual letters, numerals and common syllables (eg 'mi', 'ab'). Fortunately the French seldom enciphered the whole of a despatch. There was usually some word in clear which gave some clue to the rest of the despatch. Moreover, the cipher was so often used carelessly that informed guesses could be made at the meaning of the ciphered numbers. Naturally there was no one with experience of breaking codes in Wellington's army. Such cipher experts as Britain possessed worked at the Admiralty in London. At first, Wellington said, 'I tried — every one at headquarters tried — and between us we made it out'. He claimed that 'they had never failed to make out every cypher where there was a cypher for the letters, and had often succeeded even where there was a cypher for words.' Fortunately there was at headquarters an officer who had a natural flair for this kind of work. Captain George Scovell, Fifty Seventh, soon took over the business of deciphering and, by the autumn of 1812, it was rare for him to have to leave a single word untranslated.

Scovell was an officer of the QMG's department, and it was largely through this coincidence, despite the pretensions of Charles Stewart, that intelligence slid into the responsibilities of the QMG. With both intelligence and the movement of the troops in his province, Murray became, in effect, chief of staff to the army and was actually so titled after the battle of Waterloo. The AG's department became almost wholly concerned with 'insignificant clerking'.

Both the department of the QMG and that of the AG were, by twentieth-century standards, very small. In the autumn of 1813, when the army was more than 60,000 strong, Murray had, apart from his ADC, only four British officers with him. As Adjutant General, Pakenham had two assistant adjutants general, two deputy assistants and what would now be called a staff learner.

To some extent this smallness of staff was made possible by the fact that, for the first time in British history, Wellington had made his divisions into self-supporting tactical formations. The long-standing practice was to use no grouping higher than a brigade and that only on active service. In peacetime there was no organisation above the battalion. With a brigade there was only one staff officer, the brigade major who was normally a captain and reported direct to both the QMG and the AG at army headquarters. There were occasions on which two or three brigades had been temporarily grouped into a division under the senior brigade commander, but this was a tactical, not an administrative, grouping. On the Coruña campaign, Moore had organised his army, apart from two independent light brigades, into four divisions, one of which was known as the Reserve. The divisional generals gave the brigades their operational orders but, for administration, the brigade majors were responsible to the staff departments at headquarters. Wellington had fought the short campaigns of 1808 with a collection of brigades, although on the advance to contact he seems to have entrusted his leading brigades to his second-in-command. The Douro campaign of May 1809 was fought with brigades, divided into two 'wings' under Sherbrooke and Edward Paget, but when it came to action, Wellington manoeuvred the brigades himself, irrespective of their division into 'wings'.

It was not until 18 June 1809 that the army was formed into divisions. There were four of them at first, but by 1811 this had grown to eight, apart from the Portuguese Division, which was a permanent appendage of the Second Division. When the divisions were formed, officers of the two staff departments were attached to each. Next, batteries or troops of artillery became permanent parts of the divisions, as did an assistant commissary general and an officer of Royal Engineers. In 1810 a Portuguese brigade was attached to each division except the First, although the second did not receive its Portuguese brigade until the middle of 1811; and in the Light Division Portuguese troops were brigaded with the British regiments. By 1811 Wellington could write: 'One of our divisions is in itself a complete army, composed of British and foreign troops, artillery, departments, &c.'

The only way in which each of the divisions did not resemble 'a complete army' was that no cavalry was attached to them. Only the Light Division, which usually held the outposts, had a cavalry unit—the First Hussars of the German Legion—almost permanently under command from 1810 to 1813. The cavalry brigades were grouped into a single division, except between 1811 and 1812, when there were two cavalry divisions, one in the north and one in the south. These were largely administrative groupings, as there were very few occasions when it was possible to manoeuvre more than one cavalry brigade as a tactical formation.

As the war continued and the army expanded, it became necessary to form groups of divisions. Even Wellington found it difficult to handle nine infantry divisions and eight cavalry brigades spread over a front of 42 miles as the crow flies. One embryo corps organisation had existed since 1810, when the detachment in Estremadura, usually commanded by Rowland Hill, had been a semi-independent army. It normally consisted of two infantry divisions (Second and Portuguese) and two cavalry brigades (Second Cavalry Division). To cope with the administration problems, the staff of Second Division was augmented to four officers of the QMG's department and two from the AG's.

After Vitoria there were three corps in almost permanent existence, Hill commanding on the right and Graham (later Hope) on the left. The centre, which was as strong as the two flanking corps put together, was commanded directly by Wellington, who occasionally gave the command of half of it to Beresford. Hill's staff was already strong enough to command the right corps, and the First Division's staff was increased so as to form a corps headquarters for the left. The centre was administered by Wellington's own staff, except when he divided the force into two, when Beresford's Portuguese staff acted as a corps headquarters.

All staff officers were appointed by the Crown by special commission, on which, as was to be expected, a special fee was payable to the clerks at the War Office. Wellington could not appoint a man to the staff in the Peninsula; he could only put in orders that Captain X would act as DAQMG 'until his Majesty's pleasure is known.'

The situation of the aide-de-camp was different. Strictly speaking the ADC was not a staff officer but a member of the general's 'family'. He was paid and fed by his general, who received an allowance of 9s6d a day for doing so. Generals chose their own ADCs, subject to the officer concerned having served at least one year with his regiment. Frequently generals chose relations: Hill had a brother as principal ADC, and Andrew Hay had his son. Those who had no eligible relations frequently took a promising young officer from their own regiments. It was very much a personal choice, and Wellington remarked that he would be as careful in recommending an ADC to a general as he would 'in recommending a girl for a man to marry'.

Major-generals were permitted one ADC, lieutenant-generals two. As Commander of the Forces Wellington was entitled to three, apart from his Military Secretary, but seldom had (or required) less than seven, although the cost of subsisting the supernumeraries had to come out of his own pocket.

When Harry Smith returned to his regiment with a musket ball in his ankle, his brigadier, Sydney Beckwith, said to him: '"You are a mad fool of a boy, coming here with a ball in your leg. Can you dance?" "No," says I; I can hardly walk but with one toe turned out." "Can you be my a.d.c.?" "Yes, I can ride and eat."' There was more than riding and eating in being an ADC. Even out of battle there were long rides on unknown roads, frequently in pitch darkness and storms, always at the mercy of flooded rivers and the apolitical bandits of many nations, who beset the less frequented roads of the Peninsula. In action he was the most exposed of all the troops in the field. He was the vital link in the communications between the commander and his troops, doing the job that in the twentieth century would be done by the wireless set and the field telephone. The fate of most battles depended on the exposed figure of the young man riding from brigade to brigade with the orders. At every moment he was at the mercy of musketry, aimed or random, of artillery or of marauding cavalry. At Quatre Bras and Waterloo four ADCs to British generals were killed and fifteen wounded.

12

General Officers

In May 1811, when the British army had been fighting in the Peninsula for almost three years and had been at war with France for seventeen, Wellington wrote to London:

> I am obliged to be everywhere, and if absent from any operation something goes wrong. It is to be hoped that the general officers will at last acquire that experience which will teach them that success can be obtained only by attention to the most minute details and by tracing every part of every operation from its origin to its conclusion, point by point, and ascertaining that the whole is understood by those who are to execute it.

A year later he wrote: 'Notwithstanding all that has passed, I cannot prevail upon the general officers to feel a little confidence in their situations. They take alarm at the least movement of the enemy; and then spread the alarm and interrupt everything.'

The authorities in London were doing their best to send good generals to the Peninsula, but the talent was not available. Wellington begged them to stop: 'I hope I shall have no more new generals from England; they really do us but little good, and they take the place of officers who would be of use.' It was not until the summer of 1813 that he was permitted to discard a number of the more notable incompetents. He immediately put forward seven names, and would have suggested more if their successors would not, inevitably, have been even more incompetent: 'I do not see that the service would derive much advantage from sending to England any [general] in order that Colonel Sir Granby Calcraft may command a brigade.'

Not all Wellington's generals were incompetent. (Their capabilities are examined at greater length in my *Wellington as Military Commander*, 1968.) Some, within limits, were very good: Thomas Graham, Rowland Hill, John Hope and Edward Paget were excellent corps commanders; Carr Beresford was something more; and Stapleton Cotton 'commands our cavalry very well, though he is not exactly the person I should select to command an army'. To set against these were two officers sent out to act as Wellington's second-in-command. The first, Sir Brent Spencer, was 'exceedingly puzzle-headed . . . He would talk of the Thames for the Tagus . . . He has no mind, and is incapable of forming any opinion of his own. I cannot depend upon him for anything.' He was succeeded by Sir John Sherbrooke, 'the most violent tempered person I ever met with, and there are no bounds to his folly when he is in a passion'.

At a lower level there were generals who commanded divisions excellently but could not be trusted with a corps. Such were Cole, Craufurd and Picton, but divisions had also to be entrusted to William Stewart, who, 'with the utmost zeal and good intentions and abilities, cannot obey an order', and to William Erskine, 'upon whose sanity, I am sorry to say, much reliance cannot be placed'.

The dearth of adequate generals stemmed directly from the equitable nature of the system of promoting to the higher ranks. Purchase and patronage played their parts, for good or ill, in the promotion of officers up to the rank of lieutenant-colonel, but beyond that point seniority reigned supreme. The Horse Guards' ruling was that 'It is not consistent with the organisation of the service to appoint to the brevet of colonel out of the usual mode of progressive advancement to that rank.'

'Progressive advancement' meant that any man who became a lieutenant-colonel would inevitably become a full general if he lived long enough (not less than 23 years), provided that he did not voluntarily resign and was not dismissed by a court martial. There was no binding obligation to do any further soldiering. In June 1811 Major-Generals William Scott, Robert Tipping and Alexander Trotter were promoted lieutenant-generals. None of them had done a day's duty since 1783, the end of the American War of Independence. At that time they had all been regimental majors and, as such, they had drawn half pay ever since. 'Progressive advancement' was an escalator that carried officers upward irrespective of their abilities, their age or their physical infirmities. When the Peninsular War began, the army had one general, and he not the most senior, who had carried his regiment's colours at Culloden in the Forty Five.

The date of a man's appointment as lieutenant-colonel determined his seniority for the rest of his life. Nothing but royal birth and Wellington's unprecedented promotion to field-marshal in 1813 could disturb it. Even this last event, the reward for Vitoria and four years of victory, worried the Commander-in-Chief, who was concerned that 'the spirit of public jealousy, which might possibly have been excited by this usual promotion, would have embarrassed the public service'. The new field-marshal was only forty-four. No commoner under the age of sixty-one had previously been appointed to that rank, and sixteen of the previous nineteen appointments had been for men of more than seventy.

Most generals of all grades were elderly. An extreme example was John Prince, who served 19 years as Riding Master of the King's Dragoon Guards before he was commissioned in 1770; he became a lieutenant-general in 1814 when he could scarcely have been less than eighty and had 63 years of service. It had taken him 19 years to rise from lieutenant-colonel to lieutenant-general, three years longer than it took Wellington, who was one of a fortunate batch that, becoming lieutenant-colonels in the first half of 1793, rose to being lieutenant-generals in only 16 years.

Although there were a few exceptions, such as Blücher and Suvarov, the best generals of the Napoleonic wars were men in their thirties and early forties. Napoleon, together with Soult and Wellington, was born in 1769; Davout in 1770; and Beresford in 1768. Austria's best general, the Archduke Charles, was born in 1771, a year before Suchet and Rowland Hill. Of all Napoleon's best field commanders, only Massena was markedly older than the Emperor himself. When he took over the Army of Portugal in 1810, he said, 'I feel too old and too tired to go to war again'. He was fifty-two. In 1944 General Montgomery was fifty-seven.

If Britain wanted her commanders in their forties, the promotion escalator decreed that they must be men who had been lieutenant-colonels in their early twenties. At the time of Salamanca there were only four lieutenant-generals with the army in the Peninsula; their average age was less than forty-two and they had become lieutenant-colonels at the ages of twenty-six, twenty-four, twenty-two and twenty-one. The four of them, respectively, were Beresford, Wellington, Hill and Cotton, who had all received their early regimental promotion through a combination of purchase and patronage and, as it happened, were all excellent generals.

There should have been another lieutenant-general with the army, Thomas Graham, but he had had to go to England on sick leave. He was an exception to the rules, being sixty-four and not having joined the army until he was forty-six. He had raised the Ninetieth Foot at his own expense in 1794. This brought him the rank of lieutenant-colonel, and when, 17 months later, he added a second battalion, he became a colonel. Unfortunately for him the Duke of York's reforms were introduced at this time, so that his rank was declared only temporary and not 'progressive'.

For 14 years he took every opportunity to go on active service, serving with the Austrian army when the British were not engaged. Throughout this time he repeatedly petitioned the Horse Guards to have his colonelcy made permanent. Determined to adhere to his regulations, the Duke of York consistently refused, since, *prima facie*, Graham's was exactly the kind of instantaneous promotion that had done so much harm to the army. It was not until after the Coruña campaign, in which Graham had served as ADC to the general, that the Duke relented. 'At the dying request of the late Lieutenant-General Sir John Moore . . . his Majesty has been graciously pleased to direct that, in your particular case, the established custom of the army may be departed from by your being promoted to the rank of

Baggage Waggon, by J. A. Atkinson (NAM)

major-general . . . and that you stand amongst the major-generals in the situation you would have held had the lieutenant colonelcy to which you were appointed in February 1794 been a permanent commission.' This backdating of his commission meant that he became a lieutenant-general little more than a year later and, having meanwhile defeated Marshal Victor at Barossa, Graham became second-in-command to Wellington in the summer of 1811.

Unfortunately Graham's eyesight was poor. In June 1812 Wellington wrote: 'He complains of his right eye, for which he has been blistered in the temple; but he says with little or no effect.' Nor was he the only one of Wellington's generals with poor vision. Picton wrote in 1813 that he was 'so affected with a weakness and inflammation of the eyes as to be wholly unable to write'. When Edward Paget, who had lost an arm in 1809, was captured in 1812, Wellington 'inclined to believe that his want of sight was the immediate cause of his being taken'. Charles Stewart 'labours under two bodily defects, the want of sight and hearing', while General von Bock, who led the triumphant charge of the German dragoons at Garcia Hernandez, was so blind that he had to ask a nearby artillery officer to 'be good enough to show us the enemy'.

Blind or sighted, fit or maimed, 'progressive advancement' carried lieutenant-colonels upwards to general's rank. The saving grace of the system was that there was no limit to the number of officers who could be made generals. Thus it was possible to reach down the list to promote any man who might be useful at a higher rank. The brevet of 1813 made major-generals of eighty-two colonels, going just far enough to include Colonel Lord Aylmer, DAG in the Peninsula, who made a useful field commander. To do so meant promoting a large number of useless officers, including three who had already failed in Spain and Portugal, while three more had promptly to be sent home from there before they could take the field. No harm was done, since there was no obligation to employ generals and, until July 1814, they were not paid as generals unless they were appointed to a specific post 'on the staff'. Only two out of every five general officers were so employed.

Excluding the Royal Family and the Royal Marines, there were 518 general officers on the Army List in November 1812, but there were only 200 posts 'on the staff'. Of seventy-seven full generals only three were employed, and of 166 lieutenant-generals only forty-one. Major-generals had more chance — 161 out of 275 were 'on the staff'.

There were fifty-three staff posts for generals in Great Britain (including the Channel Islands). Few of these officers can have been overworked. How, for example, could one lieutenant-general and two major-generals fill in their time at Brighton when the *Grande Armée* was deep into Russia? And they had another major-general in close support at Hastings!

Ireland absorbed six lieutenant-generals and twenty-three major-generals. Heligoland, the British possession closest to Napoleon's troops, was only commanded by a lieutenant-colonel.

Overseas 118 general officers held posts, more than a third of them in Portugal or western Spain. Five more were stationed at Gibraltar. Sicily had an establishment of fourteen, but one of these was detached to the Ionian Isles and four were on the east coast of Spain. There were three on Malta and one on Madeira. The West

Indies had twenty-seven, and the East Indies (including Mauritius) thirteen. Canada, conducting a desperate defence against the United States, had only four, but Newfoundland and Nova Scotia shared five.

There were a variety of financial provisions for the 318 unemployed general officers. Only fourteen, who had resigned their regimental commissions, drew no pay at all. Seventy-one drew the half pay of their regimental ranks, most as majors or lieutenant-colonels, but Major General Aeneas Shaw got only 5s a day, the half pay of a captain. A fortunate few, mainly elderly officers of the Royal Irish Artillery (disbanded in 1801), had been retired on full pay.

Most of the remainder held full-pay commissions in their regiments. Major-General Horace Churchill was a full-pay captain-commissary in the Artillery Drivers, and was also entitled to draw full pay as a retired lieutenant and captain of the long-defunct Horse Grenadier Guards.

For some there were more substantial rewards. The most sought-after was the colonelcy of a regiment (see p 19), and 168 general officers had regiments.

Watering Horses, by J. A. Atkinson (NAM)

Although some of these were also 'on the staff', most of these colonels were elderly men. Sixty-nine full generals had regiments and one of them, David Dundas, had two. Colonelcies normally only became vacant with the death of the holder. During the French wars only one colonel was dismissed his regiment — General Whitelocke, who was cashiered after the fiasco at Buenos Aires. One colonel resigned. This was the Duke of Northumberland, who surrendered the Blues, the best paid colonelcy in the army at 41s a day, when the Duke of York refused to admit his claim to appoint and promote all the officers in the regiment.

Another possible source of income for senior officers was the governorship of a fortress or a colony. Some of these, such as the 'government' of the Cape of Good Hope, were active posts carrying with them the command of the troops in the garrison. Others were sinecures, given usually to reward merit or to alleviate poverty. Although such appointments were occasionally political jobs, many more were awarded as rewards for service. The governorship of Quebec is a typical example. The salary was £346 15s a year, but residence was not required, the duties being delegated to a colonel. When it fell vacant in 1797, the Duke of York wrote to the King that 'the only officers who have applied for governments are Generals [Staats] Morris, [Henry] St. John and Lieutenant General [William] Dalrymple. As I am not aware of any distinguishing feature of military merit among the three, your Majesty may prefer the eldest and poorest of them, which is General Morris, and promote him to the government of Quebec.' Quebec was one of the better paid posts. The governorship of Scarborough Castle, for instance, was worth only £15 a year.

Even with a 'government' and a regiment, generals 'on the staff' did not find it easy to make ends meet. In 1813 Wellington wrote to the Secretary of State drawing his attention to the situation of Rowland Hill and John Hope: 'They, each of them, command a large corps, and great expenses must be incurred by them; and I know the former and I believe the latter, has not the means of defraying those expenses.'

Neither Hill nor Hope were poor men. Both had the pay of lieutenant-generals. Hill was Governor of Blackness Castle (£283 3s 6d a year) and Colonel of the Ninety Fourth Foot, while Hope was Colonel of the Ninety Second. The latter found, on succeeding to the command of Graham's corps, that his annual expenses would amount to £2,140 a year, whereas his pay was only £1,861 10s.

Part of the expense was the number of horses a general required. When Graham returned to Lisbon in 1813, he shipped out ten horses, 'three for servants or draught of light baggage cart or buggy, three capital short legged hackneys (Brigton mares) and four of a superior class for chargers, from four to six years old, with good barrels, excellent action and unexceptional legs and feet for the most stony ground . . . This outfit has been very ruinous, six of them costing me alone 600 sterling.' In addition he had left in Lisbon, 'one admirable hack mare, one strong Spanish pony and an old hunter who was wounded at Barossa'. On landing, he had to buy fifteen mules for baggage and servants.

On top of this, a general was expected to provide a mess for his staff. Originally he had only been expected to 'keep a table' for his aides-de-camp, but such provision had extended to supplying all his senior staff officers. As a newly joined brigade major was told by his brigadier, 'It is your duty to post the piquets and mine to have a damned good dinner for you every day'. A divisional or corps commander would have to feed two or three ADCs, half a dozen staff officers and a commissariat officer, to say nothing of visiting generals, each of whom would be accompanied by his own ADC. Lowry Cole, commanding the Fourth Division, was known to

> live very comfortably. He now has travelling about with him ten or twelve goats for milk, a cow and about thirty six sheep, at least, with a shepherd. When you think of this, that everything is to be carried about, from salt and pepper and tea cups, to saucepans, boilers, dishes, chairs and tables, on mules, you may guess the trouble and expense of a good establishment here.

Sir Charles Oman criticised Wellington for not 'forming a school of officers capable of carrying out large independent operations. He trained admirable generals of divisions, but not commanders of armies.' This is an unjust verdict, possibly because it was made when Oman had completed only a quarter of his research into the Peninsular War. Wellington did produce a 'school of officers'. Charles Napier, John Colborne and Harry Smith all commanded armies in different and successful campaigns; each of them had been specially favoured by Wellington but, owing to 'progressive advancement', none of them was more than a lieutenant-colonel at Waterloo, when Colborne, the eldest of the three, was only thirty-seven. The men Wellington taught to be 'admirable generals of divisions' were older than this, most of them as old, or older, than Wellington himself. At Busaco, for example, six of the ten British generals present were older than their commander. Moreover, many of his generals did not survive to pass on their experience. War, in those days, was a dangerous business for generals: by the time Waterloo was won, twelve of Wellington's generals had been killed in action, two had died of disease and two had fallen to their deaths from balconies in Lisbon.

Nor can it be said with any certainty that Wellington's 'admirable generals of divisions' might not have succeeded as army commanders. Few had the chance to show their capabilities. Edward Pakenham, it is true, failed disastrously at New Orleans, but the circumstances were unpropitious and his defeat could be attributed as much to the Royal Navy as to his American enemies. On the credit side are Edward Paget's successful campaign in Burma and Stapleton Cotton's taking of the Indian fortress of Bhurtpore, which had withstood four sieges directed by General Lake, no mean general, in the previous century.

It was not the least of Wellington's achievements that he succeeded in making so many 'admirable generals of divisions' from the miscellaneous collection of officers sent out to him. A perspicacious junior officer remarked: 'Except for General Hill there is scarcely a general officer in the army of any talent and very few of any activity except Sir S. Cotton. I suppose no commander ever had so few clever men on his staff, almost all of them being coxcomical or old women.' To turn these men into the commanders of a uniformly successful army was no mean feat, and, as Wellington was fond of saying, 'I'll do the best I can with the instruments that have been sent to assist me'.

Part III

THE MACHINE IN OPERATION

13

On Active Service

It must be remembered that when they landed in Portugal, British soldiers were strangers to Europe. Apart from brief forays to Cuxhaven, Calabria and Copenhagen, no unit of the British army had landed in Europe since the turn of the century. The first sight of Lisbon was exciting, especially after weeks cooped up in a rat-infested transport. 'It stood chiefly on very precipitous hills. The general view of the city and its environs from the harbour was very beautiful, the sides of the hills being clothed with plantations and numberless vineyards, and the buildings extending for a mile and a half or two miles along the coast.' Closer inspection revealed imperfections. 'Notwithstanding that it is certainly a handsome city', wrote a surgeon, 'I dislike it more than any place I was ever in, and this altogether from the want of cleanliness of the inhabitants.' A Scottish sergeant agreed: 'The town is a dung hill from end to end'. A cavalry officer described it as 'a nasty straggling, dirty and large city. From the nature of its situation, the streets are steep. Some of them scarcely practicable for mules, and most of them too narrow for a carriage to pass. To describe the filth of all kinds which remains accumulating in these narrow passes, till swept into the river below by some heavy rain, would be impossible.' Another cavalryman commented: 'It is quite dangerous to walk in the streets after ten at night, as the people anoint you from the windows without any regard to cleanliness. They first throw the *perfume* and then cry out *"agua va"*.' 'The inhabitants', wrote an ensign, 'seem to rejoice in its nastiness.'

The Portuguese way of life was shocking to the insular and protestant British. They particularly objected to the use of garlic and oil in the cooking, and to the way in which ladies picked lice out of each other's hair in public. Above all, they were scandalised by the number of priests and monks who were to be seen in every street. They all seemed to be idle and well fed, in contrast to the poverty of most of the population. The same surgeon wrote that 'it is notorious that nine-tenths of the seductions are traced to the clergy'.

Religious disapproval was not all on one side. The priests regarded all the British as heretics. Wellington had to issue a General Order that 'As the profession of Free-masonry is contrary to the laws of Portugal, the Commander of the Forces requests that the meetings of the lodges existing in the several corps, the use of masonic badges and emblems, and the appearance of the officers and soldiers in masonic processions may be discontinued while the army is in this country.' Notwithstanding these problems 'the priests almost always stood our friends. They were commonly frank, jovial fellows. Their faith, indeed, was catholic enough; the politest among them could not in conscience give us any hope of salvation, but they damned us in the civillest terms possible.'

Of course, not all the army were heretics. Many in the ranks and a few of the officers were Catholics, though not notably conscientious in their religious observance. Wellington wrote:

The soldiers of the army have permission to go to mass, so far as this: they are forbidden to go into churches during the performance of divine service, unless they go to assist in the performance of the service. I could not do more, for in point of fact, soldiers cannot by law attend the celebration of mass, excepting in Ireland. The thing now stands exactly as it ought; any man may go to mass who chooses, and nobody makes any enquiry about it. The consequence is that nobody goes to mass, and although we have whole regiments of Irishmen, and of course Roman Catholics, I have never seen one soldier perform any one act of worship in these Catholic countries, excepting making the sign of the Cross to induce the people of the country to give them wine.

A newly arrived battalion would normally first be quartered at Belem, then a distinct little town downstream from Lisbon. The troops would be accommodated in barracks and convents, while the officers 'were billeted in the vicinity, and it was some time before anything like tolerable quarters could be procured, as in many instances we were sent to houses where there were already five or six inhabitants to a room.' Much of this overcrowding was due to the strongest corps in the army, the so-called 'Belem Rangers'.

This troop of heroes was composed of men and officers with facings of all the colours of the rainbow. Among them were those who could not fight, and those who would not; and I am sorry to say that of the latter there was a large proportion . . . Being fond of dainties, they kept within the smell of Lisbon, with its oil and garlic, the perfume of which they snuffed up with ecstasy. As for being exposed to fire, they coveted no more than sufficed for their cigars.

For the great majority of the troops, who were anxious to get to the front, the time spent at Belem was kept to a minimum, to the time needed to make the unit mobile.

The officers commanding companies, the paymaster and the surgeon must provide themselves with mules for the carriage of the camp-kettles of their respective companies, of their books, and of the medicine chest respectively; and a requisition must be made upon the Commissary for one mule to carry the entrenching tools. Requisition must likewise be made upon the Quartermaster General's department for bill-hooks, haversacks, canteens and camp-kettles to complete the battalion.

Some units needed much completing. 'I am astonished', wrote Wellington in 1809, 'that it did not occur to the commanding officer of the 2nd battalion, 87th Regiment, that their armourer would be useful to the corps on service, and that he could be no use anywhere without his tools.' Three years later it was reported that the Second Life Guards 'appear to have left England without their due staff officers, such as vetinary surgeon and paymaster'.

For the officers there was the agonising choice of what kit to take on service and what to store in Lisbon. On landing at Lisbon in 1809 the officers of the Fifty Third were ordered 'to leave all our camp equipage and every thing we had, except for one shirt, one pair of stockings and one pair of shoes for a change, which is all we have. This every officer carries on his back in a pack.' An infantry company commander took 'a portmanteau containing a few changes of linen, boots, etc., to say nothing of tea, sugar, chocolate, rice, bread, meat, a pig's skin of wine, a keg of spirits, cigars, spare horse shoes and nails.' His opposite number in the Royal Dragoons, who claimed 'to live entirely on my pay', wrote: 'I keep four horses, three baggage mules, four servants, beside a woman cook, and can give my friends port wine, claret, Madeira and *vin de Grave*, any day, either in camp or town, carrying all this about with me.' A gunner captain's baggage included '1 large chest, 2 portmanteaus, 1 carpet bag with liquor containers, 1 cheese in a bag, 2 canteen baskets, a tent, bedding, and a box with papers and orderly books.'

In the infantry, subalterns were allowed the forage for one mule between two officers. This meant that they had to make do with their blankets, a change of linen and 'a clasp knife, which was both fork and spoon. Our little stock of tea, sugar and brandy was carefully hoarded in a small canteen, wherein dwelt a little tin kettle, which also acted the part of teapot; *two* cups and saucers (in case of company), two spoons, two forks, two plates of the same metal, a small soup-tureen, which on fortunate occasions acted as a punch-bowl, but never for soup.' There was more scope for the cavalry subaltern. A lieutenant of the Eighteenth Hussars in February 1813 spent

> . . . most of the day arranging packing up my clothes preparatory to marching up country. Had the whole of my baggage on the mule and find he can carry it well. I take the following articles with me:- 2 pelieces [sic]; 1 dress waistcoat; 4 regimental pantaloons; 3 white pantaloons; 1 leather pantaloons; 2 blue waistcoats; 2 white waistcoats; cotton drawers; 2 flannel drawers; 3 flannel waistcoats; 12 hose; 4 black silk handkerchiefs; 6 pocket handkerchiefs; 2 foraging caps; 1 hussar cap with oil skin cover; 1 cap line; 1 sash; 1 peliece [sic] line; 3 pr. gloves; 2 night caps; canteen; breakfast and dinner service complete; 1 leather trunk; double saddle bags; basket with socks etc.; spy glass; great coat; flannel jacket; leather bucket; 15 cakes soap; boot jack; 1 dressing gown; two blankets; 1 rug; 1 bearskin bed; dressing case; writing case; ten books; 1 pr. hussar pistols; 1 pocket pistol; 1 powder flask; 1 pouch belt (plain); dress sword; dress sabretache; boots; 1 pr. shoes; 2 pr. slippers; 1 hussar pipe (complete); hussar horse accoutrements (complete); 2 horse cloths; 2 horse blankets; 1 plain saddle; 2 plain bridles; pack saddle; bridle, etc. (complete); 3 shoe brushes and black J.; 2 clothes brushes; oil skin and traps (to go over baggage).

When at last all was ready, the battalion would move off towards the frontier. It was a long haul, frequently done in blazing heat and choking dust.

Soldiers Drilling, by J. A. Atkinson (NAM)

It will be considered as a Standing Order, when not near the enemy, that each regiment will be preceded by two officers for the purpose of taking up quarters; one of whom will march 24 hours before the regiment, and on his arrival will receive the necessary information from the Assistant Quartermaster General, or from the quartermaster of the regiment preceding that to which he belongs. The other officer will march on the same day as the regiment does, but sufficiently early to arrive at 10 o'clock in the forenoon, when he will have the quarters pointed out to him by the officer who went the day before, and who, after having done this, will proceed to the next station.

The camp colour men — viz. one man per company under the command of the quarter master sergeants of each regiment, and one officer per brigade — will assemble at the brigade major's quarter every morning, one hour and a half before the hour appointed for the march of the brigade. The commissary and the cattle, with two butchers per regiment, under the charge of the commissary's storekeeper, will, when possible, be one march ahead of the brigade. Thus, the meat will be slaughtered and all the provisions will be in perfect readiness to be delivered over to the quartermasters before they arrive. The quartermasters will march two or three hours before the brigade or, if possible, the preceding evening. They will ride on as fast as they can, and as soon as they arrive, which will be early in the forenoon, the commissary's storekeeper, butchers and cattle will proceed to the next station.

Most of the marching was done before the heat of the day. Usually the columns would start at sunrise. 'When marching at ease, the ranks may be opened and the files loosened, but each rank, section or division must be kept distinct, and every man must remain exactly in his place. The officer commanding the leading regiment will sound the halt half an hour after it marches off, and afterwards once an hour after it marches off; each halt to last at least five minutes.' On very hot days, when there was no pressing urgency, the day's march might end as early as 10am. On other days it might continue until the middle of the afternoon. At the end of it the troops might either bivouac or be put into billets.

In good weather bivouacking was an idyllic occupation.

See the old soldiers come to their ground. Let their feelings of fatigue be great or small, they are no sooner suffered to leave the ranks than every man rushes to secure whatever comforts the neighbourhood affords as likely to contribute to his comforts for the night. Swords [bayonets], hatchets and bill-hooks are to be seen hewing and hacking at every tree and bush within reach — huts are quickly reared, fires are quickly blazing, and while the camp kettle is boiling, or the pound of beef frying, the tired and happy souls are found toasting their toes around the cheerful blaze until the fire has done the needful, when they fall on like men. The meal finished, they arrange their accoutrements for any emergency, when they dispose themselves for rest.

The story was different in bad weather.

The rain poured down in torrents. Wind and hail in all their varieties beat unmercifully upon us. To increase our sufferings, the personal baggage had been sent on some days in advance, so we had no covering whatever save the garments we wore; and as to subsistence, our only recourse was the contents of a lank and miserable haversack, wherein were jumbled up together, in a sort of medley, the various remnants of ration leather (falsely called beef), and mouldy biscuits, hard and jaw-breaking, of which the maggots contended for a share. At the determination of each day's march, down came the branches of the forest, and loudly clashed the bill-hooks and the axe, to put in requisition materials for the long wished-for fire, to establish which was a labour of no trifling nature, for the timber, thoroughly saturated with rain, lay in smoking heaps long after the light had been communicated, while we with haggard looks stood collected round the smouldering pile.

An ensign of the Guards, on his first night with the army, 'slept close to my company, in the gentle declivity of a ploughed field; and having taken up my berth in a furrow, found, when I woke next morning, that it had been turned into a purling stream, which had run in at my stock and out at my boots.'

Whenever possible the troops were billeted. Wellington believed that 'the custom of bivouacking was extremely bad for the troops. It prevented men from getting regular rest: that they got into the habit of sleeping for an hour at a time, or when they felt drowsy; and that nothing wears [them] out so effectively.' Many officers disagreed with him. 'A clean hut was far preferable to a dirty house. A good tree became a matter of moment and, on halting, the officers took their choice by seniority with great gravity.'

Some houses in the countryside were extremely dirty. As a hussar officer wrote, 'Edwin and I slept in a cottage. Three different families live in it, besides the cows, mules, pigs, fowls, &c., &c., without any partition. We lay in our blankets and clothes in one corner of this wretched hut on a bundle of straw.' A light infantryman said: 'If you go into any house, you stand a chance of coming out lousy and flea bitten.' This was echoed by another hussar: 'The house I am in, is swarming with bugs and fleas. They made a most *terrible example* of me so that I am spotted like a *trout*.'

Another trouble with billets was that they were almost always overcrowded. On the night after the action at Sabugal, a Guards officer remembered that 'five of us, including the A.Q.M. General of the division, were stowed away, or confined, in a space about the size, colour and appearance of a respectably proportioned coalhole in the neighbourhood of Berkeley Square.'

Portuguese houses might be dirty but the inhabitants were usually welcoming. Assistant Surgeon Brookes wrote after Talavera: 'Since I have been in Spain I have met with but meagre civility. When you are billeted in a genteel house you are just shown a miserable place to lay down. They walk off & come near you no more. The Portuguese are ten times as hospitable.'

Whenever possible, the troops were put into convents or other large buildings, but every available piece of accommodation had to be pressed into service. A cavalry officer left a description of the little town of Azambuja when the Fourth Division was quartered on it:

When four or five thousand men with a proportionate number of horses occupy a small town, it may be imagined that there is very little superfluous space, either within doors or without. The whole was, in fact, a thick compost of military bustle. Baggage waggons and artillery parked in the square; bugles sounding the various calls; the dingy streets thronged with soldiers, some hastening to their respective parades, others lighting fires and cooking in the open air; orderly sergeants hastening to and fro with looks of steady importance; soldiers' wives in gay attire with looks of no steadiness at all. The interior of the churches exhibited a curious spectacle; they were converted into barracks. The gilded shrines were torn down for firewood, and instead of frankincense and myrhh, the high altar reeked with the steam of ration beef. If churches were thus treated, private houses scarcely fared better. Twenty or thirty were crammed into each room, against the bare walls of which they made their fires, with the aid of whatever relics of firewood friend and foes had spared; in default of movables, which had in most cases moved off, recourse was had to doors, window-frames and flooring, and where these too failed, rafters and roof-timbers were put into requisition, a process by which numbers of houses were daily converted into ruins.

Wellington issued order after order in an attempt to prevent the troops destroying their billets in order to cook their meals:

The Commander of the Forces is ashamed to acknowledge that the British troops have, in many instances, done more mischief to the country in this manner than has been done by the enemy . . . Very recently the troops on their passage through Coimbra to the army, have burned the timbers of the convent which was allocated for their accommodation. Experience has shown that when the non-commissioned officers and, particularly, the officers of regiments do their duty, these crimes cannot be committed. It is impossible that a soldier, or any number of soldiers, can take down the large beams of the roof of a convent, or even of a house, and burn them, without the knowledge of the non-commissioned officers of their companies, and even of their officers, if the latter do their duty and attend to their men as they ought.

The troops continued to tear down their billets and the officers and NCOs did little or nothing to stop them. It was in everyone's interest that the ration beef should be cooked, and neither Spain nor Portugal abound with firewood. As the war continued, the supply of firewood became shorter and shorter. So did the number of available billets.

The campaigns of the Napoleonic wars were intermittent affairs. It was not unusual for the British and French armies in the Peninsula to be out of sight of one another for months at a stretch, as was the case, for example, between 21 August 1809 and 17 February 1810. All ranks had a good deal of time on their hands, and boredom was a constant danger, increasing the tendency of all ranks to drunkenness. One of the less harmful ways of passing the time among the officers was in letter-writing but, since the army had got itself into a frame of mind where all British campaigns were expected to end in an inglorious re-embarkation, the effect on public opinion in England was deplorable. This was particularly serious in 1809. Soon after Talavera an Engineer officer attached to headquarters was writing home: 'I have little doubt that we shall soon see England again. No good, I am convinced, can ever be done for these people here.' A few months later a brigadier, who should have known better, wrote: 'People seem to think that the time spent in preparations for a defence [of Lisbon], which will in all probability be ineffectual, might be more usefully employed in taking timely measures for the removal of the immense personal property in plate and money which is in Lisbon, and would naturally find its way to England.'

This kind of defeatism made Wellington's task more difficult, since one of his greatest problems was convincing his own government that the war could be won. He wrote in disgust: 'As soon as an accident happens every man who can write, and has a friend who can read, sits down to write his account of what he does know and his comments on what he does not understand.' All he could do was to urge the officers to be more careful. Censorship was unthinkable. 'I am sure your Lordship does not expect that I, or any other officer in command of a British army, can pretend to prevent the correspondence of the officers with their friends. It could not be done if attempted.'

There were other ways of passing the time. All ranks did a good deal of poaching. The officers hunted, shot, coursed their greyhounds and gave balls for the local beauties, such as they were. An officer commented after attending a ball given by Wellington in Madrid, 'A good sprinkling of black eyes and, I am forced to state, black teeth also'. Things improved when the army entered France, perhaps because the girls smelled less strongly of garlic. A cavalry man asserted that 'they swear that [the French army] are no longer Frenchmen, and I can assure you that if, sixteen or eighteen years hence, the breed has not very materially improved in this part of France, it is not the fault of the fair sex who do their best to regenerate the nation.'

The Spanish and Portuguese women may have had their defects, but they followed the army in quantity. By December 1813, when the army was firmly established on French territory, the Judge Advocate General reckoned that there were with the army '700 Portuguese and 400 Spanish women as suttlers, *vivanderas*, washerwomen etc.' Inevitably there were problems. Lieutenant Kelly of the grenadier company of the Fortieth ran away with the daughter of a Portuguese general. The lady's family gave chase but Kelly had taken the precaution of taking some of his grenadiers with him. 'The pursuers being armed with sticks, an altercation took place in which the Portuguese succeeded in capturing [the lady's horse and baggage]; but the officer fought bravely for his spouse and was well backed up by his men, so that he succeeded in carrying her off at any rate and getting to the cantonments, and on the following morning married her.' Next day, the bride's mother descended on Wellington who 'said he would give [the bride] up to the laws of Portugal but, as [Kelly] had married her, Lord Wellington swears he

Lisbon and the aqueduct of Alcantara, by W. Bradford (NAM)

will not interfere at all. The woman swears she will get the priest who married them transported for life, as well as the officer and has moreover declared that she will kill her daughter if she meets her.' All, however, ended happily. The bride's father, 'after a fortnight's consideration, gave in and made it up with his new son in law'. The grenadiers of the Fortieth were given a pint of wine each.

Less happy was the story of Captain the Hon Sanders Gore of the Ninety Fourth, who

> . . . was quartered in Vitoria, and had some intrigue with a girl. He at first took her home to his quarters. Her friends had recourse to the police. The armed police came, and were in the house to take the girl: Captain Gore resisted and the police were fairly turned out again by him and his servant. When out of the house they are said to have formed, as it were, and then to have fired in through the door in cold blood, and with no particular object as to taking Captain Gore. The latter was shot and died almost immediately.

Apart from the Spanish and Portuguese women with the army, there were some 4,500 British 'wives on the strength'. At one end of the social scale was the lady Captain Landman found close behind the forward troops at the battle of Rolica.

> I overtook a lady dressed in a nankeen riding habit and straw bonnet, and carrying a rather large rush hand basket. The unexpected sight of a respectably dressed woman in such surroundings greatly perplexed me; for the musket shot showering about pretty thickly and making the dust fly on most parts of the road. Moreover, at this place, several men were killed, and others mortally wounded, all perfectly stripped, were lying scattered across the road, so that, in order to advance, she was absolutely compelled to step over them. I, therefore, could not resist saying to her, *en passant*, that she had much better go back for a short time, as this was a very unfit place for a lady to be in, and was evidently a very dangerous one. Upon this, she drew herself up, and with a very haughty air, and, seemingly, a perfect contempt for the danger of her situation, she replied, 'Mind your own affairs, Sir, — I have a husband before me.'

Quite different, but no less courageous, was Mrs Dan Skiddy of the Thirty Fourth, who did Ensign George Bell's washing. When he said,

> 'No money yet, Mrs Skiddy; I owe you a long washing bill,' she replied, 'Och, never mind that, jewil [sic], if you never paid me; sure, you're always mindful of Dan on the march, and carry his firelock sometimes a bit when the *crather's* going to drap wid all the leather straps on his back, and nearly choked wid that stock round his *thrapple*.' 'Well, we march tomorrow, and so go and get ready.' 'O worra-worra, march the morrow, and not a shoe to me wee donkey. The curse of the crows be on the French; may they never see home again,' and away she went storming *agin* the French.

On the retreat from Burgos she carried her exhausted husband 'on me back, knapsack, firelock and all, strong as Sampson, for the fear I was in, I carried him half a league after the regiment into the bivwack.'

The women, wives or otherwise, were a constant source of trouble. They refused to accept that they were subject to military law, and many of them looted abominably. They also drank as heavily as their menfolk. On occasions a rabble of women and children caused a tiresome obstruction to the march of the troops, particularly on a retreat, when they would be in front of the columns.

Undoubtedly the wives, particularly the wives of the private soldiers, had a wretched time when the army was on the move and, although their conduct often drew down most adverse comments from the more 'respectable' of their husbands' comrades, reports of their infidelity are, all things considered, remarkably few. The most squalid incident was the court martial of another Lieutenant Kelly of the Fortieth, who was sentenced to be cashiered for 'co-habiting with the wife of Private Noah Cooper and for assaulting Private Cooper' when he requested the return of his wife. When the sentence was referred to London, the Prince Regent reduced the sentence to a reprimand, possibly because Kelly had been promoted from the ranks. He left the army soon afterwards. As another officer remarked, 'Commanding officers had almost unlimited powers to dismiss officers without court martial for grave offences. It saved a good deal of trouble.'

Troublesome as the soldier's wives so frequently were, they almost all shared with their husbands a fierce loyalty to their regiment and its officers. The regiments were, after all, the only home they had. Charles Diggle remembered, when he was a young lieutenant on the retreat to Coruña,

> . . . the kind act of a worthy woman, Sally Macan, the wife of a gallant soldier in my company, who, observing me to be falling to the rear from illness and fatigue, whipped off her garters and secured the soles of my boots, which were separating from the upper leathers, and set me on my feet again . . . A year or so after this, I had the opportunity of requiting her kindness by giving her a lift on my horse the morning after she had given birth to a child in the bivouac.

Nelly Carsons, though unconsciously, performed an even greater service to William Grattan after the storming of Badajoz. Grattan had been wounded in the left breast near the ravelin of San Roque, and was led back to his tent by two men of his regiment, the Connaught Rangers. He found

> . . . my truss of straw occupied by Mrs Nelly Carsons, the wife of my batman, who by way of banishing care, had taken to drinking divers potations of rum to such an extent that she lay down on my bed, thinking, perhaps, that I was not likely again to be its occupant. Macgowan attempted to wake her, but in vain — a battery of a dozen guns might have fired close to her ear without danger of disturbing her repose. 'Why then,' says he, 'sure the bed's big enough for yees both, and sure she'll keep you nate and warm, for, be the powers, you're kilt with the cold and the loss of blood.' I was in no mood to stand on ceremony or, indeed, to stand at all. I allowed myself to be placed beside my partner, without further persuasion; and the two soldiers left us. I soon fell

into a doze in which I might have remained very comfortable had not my companion awoke sooner than I wished; discharging a huge grunt, and putting her hand upon my leg, she exclaimed, 'Arraj! Dan, jewel, what makes you so stiff this morning'.

It is hard to say what, apart from cooking and drinking, the soldiers and their wives did in the long periods between active campaigning. They were seldom permitted to wander far from their camp or billet; usually a soldier required a special pass, rarely granted, to go beyond the outlying piquets of his brigade. Some effort was made to educate the soldier and his children. In 1811 a schoolmaster sergeant was added to each battalion, and given £10 for the purchase of educational stationery. Two months later a General Order announced that 'a school is already established at Belem for the instruction of the children of soldiers who are there; but should there be any children with the regiments, commanding officers should take measures to establish schools in the regiments in order that the children may be educated as opportunities may offer.'

There were some organised games. Cricket is mentioned occasionally, football more frequently. The Connaught Rangers and the Seventy Third Highlanders each seem to have evolved a species of fives. The British regiments of the Light Division, the heirs to Moore's training, were particularly noted for their devotion to games, with all ranks taking part. On the whole, however, there can be no doubt that the long spells between active operations must have been agonisingly dull for the soldiers and scarcely less so for the officers. There must have been many who, remembering their youth as ploughboys, were glad when, in July 1810, the following order was read to them: 'The Commander of the Forces requests that the General Officers commanding divisions will direct that those soldiers who may be inclined to reap the harvest may have leave to do so.'

14

In Action

At the most dangerous phase of the battle of Waterloo, Wellington remarked, 'Hard pounding, gentlemen; try who can pound the longest'. After Sorauren he wrote, 'The battle was fair bludgeon work'. 'Hard pounding', 'fair bludgeon work' — both were accurate descriptions of battle in the early nineteenth century. The weapons were inaccurate, their lethal range was short, but to stand shoulder to shoulder, going through the complicated procedure of loading, priming, aiming and firing a musket at a steady three rounds a minute while, 50yd away, another packed mass of men was firing back with the same well drilled regularity must have called for a courage and discipline no less great than that needed in the first half of the twentieth century to walk steadily forward under the ripping hail of machine guns. If Wellington's men, when only moderately wounded, were unlikely to drown in mud, as their descendants did at Passchendaele, they stood a much higher chance of dying in the foetid hospitals with 'next to no ventilation; small windows; great tubs or barrels for all purposes; the stench horrible'.

Albuera was the worst of the pounding matches. Of the 7,640 British infantry present, 3,933 were casualties. A sergeant of Fusiliers wrote that 'The orders were "Close up! Close up! Fire away!"' The survivors never forgot the moment when the Second Division went forward to support the hard-pressed Spaniards. A week later one of the officers wrote:

> During our advance in open column, the French artillery played on us, and did great execution. When the British line was formed, the Spaniards retired through us, and we advanced through a heavy fire of musketry and artillery which soon thinned our ranks. Very soon we had a glimpse of a massive column of the enemy advancing upon us. We kept up a lively fire as we advanced against them, they as briskly returned it until we came within twenty or thirty yards. We then gave three cheers and prepared to charge.

The story is taken up by other officers:

> A body of the enemy's horse was discovered under the shoulder of rising ground [and this] not permitting us to pursue, we halted and recommenced firing at them. The slaughter was now, for a few minutes, dreadful; every shot told . . .
> This was the moment at which the murderous and desperate battle really began. A most overwhelming fire of artillery and small arms was opened upon us, which was vigorously returned: there we unflinchingly stood, and there we fell; our ranks were at some places swept away by sections. This dreadful

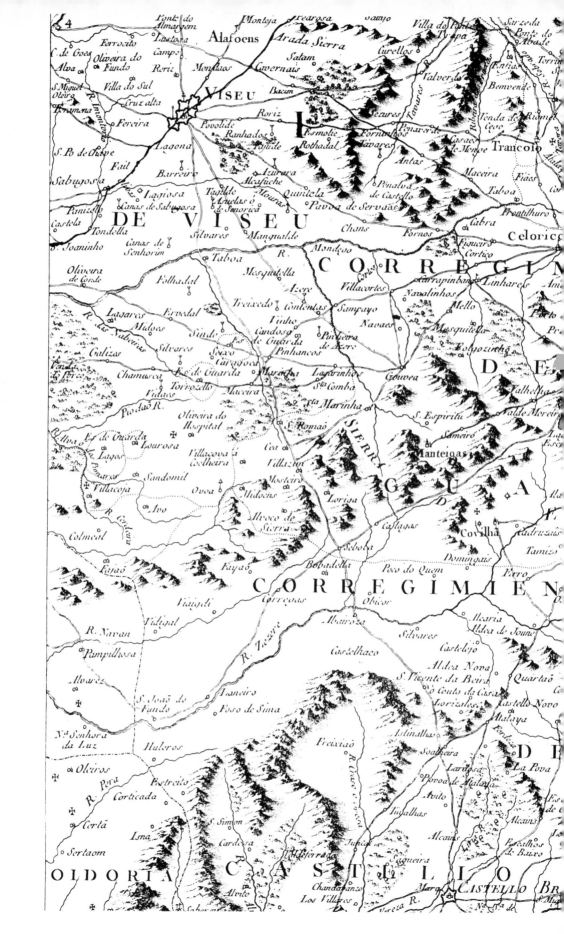

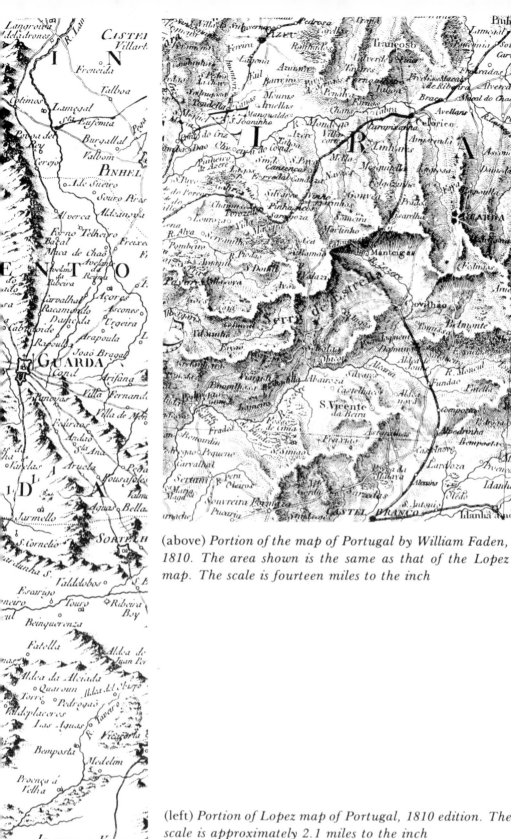

(above) *Portion of the map of Portugal by William Faden, 1810. The area shown is the same as that of the Lopez map. The scale is fourteen miles to the inch*

(left) *Portion of Lopez map of Portugal, 1810 edition. The scale is approximately 2.1 miles to the inch*

contest had continued for some time when an officer of artillery came up and said he had brought two or three guns, but that he could find no one to give him orders (our superior officers being all wounded or killed). It was suggested to him that he could not do wrong in opening directly upon the enemy, which was accordingly done. Our line at length became so reduced that it resembled a chain of skirmishers in extended order, while, from the necessity of closing in towards the Colours, and our numbers fast diminishing, our right flank became still further exposed.

It was always round the Colours that the heaviest casualties occurred. The two junior subalterns, guarded by sergeants, stood in the centre of the battalion's line with them. There was little they could do to defend themselves, since, especially in any kind of wind, it needed both hands to control the Colour, a 6ft square of embroidered silk that was both the battalion's rallying point and the physical manifestation of the pride and devotion even the most drunken and disreputable soldier felt for his regiment.

At Albuera the King's Colour of the Buffs was carried by Lieutenant Matthew Latham.

He was attacked by several French hussars, one of whom, seizing the staff and rising in his stirrups, aimed a stroke at Latham's head, which failed at cutting him down, but which sadly mutilated him, severing one side of his face and nose; he still struggled with the hussar, and exclaimed, 'I will surrender it only with my life.' A second stroke severed his left arm and hand, in which he held the staff, from his body. He then seized the staff in his right hand, throwing away his sword, and continued to struggle with his opponents, now increased in numbers; when ultimately thrown down, trampled upon and pierced by the spears of the Polish lancers, his last effort was to tear the flag from the staff, as he lay prostrate, and thrust it into the breast of his jacket.

Although left for dead, Latham eventually recovered and, two years later, was rewarded with a captaincy in the Canadian Fencibles; but it is not surprising that when, at Waterloo, Sergeant Lawrence, 'at about four o'clock was ordered to the Colours, this was a job I did not like at all. There had been before me that day fourteen sergeants already killed and wounded while in charge of the Colours, with officers in proportion.'

Albuera also included another horrifying, though fortunately rare, event — cavalry charging into an unprepared brigade of infantry. The 1er Lancers of the Vistula and the 2me Hussars charged into the rear of Colborne's brigade while it was in line. 'Our men now ran into little groups of six or eight to do as best they could. The officers snatched up muskets and joined them, determined to sell their lives dearly. Quarter was not asked, and rarely given.' Out of three battalions, 1,650 strong, 1,250 men were killed, wounded or made prisoner.

This was the kind of disaster that every infantryman feared and against which every precaution was taken. On the retreat from Burgos a surgeon noted than on 26 October, 'as the country was advantageous for cavalry, and the enemy greatly outnumbering us in this arm, we expected the enemy would harass us much. Accordingly, before we marched, the men practiced a little drill in forming squares with celerity to repel the charge.' Albuera was the result of an unfortunate combination of circumstances, driving rain and a misunderstood order. Alerted infantry had nothing to fear. At Fuentes de Oñoro six battalions of the Light Division retired three miles across a plain unscathed although beset by 3,500 horsemen. One of the young officers regretted in a letter home that they had not been 'heavily engaged'.

Isolated men on foot were extremely vulnerable to cavalry, although a single man who kept his head could deal with a single horseman. At San Milan an officer of the Rifles 'was chased round and round a tree by a French hussar, who cut at him repeatedly, 'and would have cut him down had he not spied the rifle of a man who had been killed; and as it was fortunately loaded, he shot his antagonist.' Private William Brown told how the Forty Fifth was charged by dragoons at Salamanca:

We had not time to form square and suffered severely; ranks were broken and thrown into confusion. Several times the enemy rode through us, cutting down with their sabres all that opposed them — among the rest I received a wound, but comparatively light although well aimed. One of the enemy brandished his sword over me and, standing in his stirrups, prepared to strike. But pricking his horse with my bayonet, it reared and pranced when the sword fell, the point striking my forehead. He was, however, immediately brought down.

On the other British flank at Salamanca the Fifty Third were also attacked by dragoons. According to their adjutant, 'Our regiment was formed on the left of the line, and a little off from the division to prevent the enemy flanking us. We had fired about 10 rounds with our small regiment of 245 rank and file, when about two or three hundred of the enemy's cavalry, supported by infantry, made a charge and totally surrounded us. They called out "Surrender". We answered "No"'. The commanding officer of the battalion continues:

We retired in good order, in line, and twice stopped the enemy by halting and firing. At last a circular rocky hill, about two hundred yards in the rear, offer'd an advantage; I determined to profit by it; the dragoons being too near, and the ranks too much thinn'd to attempt a square, we made a dash for the hill. The dragoons came thundering on in the rear, and reached the hill just as our people faced about. The fire checked them, and it was soon obvious that they would make no impression. At this moment, I saw part of the regiment, which had not reached the rock, running down the hill in great confusion, without, however, being pursued by the dragoons. Giving the charge of the hill to [Brevet Lieutenant-Colonel] Mansell, I dashed through the dragoons, who made way for me, and succeeded in rallying the men round the King's Colour, which I had with me. The several attacks of the dragoons failed, though at one time they seized the end of the King's Colour and there was a struggle who should have it; when a sergeant of grenadiers wrested it from the dragoon who held it, or rather tore the silk from the pole, which, I think, remained with the enemy; at the same time our people **gained** ground on the right, and the dragoons retired in confusion. They would not have been with us so long, had our men not been left almost without ammunition.

Not all great battles were pounding matches. Busaco had an apocalyptic character. The right-hand French attack came up the steep slope aiming directly towards the point where the two brigades of the Light Division joined. George Napier, Fifty Second, described how,

> . . . we were retired a few yards from the brow of the hill so that our line was concealed from the view of the enemy as they advanced up the heights, and our skirmishers retired, keeping up a constant and well directed running fire upon them; and the [troop] of horse artillery under Captain Hew Ross threw such a heavy fire of shrapnel shell, and so quick, that their column, which consisted of about 8,000 [6,500] men, was put in a great deal of confusion and lost great numbers before it arrived at a ledge of ground just under the brow of the hill, where it halted a few moments to take breath, the head of the column exactly fronting my company, which was the right company of our brigade, and joining the left of the Forty Third, where my brother William was with his company. General Craufurd himself stood on the brow of the hill watching every movement of the attacking column, and when all our skirmishers had passed by and joined their respective corps, and the head of the enemy's column was within *a very few yards of him*, he turned round, came up to us

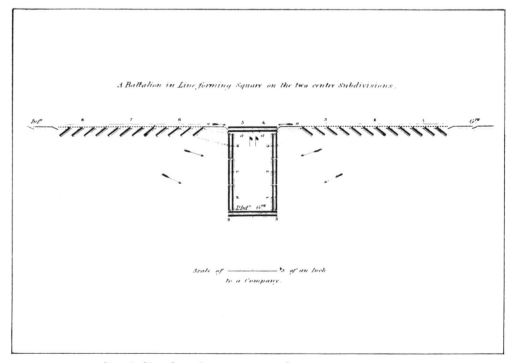

Battalion in line forming square on the two centre sub-divisions
('Field Exercise & Evolutions of the Army', edn of 1833) (NAM)

and called 'Now, Fifty Second, revenge the death of Sir John Moore! Charge! Charge! Huzza!', and waving his hat in the air, he was answered by a shout that appalled the enemy, and in one instant the brow of the hill bristled with two thousand British bayonets. My company met the head of the French column, and immediately calling on my men to form column of sections in order to give more force to our rush, we dashed forward; and as I was in front of my men a yard or two, a French soldier made a plunge at me with his bayonet, and at the same time his musket going off, I received the contents under my hip and fell. At the same instant the French fired into my front section, consisting of about nine men in the front rank, *all of whom fell*, four of them dead, the rest wounded. I got to my legs immediately again and pursued the enemy down the hill, for by this time they had been completely repulsed and were running down the hill as fast as their legs could carry them. William and Captain Lloyd, who were upon my right, seeing that the French were still in column and in great confusion from the unexpectedness of the charge and the shout which accompanied it, had wheeled up their companies by the left, and thus flanked the French column and poured a well directed fire right into them. Major Arbuthnot, who was on my left, did the same with the remaining companies of the Fifty Second, so that the enemy was beset on both flanks of his column and, as you may suppose, the slaughter was great. We kept firing and bayonetting them till we reached the bottom and the enemy passed the brook and fell back upon their main body. All this was done in a very short time from the charge till the French were driven from the top to the bottom, like a parcel of sheep.

At Busaco bayonets were used only to speed an enemy already in flight. It seems that the only occasion in the Peninsula when bayonets actually crossed was near Roncesvalles on 25 July 1813. The story is told by Captain George Tovey of the Twentieth:

The division had been expecting an attack that morning and the Twentieth were lying in column by their arms. It was daylight when a German sergeant of the Brunswick Oels corps, who had been out in front, came in haste to tell us that the French had made the Spanish piquet (who were posted to give us intelligence) prisoners without firing a shot. The left wing of the Twentieth was moved instantly to form on some strong ground in the direction they were coming, and while doing so the enemy's light troops opened so galling a fire, that Major General Ross, who was on the spot, called for a company to go in front [in the following year Robert Ross sacked Washington, DC, and was killed at Baltimore]; without waiting for orders, I pushed out with mine, and *in close order and double quick* cleared away the skirmishers from a sort of plateau. They did not wait for us, and, on reaching the opposite side, we came so suddenly on the head of the enemy's infantry column, who had just gained a footing on the summit of the hill, that the men of my company absolutely paused in astonishment, for we were face to face with them, and the French officers called on us *to disarm*; I repeated '*Bayonet away! Bayonet away!*', and rushing headlong among them, we fairly turned them back into the descent of the hill; and such was the panic and confusion occasioned among them by our sudden onset that our small party, for such it was compared to the French, had time to regain the regiment. The enemy had many men killed and their leading officer fell at my feet with two others, all bayonetted. The company, with which I was the only officer present on this occasion, did not amount to more than between seventy or eighty men, and we had eleven killed and fourteen wounded . . . A powerful man of the name of Budworth returned with only the blood-soiled socket of his bayonet on his piece; and he declared that he had *killed away* until his bayonet broke; and I am confident, from the reckless and intrepid nature of the man, that he had done so.

The assault of a fortress was even worse than a pounding match. An officer of the Thirty Ninth described the breaches at Badajoz after they had been taken. They 'were fortified in a manner so singularly strong that I do not think any army in the world could have entered by force. From the upper part of each, and resting on the slope, were hung planks thickly studded with iron spikes six inches long. These covered the whole front of the breach. On top was a *chevaux de frise* formed of sword blades, thirty six of which I counted on each frame, and immediately behind that was a breastwork where the enemy was posted.' The men moving to the attack of these frightful obstacles were noted as being, 'in the highest spirits, but without the slightest appearance of levity in their demeanour — on the contrary, there was a cast of determined severity thrown over their countenances that expressed in legible characters that they knew the sort of service they were about to perform, and had made up their mind to the issue. They had no knapsacks, their firelocks were slung over their shoulders, their shirt collars were open, and there was an indescribable *something* about them.' When

> . . . a tremendous fire was opened upon us the troops were in *no way daunted*. The ladders were found exactly opposite the centre breach and the whole [Light] division rushed to the assault with amazing resolution. There was no check. The soldiers flew down the ladders, and the cheering from both sides was loud and full of confidence. While descending the ladders [into the ditch], a soldier of the 52nd growled out a hearty curse, and was very angry at my preceding him, and furious blows were exchanged among the troops in their eagerness to get forward; while the grape shot and musketry opened their ranks . . . The ditch was very wide and when I arrived at the foot of the centre breach eighty or ninety men were formed. One cried, 'Who will lead?'. This was the work of a moment. Death and the most dreadful sounds encompassed us. It was a volcano! Up we went; some killed, and other impaled on the bayonets of their own comrades.

The Light Division failed at the breaches but the Third Division took the castle by escalade after being exposed to 'a dreadful fire of musketry, while from the body of the wall the enemy continued to pour, by means of boards placed in the parapet, whole showers of grenades, which they arranged in rows, and being lighted with a match, the whole was upset, exploding amongst us in the ditch.'

Despite these horrors, men could scarcely be restrained from volunteering. When George Napier asked for 100 volunteers from each regiment of the Light Division to form the storming party at Ciudad Rodrigo, 'instantly there rushed out nearly half the division, and we were obliged to take them at chance'. Even more remarkable is the story of Sergeant Ball of the Twenty Eighth in 1813. Being a steady soldier he had been sent to Passajes to buy tobacco for the men and tea for the officers of the regiment, which was posted in the Pyrenees. Two thousand dollars had been subscribed by the officers and Ball was given a party of six men to assist him. They

> . . . arrived at Passajes on the 30th August, and learning that San Sebastian was to be stormed next day, the sergeant addressed his men, telling them that there was hardly an action in the Peninsula in which the 28th had not a share, and proposed to them to volunteer on the storming party, for the credit of the regiment. To this the men joyfully assented, and the next question was, how to dispose of the money safely, with which they had been entrusted? It was determined to place it in the hands of a commissary, taking his receipt for the amount, which document the sergeant lodged in the hands of a third person. Having thus provided for the property of their officers, those brave fellows volunteered for the desperate enterprize. It would be superfluous to say that they did their duty, and, most fortunately—indeed singularly—none of them were hurt. After the town was taken, the sergeant collected his men, reclaimed the money, purchased the supplies, and returned to his regiment.

Battles were rare occurrences. Most of the time in which the armies were in contact only the outposts were within sight of each other. They adopted a civilised policy of live and let live, it was regarded as bad form for sentries to fire at each other. If something was about to happen, due notice was given. Before their attack at the Nive, 'The French called out to our sentinels to retire in French and Spanish. At half past nine a.m., the enemy's skirmishers came forward in a careless fashion, talking to each other, and good-naturedly allowed our sentinels to retire without firing at them.' As Wellington said, 'I always encouraged this; the killing of a poor fellow of a vidette or carrying off a post could not influence the battle, and I always when I was going to attack sent to tell them to get out of the way.'

Sentries were often very close to each other. On the night after Fuentes de Onoro, a Rifleman remembered that 'the French were divided from us only by a narrow plank thrown across a stream. The French sentry crossed the plank for a light for his pipe and stood chatting carelessly to me.' A brigade major was posting his piquets one night when 'I saw a French officer doing the same. We civilly greeted each other. I said I wished to speak to him. He came up with the greatest confidence and good humour. I showed him my vidette and then remarked that his was far too far in advance and might create an alarm at night while relieving. He said he could not see that, but to please me, if I would point out where I wished he should be, he would immediately move him—which he did.' When the two armies faced each other across the Douro in July 1812, it was 'not uncommon to see five hundred of the enemy, and as many of our men bathing together in the river in the most perfect good humour possible. At the same time the cavalry of the two armies come down on their respective sides to water their horses, it being perfectly understood that neither party shall ever approach the river armed.' 'We are,' wrote a Guards officer, 'wonderfully polite at the outposts; and, in short, are cutting each others' throats quite in a friendly way.'

Flags of truce frequently passed between the lines. In June 1810. when the French siege of Ciudad Rodrigo was beginning, 'A flag of truce, by a colonel, has just come in to Carpio; he delivered letters for Lord Wellington and gave Marshal Ney's compliments to General Craufurd, hoping he is well; also a message to Captain Krauchenberg [First Hussars, King's German Legion], saying that his dog is safe and shall be returned at the first opportunity. The dog followed a party of French when skirmishing with Krauchenberg some days back.' A few months later, a British officer took a letter from the Adjutant General into the French lines: 'I herewith send a sword which you will deliver to Monsieur Le Doux, with my

Cut Two against Infantry ('Rules & Regulations for the Sword Exercise of the Cavalry', edn of 1796) (NAM)

compliments to Monsieur le Général de Division Fririon, Chef de l'État Major. He will be pleased to state that the sword was taken with Adjutant Oberlet, of the 22nd regiment of infantry. The Adjutant declares that it was lent to him by the captain of his company, and under such circumstances I have much pleasure in returning the captain of the 22nd regiment his sword.'

Being taken prisoner was, as always, a risky business. At best all one's personal possessions would be rifled. Judge Advocate General Larpent was luckier than most when he was captured at San Marcial.

> In a moment my two horses, and cloak, pistols, sword, telescope, handkerchief, were all gone. Having received some money just before, I had about fifteen doubloons about me. One half they found instantly, and were so pleased that they scarcely searched more, except to take my knife, comb, &c. I then told them that I was only a civil officer, a non-combatant; but that I had some more money, and that if they would then, when they had got everything from me, release me, I would tell them where it was, and give it to them. This I did, thinking as they had got so much booty, they would wish to keep it secret, not to be called upon to refund any part, and that therefore they would not be sorry to say I had escaped, and let me go that I might not have to tell the story. They promised to do this, so I produced the rest, and at the same time contrived to give my watch a twist up above my waistcoat, that when they felt for it, they found nothing, and by this means I contrived to save that.

As might have been expected, his captors refused to release him, but he did admit that 'upon the whole they behaved very civilly, and without any violence'.

Quite different was the treatment of Lieutenant John Brooke, Forty Eighth, who was one of those captured when the lancers overwhelmed Colborne's brigade at Albuera. He believed many of the lancers

> . . . to have been intoxicated, as they rode over the wounded prisoners barbarously darting their lances into them. Several unfortunate prisoners were killed in this manner while being led from the field to the rear of the enemy's lines. I was an instance of their inhumanity; having been plundered of everything I had about me, I was being led as a prisoner between two French infantry soldiers, when one of these lancers rode up and deliberately cut me down. Then taking the skirts of my regimental coat, he endeavoured to pull it over my head. Not satisfied with his brutality, the wretch tried by every means in his power to make his horse trample upon me, dragging me along the ground and wheeling his horse over my body. But the beast, more merciful than the rider, absolutely refused to comply with his master's wishes and carefully avoided putting a foot on me. From this miserable situation I was rescued by two French infantry soldiers and a dragoon, who guarded me to the rear.

In earlier wars it had been customary to exchange prisoners-of-war on a rank for rank basis at the earliest possible moment. This became difficult in the

Peninsula, owing to what the British regarded as sharp practice on the French side. Massena seems to have been the chief offender. In April 1811 Wellington wrote than the marshal 'executed with so little faith the only agreement that I ever made with him that it is impossible to propose another to get out of his hands the few prisoners that he may have. Upon that occasion, having, as he stated, 120 British soldiers, and Captain Percy and Lieutenant Carden and a midshipman of the navy as prisoners, he detained the three officers and sixty of the soldiers, and sent instead of them Portuguese militia and *ordenanza* [a Portuguese form of Home Guard] to be exchanged for French prisoners.' After Massena's departure some exchanges did take place, but the system was never as satisfactory as it should have been and, within three months of the end of the war, Wellington was still complaining that 'There is no dealing with these people, excepting at arm's length'.

As can be seen, the war fought between the British and the French varied between savage barbarity and civilised courtesy. There was a sharp contrast between the scene in the breaches of Badajoz where, on the morning after the storm, 'there lay a frightful heap of thirteen or fifteen hundred British soldiers, many dead but still warm, mixed with the desperately wounded. Body piled on body, involved and intertwined into one mass of carnage,' and the incident in which a reconnoitring officer of the Sixteenth Light Dragoons jetisoned his rain-soaked cloak when shaking off his French pursuers. 'Some days afterwards, a French dragoon was seen to advance near our outposts; he approached one of our videttes as near as he thought prudent and, making a sign to him, let something fall to the ground and rode back to his own advanced posts. On examination it was found to be the cloak abandoned by the officer of the 16th, his name and regiment being marked on it.'

EPILOGUE

15

The Commander of the Forces

At the top of the military structure in the Peninsula was an unmistakable figure. A young officer, newly arrived in Spain saw

> four mounted officers, one of them riding a little ahead of the rest. He was a thin well-made man, apparently of the middle stature, and just past the prime of life. His dress was a plain grey frock, buttoned close to the chin; a cocked hat covered with oilskin; grey pantaloons, with boots buckled at the side, and a steel-mounted light sabre. Though I knew not who he was, there was a brightness in his eye which bespoke him more than an aide-de-camp or a general of brigade; nor was I left long in doubt. There were in the ranks many veterans who had served in the Peninsula during some of the earlier campaigns; these instantly recognized their old leader; and the cry of *Douro! Douro!*, the familiar title given him by the soldiers was raised. This was followed by reiterated shouts, to which he replied by taking off his hat and bowing.

'Often,' wrote another officer, 'he passes on in a brown study, or only returns the salutes of the officers at their posts; but at other times he notices those he knows with a hasty "Oh! how d'ye do", or quizzes good humouredly one of us with whom he is well acquainted. His staff come rattling after him, or stop to chat with those they know, and his *cortège* is brought up by his lordship's orderly, an old Hussar of the first Germans, who has been with him during the whole Peninsular War.'

He was known to his troops in a way that is inconceivable to a modern general, and had an uncanny knack of turning up whenever he was most needed. His presence gave the troops the confidence that they needed for victory. 'Our people', wrote a battalion commander, 'were not at all daunted by the force opposed to them, and seemed to think Lord Wellington's presence equal to two divisions.' 'I cannot,' wrote an officer of the Fortieth, at the battle of the Pyrenees, 'adequately express the sense of confidence and assurance that was revived by his presence among a single division of the army; cheers upon cheers were vehemently raised along the whole line.'

At the battle of the Nive the situation was desperate. The allied forward positions had given way and 'the French came on with loud shouts and great courage — our Portuguese allies fairly fled the field — one or two of the British regiments were overpowered; and even we [the (reformed) Eighty Fifth] whose ranks had hitherto been preserved, began to waver, when Lord Wellington himself rode up. The effect was electrical. "You must keep your ground, my lads," cried he, "there is nothing behind you — Charge! Charge!" Instantly a shout was raised. Many fugitives who had lost their own corps, threw themselves into line on our flank; we poured in but one volley, and then rushed on with the bayonet. The enemy would not stand it; their ranks were broken, and they fled in utter confusion.'

Wellington's ability to survive in the hottest fire was a legend in the army. In fact he was wounded three times in the Peninsula. At Talavera, 'I was hit in the shoulder at the end of the action, but not hurt, and my coat shot through.'

> After dusk, at the battle of Salamanca, the Duke rode up *alone* behind my regiment [Forty Third], and I joined him . . . the flush of victory was on his brow and his eyes were eager and watchful, but his voice was calm and gentle. He was giving me some orders when a ball passed through his left holster and struck his thigh; he put his hand to the place, and his countenance changed for an instant, but only for an instant; and to my eager inquiry if he was hurt, he replied, sharply, 'No' and went on with his orders.

His third wound was at Orthez in February 1814. He was standing with Alava, the Spanish liaison officer, 'having just dismounted and were laughing at a Portuguese soldier who had just passed saying that he was "*offendido*", when the Duke was struck down, but immediately rose and laughed all the more at being *offendido* himself.' A musket ball had driven the hilt of his sword into his thigh, breaking the skin and making riding painful. This did not keep him from his work or even from making a long ride that night to visit the bedside of a former ADC who had been seriously wounded. As he stood beside the bed it was observed that 'his cheeks were wet with tears'.

In theory, Wellington disapproved of generals exposing themselves to unnecessary risks and complained that Sir John Hope 'places himself among the sharpshooters, without, as they do, sheltering from the enemy's fire.' In practice, he did much the same himself. On the advance beyond the river at Vitoria, he rode among the leading Riflemen 'calling out, "That's right, my lads; keep up a good fire!"' From the south of France, a dragoon officer wrote that Wellington was being criticised for 'riding too far forward . . . We are anxious that he should take care of himself.'

His style in action was quiet and undemonstrative. 'Lord Wellington's simplicity of manner in the delivery of orders, and in command, is quite that of an able man. He has nothing of the truncheon about him; nothing full-mouthed, important or fussy: his orders on the field are all short, quick, clear and to the purpose.'

He must have been the most relaxed of great commanders. On the morning of Salamanca he was observed to be 'a little nervous' but, once he had taken his decision, his orders were almost casual. He galloped across to the Third Division and rode up to his brother-in-law who was in command. 'He looked paler than usual but was quite unruffled in his manner. Tapping Pakenham on the shoulder, he said, "Edward, move on with the Third Division—take the heights in your front—and drive everything before you".' Then he rode back to the Fifth Division where, 'on this, as on all occasions [he] gave his orders in a concise and spirited manner: there was no appearance of contemplating a doubtful result; all he directed was to time and foundation, and his instructions concluded with commands that the enemy should be overthrown and driven from the field'. Towards the end of 21 June 1813 when 'the bright evening sun was streaming on the towers of Vitoria, the battle still raged in our front, and on our left, towards the city, it was all confusion and smoke. At this moment Lord Wellington rode up with all his staff; as he passed [the Fifty Third], which was halted, he desired us to move on: I asked, "in column or in line?" Never shall I forget the animation of his countenance, "Any how, but get *on!*" was the reply.'

Wellington once remarked to his brother that 'It is useless to lament what cannot easily be remedied'. Whatever his worries, he had the ability to sleep at any time. 'When I throw off my clothes, I throw off my cares, and when I turn in my bed it is time to turn out.' During the battle of the Pyrenees, one of the tensest periods of the war, his headquarters were in a small cottage and, having eaten a meal, he 'went into the next room and threw himself upon a bed without a mattress, on the boards of which he presently went to sleep, with his despatch box for a pillow. The aides-de-camp slept on chairs or on the floor, scattered about. Presently arrived, in great haste and alarm, two officers of artillery, Captain Cairnes and another, who begged to see the Duke, the former saying he had just brought up some guns from the rear, and that he had suddenly found himself close to the enemy, and did not know what to do. They went and woke the Duke, who desired him to be brought in. The officer entered and told his story, when the Duke said, very composedly, "Well, sir, you certainly are in a very bad position, and you must get out of it the best way you can," and turned round and was asleep again in a moment.'

It is hard to say to what extent this unruffled appearance was a deliberate façade. Occasionally he was seen in real distress. Dr McGrigor remembered him when he heard the news that the assault on the breaches at Badajoz was ending in bloody stalemate. 'At this moment I cast my eyes on the countenance of Lord Wellington, lit by the glare of a torch held by Lord March; I shall never forget it to the last moment of my existence. The jaw had fallen and the face was of unusual length, while the torchlight gave his countenance a lurid aspect; but still the expression of the face was firm.' 'When the extent of the night's havoc was made known to Lord Wellington, the firmness of his nature gave way, and the pride of conquest gave way to a passionate storm of grief for the loss of his gallant soldiers'. When Creevey called on him on the day after Waterloo he 'was walking distractedly about the room exclaiming "Those Guards—those Guards, what fine fellows!" During dinner, the tears rolled down his cheeks and he could not recover his spirits at all.'

When Wellington died in 1852, Greville wrote that he 'was not an amiable man; he had no tenderness in his disposition.' That may have been true of the aged Duke, the man who had become a legend in his own lifetime, but it was far from being true of the young general who fought in the Peninsula. Being shy, he was rather stiff on first acquaintance. Lady Shelley, who first met him in 1814, noted that his 'manner is formal and, at first introduction, very imposing'. George Napier wrote that 'he has a short manner of speaking and a stern look, which people mistake for want of heart; but I have witnessed his kindness to others, and felt it myself in so many instances and so strongly, that I cannot bear to hear him accused of wanting what I know he possesses.'

He could be terrifying to those who disobeyed his orders or neglected their duties but these displays of irritability were rare and usually the product of a period of intense strain. More usually he would shrug the nuisance off and set about putting matters right by his own exertions. When three of his divisional commanders decided to take a short cut, in defiance of his orders, and found themselves, with their men, faced by an impassable river, his comment was 'Oh! by God, it was far too serious to say anything'. When Robert Craufurd embroiled his division in an unnecessary and costly action on the Coa, Wellington's comment was, 'Though I am to be hanged for it, I cannot accuse a man who I believe has meant well, and whose error is one of judgement and not of intention; and indeed I must add that although my errors, and those of others also, are visited heavily upon me, this is not the way in which any, much less a British, army can be commanded.'

He was a strict disciplinarian but his army would not have had it otherwise. Sergeant Cooper of the Fusiliers wrote:

> It has often been stated that the Duke of Wellington was severe. In answer to that I would say that he could not be otherwise. His army was composed of the lowest orders. Many, if not most of them, were ignorant, idle and drunken . . . Could a general, so wise, just and brave as he was, suffer the people to be robbed with impunity?

At the same time he was always ready to temper severity with mercy. There are dozens of examples of his finding an excuse to pardon a convicted criminal. When, just after the taking of Ciudad Rodrigo, two Connaught Rangers were sentenced for robbery, he issued a General Order: 'In consideration of the good conduct of the Eighty Eighth regiment in the recent operations, the Commander of the Forces remits that part of the sentence of the General Court Martial under which the prisoners Smith and Reilly are to receive a corporal punishment but they must be put under a stoppage to repay the money which they took respectively.' Even after Vitoria, when he was at his most bitter against the troops who had plundered 'about a million sterling', he made excuses for them. 'Many of their outrages are certainly to be attributed to want of money.'

Frequently his rebukes were cutting rather than severe. When Colonel the Hon Edward Stopford, commanding a brigade of Guards, started a major fusillade at nothing, Wellington rode up and 'asked what had occasioned the firing; the brigadier had an awkward excuse to make, and had to avow his incorrectness of vision; Lord Wellington, turning sharply aside, asked him how old he was; the brigadier replied, "Fory four." "Ah!" said Lord Wellington, "you will be a great soldier by the time you are as old as I am." The future Duke at that time was forty-one.'

Even if he felt it necessary to be strict in matters of discipline, Wellington was no martinet. The adjutant of the Fifty Third wrote that 'He is a good soldier and much beloved by the army. He gives no unnecessary trouble if people conduct themselves as they ought, but otherwise he is very severe.' He cared nothing for the minutiae of uniform. 'Provided we brought our men into the field well appointed, with sixty rounds of good ammunition each, he never looked to see whether their trousers were black, blue or grey.'

This is not to say that he was not particular, even fastidious, about his own dress. The officers did not refer to him as 'Beau Douro' for nothing. Larpent wrote that 'he is remarkably neat, and most particular in his dress, considering his situation. He is well made and knows it, and is willing to show off to the best what nature has bestowed. He cuts the skirts of his own coats shorter to make them look smarter: and only a short time since, on going to see him on business, I found him discussing the cut of his half boots and suggesting alterations with his servant.' Whenever possible he wore civilian clothes but, when occasion demanded, he could cut a splendid figure in uniform. At a review of the Household Cavalry brigade near Ciudad Rodrigo in 1813, he appeared in the full dress of the Blues, 'wore a star, and looked very well. His horse was most beautifully caparisoned, and had a net of embroidered gold and purple of uncommon beauty, which had been worked and presented to him by the ladies of Cadiz'. When he put on all his decorations in order to invest Sir Stapleton Cotton with his KB, he remarked, 'Why, I look like a ribbon merchant'.

Except when actually in the presence of the enemy, he had to spend most of his time at his desk.

> Lord Wellington rises at six o'clock every morning, and employs himself until nine (the breakfast hour) in writing. After breakfast he sees the heads of departments, viz: Quartermaster General and Adjutant General, Commissary General, Commander of the Artillery and any other officer coming to him on business. This occupies him until 2 or 3 p.m., and sometimes longer, when he gets on his horse and rides to near six. At nine he retires to write again, or employs himself until twelve when he retires for the night. His correspondence with England, and the Portuguese government, is very extensive.

Wellington's interviews with the heads of departments could be harrowing experiences for those not accustomed to the great man's ways. When he first arrived, Judge Advocate Larpent found him 'very ready and decisive and civil', but confessed that 'going up with my charges and papers for instructions, I feel something like a boy going to school.' Dr McGrigor wrote:

> At first, it was my custom to wait upon Lord Wellington with a paper in my hand, on which I had entered the heads of business about which I wished to receive his orders, or lay before him. But I shortly discovered that he disliked my coming with a written paper; he was fidgetty and evidently displeased when I referred to my notes. I therefore discontinued this, and came to him daily, having the heads of business arranged in my head.

His correspondence was vast and almost all of it was written in his own hand, the Military Secretary and the ADCs doing the copying. Peel considered him to be one of the most powerful writers in the English language and his letters are models of clarity, a sure reflection of the quality of his mind since, 'Excepting on very important occasions, I write my despatches without making a draft.' He had a ready wit and a taste for irony. When disputing with the Horse Guards about the promotion of the officers of a cavalry regiment that had misbehaved at the battle of Vitoria, he wrote:

> The question is, whether to refrain from promoting officers of a bad regiment, is to improve it: if it is, they ought not to be promoted, and I will not recommend them until I find the regiment is improved, whatever may be the extent to which private interests may, in consequence, be affected; if it is not the sooner the officers of the Eighteenth Hussars are promoted the better.

No man was less pompous than Wellington. When he heard that he had been given a step in the peerage as a reward for his victory at Salamanca, he said, 'What the devil is the use of making me a marquess?' At his headquarters 'everything was strikingly quiet and unostentatious. No one would have suspected that he was quartered in the town. Just a few aides-de-camp who went about the streets alone and in their overcoats, a few guides, and a small staff guard; that was all.' A sapper officer who had to report to him during the night near Burgos found headquarters 'in a detached straggling building on the edge of the village . . . without a guard or even a sentry at the door; neither orderly sergeant nor servant could be routed up and he reached the bedroom door unperceived. He knocked several times in vain but at length, on lifting the latch and opening the door, a sharp "Who's there?" greeted his ears. The name being returned he was desired to enter.'

As a result Wellington and his senior staff officers were almost always accessible to any officers who wished to see them. When Captain Dyneley, Royal Horse Artillery, escaped from a short period of French captivity in 1812, he reported himself to Wellington at Madrid.

> His lordship was sitting in the palace by himself. Colonel Gordon took me to him. He was exceedingly glad to see me, got me a chair and seated me by him. 'By-the-by,' said his lordship, 'you cannot have had anything to eat lately; order dinner for him and see he has a comfortable bed for he should be put to bed instantly, as he appears much fatigued.' I said, if his lordship would allow me to ask for some tea, I should prefer it to dinner. He said, 'Certainly,' and ordered it: He then entered into conversation and I told him everything I knew of the enemy's strength, their route, etc. This being finished, he said he was going to write letters to England and desired me to go into his secretary's room, and let my friends in England know that I had returned; in fact nothing could have been kinder than he was.

Any officer who happened to meet 'the Beau' was liable to get a casual 'If you will dine with me, I dine at six'. He made a point, wrote Lieutenant Anderson of the Twenty Fourth, 'of asking juniors as well as seniors'. Ensign Stepney Cowell

frequently dined with Lord Wellington and my attention was frequently fixed on observing the manners and customs of our chief; they seemed perfectly natural, straightforward and open. He conversed with liveliness on most subjects. There was a lightheartedness of manner about him, which betokened more of self-confidence than of anxiety or care, and which gave an agreeable tone to the society around him. Although upon his acts depended the fate of nations, few, from observation, could discover that he felt himself in a more responsible position than the youngest subaltern in his army. He seemed to enjoy the boyish tricks of those around him: weighty affairs did not appear to have impaired his zeal for the playfulness or jokes of his followers. At table he seldom spoke of military matters, and never of passing events in Portugal; the news of the day in England, the amusements or social state of Lisbon, or allusions to foreign countries, most frequently formed the topics of his conversation.

He greatly enjoyed any kind of party, official or unofficial. When the officers of the Light Division staged a performance of *The Rivals* in a barn at Gallegos, Wellington and his staff rode over from Freneda. When one of the leading actors forgot his lines, there was an awkward silence until 'the Commander of the Forces rose up and began clapping and crying *Bravo!* Instant confidence was restored and the part recollected'. He remained to the end when 'a variety of comic songs were sung' and then 'galloped back through the worst roads in Europe, twelve miles'.
There was a more formal occasion when he

desired to invest General Cole with the Order of the Bath in a suitable manner; and as he had never done anything for Ciudad Rodrigo, of which he is Duke [in the peerage of Spain], he determined to give a grand fête in the midst of the ruins—a grand dinner, ball and supper. All the heads of departments, generals, public authorities, Spanish and English, were invited to dinner, to the amount of sixty five. In the evening ladies, about forty, and men, about a hundred and fifty, came to a ball and supper. The dinner and supper were half cooked at Freneda and carried over in military waggons and mules. All the plate at headquarters was out in requisition, and there was enough to afford a change of silver at dinner. The whole went off very well, except that it was excessively cold, as a few balls during the siege had knocked in several yards of the roof, and it was a hard frost at the time. Lord Wellington was the most active man at the party . . . He stayed at business at Freneda until half past three, and then rode full seventeen miles to Rodrigo in two hours to dinner, dressed in all his orders, was in high glee, danced, stayed supper, and at half past three went back to Freneda by moonlight and arrived before daybreak at six; so that by twelve he was ready again for business.

Riding was his great relaxation. He kept a pack of hounds at headquarters and rode to them two or three times a week. The QMG said

that on hunting days he could almost get anything done, for Lord Wellington stands, whip in hand, ready to start and soon despatches all business. Some of the generals, Lord Wellington observed one day, used to come and hunt and then get on business, and get him to answer things in a hasty way which he did not intend, but which they acted upon. 'Oh, d--- them', said he, 'I won't speak to them again when we are hunting' . . . When the hounds are out, he is no longer the Commander of the Forces, the General in Chief of three nations, and the representative of three sovereigns; but the gay, merry country gentleman, who rode at everything, and laughed as loud when he fell himself as when he witnessed the fall of a brother sportsman.

He did fall often and in February 1813 a staff officer noted that 'only yesterday Lord W. himself (and mare) rolled neck and crop into the river'. Minor mishaps never worried him, even when he was quartered near the Pyrenees and the chimney 'was on fire from the dressing of his Lordship's dinner. Lord Wellington was out in the rain with his hat off, a silk handkerchief over his head, giving directions.'

Transcending all his hard work, his genius, his gaiety, his occasional flashes of ill-temper, was his pride in his army and his sense of duty. 'There is only one line to be adopted in opposition to all trick; that is the steady, straight line of duty, tempered by forbearance, lenity and good nature.' He knew, better than anyone, the faults and weaknesses of his men. On occasions he spoke harshly of them. He believed that drunkenness and plundering were a species of military original sin, but he also believed that the soldiers were not to be blamed for their excesses. It was his job, and that of every officer, to protect the man in the ranks from the assaults of the enemy, the neglect of the British government and his, the soldier's, own vices. 'I know of no point more important than closely to attend to the comfort of the soldier: let him be well clothed, sheltered and fed. How should he fight, poor fellow, if he has, beside risking his life, to struggle with unnecessary hardships. One ought to look sharp after young officers and be very indulgent to the soldiers.'

There are countless examples of his kindness and concern for the ordinary soldier. One private of the Ninety Second never forgot when, at Quatre Bras, he had kept his place in the line after being wounded. Wellington saw him and said, 'You have done enough, my man. Make your way to the rear while your blood is still warm'.

Wellington knew that, thanks to the care he had taken of it, the Peninsular army was 'the most complete machine for its numbers now existing in Europe'. He 'had the satisfaction of reflecting that, having tried them frequently, they have never failed me'. Working with excellent raw material but within the bounds of a system that made any kind of coordinated effort impossible, Wellington created one of the finest armies of any country at any time in history. It was essentially a personal achievement. Other British generals at the same time — Graham at Bergen-op-Zoom, Murray at Tarragona, Pakenham at New Orleans — met nothing but calamity. Only Wellington could conjure up victory. 'When I come myself, the soldiers think that what they have to do is the most important, since I am there, and all will depend on their exertions. Of course, these are increased in proportion, and they will do for me what, perhaps, no one else can make them do.' As he said on the morning after Waterloo, 'I don't think it would have done if I had not been there'.

Bibliography

Note: The abbreviation AHR is used for the Journal of the Society for Army Historical Research.

Part 1. *Biographies, Letters & Memoirs* (arranged in alphabetical order of the name of the biographee)

Recollections of a Military Life. Joseph Anderson. Ed. Acland Anderson, 1913

Retrospect of a Military Life. James Anton, Quartermaster Sergeant, 1841

A Light Dragoon in the Peninsula, The Diary of Capt. Lovell Badcock, 14th Light Dragoons. Ed: C. T. Atkinson. AHR, xxxiv

The Barnard Letters. Ed: A. Powell, 1928

Rough Notes of an Old Soldier. George Bell (2 vols), 1867

The Letters of William Bell, 89th Foot, 1808-10. Ed: B. W. Webb-Carter. AHR, xlviii

Transcript of Letters from Marshal Beresford to Lady Anne Beresford in the library of the British Council, Lisbon

'The Bingham Papers and the Peninsular War'. Ed: T. H. McGuffie. *Army Quarterly,* Apr 1949 — Oct 1951

A Boy in the Peninsular War: The Services, Adventures and Experiences of Robert Blakeney. Ed: J. Sturgis, 1899

Twelve Years Military Adventure. John Blakiston (2 vols), 1840

Manuscript Letters of Henry, William and Charles Booth in the possession of Peter Booth, Esq

Journal of an Army Surgeon during the Peninsular War. Charles Boutflower, nd

Letters of Lieut & Capt George Bowles, in *Letters of the 1st Earl of Malmesbury, his Family & Friends*. Ed: 3rd Earl of Malmesbury (2 vols), 1870

Peninsular Portrait. The Letters of Capt. William Bragge. Ed: S. A. Cassels, 1963

'Letters of Lieut. William Brereton, R.H.A.' *Proceedings of the R.A. Institution*, 1895

Manuscript Letters of the Rev Samuel Briscall in the author's possession

A Prisoner of Albuera: William Brooke, 2/48th Foot, in Sir Charles Oman's *Studies in the Peninsular War, 1929*

Personal Narrative of Adventures in the Peninsula. [E. W. Buckham], 1827

Life and Correspondence of Field Marshal Sir John Burgoyne. Ed: G. Wrottesley (2 vols), 1873

A Narrative of the Retreat of the British Army from Burgos in a Series of Letters. George Frederick Burroughs, late Asst Surgeon, Royal Dragoons, 1814

Lord Cardwell at the War Office. Robert Biddulph, 1904

The 2/53rd in the Peninsular War. Letters of Lieut. John Carss. Ed: S. H. F. Johnston. AHR, xxvi

Memoirs & Correspondence of Viscount Castlereagh. Ed: 3rd Lord Londonderry (12 vols), 1848-52

Letters of a Peninsular War Brigadier. Brig-Gen. Catlin Craufurd. Ed: M. C. Spurrier. Transcript in Old War Office Library

Life of Colin Campbell, Lord Clyde. Lawrence Shadwell (2 vols), 1881

Life of John Colborne, Lord Seton. G. C. Moore Smith, 1903

Memoirs of Sir Lowry Cole. Ed: M. L. Cole & S. Gwynn, 1934

Memoir of the Late War. John Cooke (2 vols), 1831

Rough Notes of Seven Campaigns. John Spencer Cooper, 2nd Edn, 1914

Adventures of a Soldier. Edward Costello. Ed: Antony Brett-James, 1967

Creevey. Ed: John Gore, 1938

The Croker Papers. Ed: L. W. Jennings (3 vols), 1884

Journal of an Officer in the Commissariat Department of the Army. [J. G. Danniell], 1820

The Dickson Manuscripts. Ed: J. H. Leslie, 1908-09

Recollections of the Eventful Life of a Soldier. Joseph Donaldson, new edn, 1841

The Diary of Capt. Neil Douglas, 79th Foot, 1809-10. Ed: Antony Brett-James. AHR, xli

Diary of Maj. Thomas Downman, R.H.A. Apr-Jul 1811. AHR, vi

Peninsular Journal of Maj.-Gen. Sir Benjamin D'Urban. Ed: I. J. Rousseau, 1930

'Letters written by Lieut.-Gen. Thomas Dyneley, 1806-15.' Ed: E. Whinyates. *Proceedings of R.A. Institution,* 1896

Dyott's Diary 1781-1845. Ed: R. W. Jeffery (2 vols), 1907

Memoirs of George Elers. Ed: Monson & Leveson Gower, 1903

Military Memoirs of Four Brothers by the Survivor. [Robert Fernyhough], 1829

With the 10th Hussars in Spain. Letters of Edward Fox Fitzgerald. Ed: D. J. Haggard. AHR, xliv

Vie Militaire de Général Foy. Ed: Girod de l'Ain, 1900

Letters of Sir Augustus Frazer. Ed: E. Sabine, 1859

A Subaltern in the Peninsular War. Letters of Lieutenant Robert Garrett. Ed: A. S. White. AHR, xiii

The Correspondence of King George III. Ed: Sir John Fortescue (6 vols), 1928

Later Correspondence of King George III. Ed: A. Aspinall (5 vols), 1962-70

Correspondence of George, Prince of Wales, 1770-1812. Ed: A. Aspinall, 1962-71

The Subaltern. G. R. Gleig. Ed: Ian Robertson, nd

General Graham. Antony Brett-James, 1959

Life of Thomas Graham, Lord Lyndoch. Alex. M. Delavoye, 1880

Adventures in the Connaught Rangers. William Grattan. Ed: Sir John Fortescue, 1902

Vicissitudes of a Soldier's Life. John Green, 1827

The Greville Memoirs. Ed: H. Reeve (8 vols), 1896

Peninsular War Letters of Major Edward Griffith. Ed: Norman Tucker. National Library of Wales Journal xii (1961)

Recollection in Portugal & Spain in 1811 & 1812. Cornet Francis Hall, 14th Light Dragoons. Ed: E.G.H., RUSI Journal lvi (1912)

The Recollections of Rifleman Harris. Ed: Christopher Hibbert, 1970

Reminiscences under Wellington. William Hay. Ed: S. C. I. Wood, 1901

Memoirs of an Assistant Commissary General. George Head, 1837

Letters of a Young Diplomat and Soldier during the time of Napoleon. Ralph Heathcote. Ed: Gröben, 1907

Seven Years' Campaigning in the Peninsula & Netherlands. Richard D. Henegan (2 vols), 1846

Events of a Military Life. Walter Henry, 1843

Letters from Headquarters. Letters of H. A. Johnson. Ed: Michael Glover. AHR, xliii

Adventures in the Rifle Brigade. John Kincaid, 1830

Random Shots of a Rifleman. John Kincaid, 2nd Edn, 1847

Recollections of my Military Life. George Landman (2 vols), 1854

Private Journal of Judge Advocate Larpent. Ed: G. Larpent, 3rd Edn, 1854

Autobiography of Sergeant William Lawrence. Ed: G. N. Bankes, 1886

Rough Notes of an Old Soldier. Jonathan Leach, 1831

A Narrative of the Peninsular War. Andrew Leith Hay (2 vols), 2nd Edn, 1831

Some Letters of Commissary General Havilland Le Mesurier and his son Colonel Havilland Le Mesurier during the Wars of the French Revolution and the Peninsula. (Printed Bankipur), nd

Military Journal of Colonel Leslie of Balquhain, 1887

Peninsular Cavalry General: The Correspondence of Robert Ballard Long. Ed: T. H. McGuffie, 1951

Scarlet Lancer: John Luard. James Lunt, 1964

The Memoirs of Baron Marbot. Tr: A. J. Butler, 1893

Autobiography & Services of Sir James McGrigor, 1861

Sir John Moore. Carola Oman, 1953

Thomas Morris. The Napoleonic Wars. Ed: John Selby, 1967

Passages in My Life. Baron von Müffling, Trans & Ed: P. Yorke, 1853

Life & Opinions of General Sir Charles Napier. Ed: William Napier (4 vols), 1857

Early Military Life of Sir George Napier. Ed: W. C. E. Napier, 2nd Edn, 1886

Life of General Sir William Napier. Ed: H. A. Bruce (2 vols), 1864

The Pakenham Letters, 1800-15. Ed: Lord Longford, 1914

The Adventures of Captain John Patterson, 50th Regiment. John Patterson, 1837

Camp and Quarters. John Patterson (2 vols), 1843

Spencer Perceval, the Evangelical Prime Minister, 1762-1812. Denis Grey, 1963

Memoirs of Lieutenant General Sir Thomas Picton. H. B. Robinson (2 vols), 1835

An Engineer Officer under Wellington. The Diary & Correspondence of Lt. Rice Jones, R.E. Ed: H. V. Shore. *R.E. Journal 1912-13*

A Peninsular Brigadier. Letters of Maj.-Gen. Sir F. P. Robinson. Ed: C. I. Atkinson. AHR, xxxiv

Memoir of Sir Hew Dalrymple Ross, 1871

On the Road with Wellington. A. E. F. Schaumann. Ed: A. M. Ludovic, 1924

Waterloo Arthur. The Letters of Arthur Shakespeare. Ed: C. T. Atkinson. AHR, xxxvi

The Diary of Frances, Lady Shelley. Ed: R. Edgcumbe, 1912

Recollections of the Peninsula. [Moyle Sherer], 1823

A British Rifleman: The Journals & Correspondence of Major George Simmons. Ed: W. Verner, 1899

Memoirs of a.Serjeant, late of the 43rd Light Infantry Regiment. 2nd Edn, 1839

Autobiography of Sir Harry Smith. Ed: G. C. Moore Smith, 1901

James Smithies, 1787-1868, 1st Royal Dragoons. Ed: E. Robson. AHR, xxxiv

Reminiscences of my Military Life. Charles Steevens. Ed: Nathaniel Steevens, 1878

Leaves from the Diary of an Officer of the Guards. Stepney Cowell Stepney, 1854

Twenty One Years in the British Foot Guards. John Stevenson, 1830

'Diary of Lieutenant William Swabey, R.H.A.' Ed: F. A. Whinyates. *Proceedings of R.A. Institution* 1897-98

Diary of a Cavalry Officer. William Tomkinson. Ed: J. Tomkinson, 1894

Journal of a Soldier in the 71st Regiment. [T.S.], 3rd Edn, 1822

'Diary of Captain Exham Vincent, 39th Regiment.' Transcript in the Dorchester Military Museum

The Last Journals of Horace Walpole, 1771-83. Ed: Francis Steuart (2 vols), 1900

Letters from the Peninsula, 1808-12. William Warre. Ed: E. Warre, 1909

The Letters of Private Wheeler. Ed: B. H. Liddell Hart, 1951

The 18th Hussars in 1813. Diary of Lieut. George Woodberry. Ed: W. Y. Carman. AHR, xxxvi

Part 2. *Wellingtoniana*

The Despatches of Field Marshal the Duke of Wellington. Ed: J. Gurwood (12 vols), 1834-9

Supplementary Despatches & Memoranda of Field Marshal the Duke of Wellington. Ed: 2nd Duke of Wellington (14 vols), 1858-72

The General Orders of F.M. the Duke of Wellington. Ed: J. Gurwood, 1837

186

General Orders, Portugal, Spain & France, 1809-14. (5 vols), 1810-15
'Some Letters of the Duke of Wellington to his brother, William Wellesley Pole.' Ed: Sir
    Charles Webster. *Camden Miscellany,* xviii
Personal Reminiscences of the Duke of Wellington. Francis, Lord Ellesmere. Ed: Countess
    of Stafford, 1904
The Gascoyne Heiress. Carola Oman, 1968
'Notes of Conversations with the Duke of Wellington.' Earl of Stanhope, 1889
Words on Wellington. William Fraser, 1902

Part 3. *Histories &c.*
History of the King's German Legion. N. Ludlow Beamish (2 vols), 1832
Narrative of the Campaigns of the 28th Regiment. Charles Cadell, 1835
Proceedings upon an Inquiry relative to the Armistice and Convention made & concluded
    in Portugal in 1808. 1809
The Military Forces of the Crown. Their Administration & Government. C. M. Clode
    (2 vols), 1869
History of the Royal Sappers & Miners. T. W. J. Connolly (2 vols), 1837
The History of the Rifle Brigade. William H. Cope, 1877
The Army of Frederick the Great. Christopher Duffy, 1974
History of the Royal Regiment of Artillery. F. Duncan (2 vols), 1878
History of Lord Farringdon's Regiment (29th Foot). H. Everard, 1891
History of the Army Ordnance Services. A. Forbes (3 vols), 1929
A History of the British Army. Sir John Fortescue (13 vols), 1899-1930
The County Lieutenancies & the Army. Sir John Fortescue, 1909
The Life of a Regiment. The Story of the Gordon Highlanders. Vol i. C. Greenhill
    Gardyne, 1901
Britain at Bay. Richard Glover, 1973
Peninsular Preparation. The Reform of the British Army, 1795-1809. Richard Glover, 1963
Journal of the Sieges carried out by the army under the Duke of Wellington. John T. Jones
    (3 vols), 3rd Edn, 1846
List of the Officers of the Royal Artillery. John Kane, 1815
A Social History of the Navy, 1793-1815. Michael Lewis, 1960
Origin & Services of the Coldstream Guards. Daniel Mackinnon (2 vols), 1833
Peninsular Sketches by Actors on the Scene. Ed: W. H. Maxwell (2 vols), 1845
Historical Records of the Fifty Second Regiment. W. S. Moorsom, 1860
The Structure of Politics at the Accession of George III. Lewis Namier, 2nd Edn, 1961
History of the War in the Peninsula & South of France. William Napier (6 vols), cabinet
    Edn, 1852
The Emperor's Chambermaids. The Story of the 14th/20th King's Hussars. L. B. Oates,
    1973
History of the Peninsular War. Sir Charles Oman (7 vols), 1902-30
Wellington's Army. Sir Charles Oman, 1913
History of the Corps of Royal Engineers. Whitworth Porter (2 vols), 1889
Celer et Audax. A Sketch of the Services of the 5th Battalion, 60th Regiment (Rifles).
    Gibbes Rigaud, 1879
Records of the Royal Military Academy 1741-1892. 2nd Edn, 1892
Royal Military Calendar or Army Service & Commissions Book. (5 vols), 3rd Edn, 1820
Royal Military Chronicle or British Officers' Monthly Register. Vols 1-5, 1810-1815
In this Sign Conquer. J. Smyth, VC, 1968
Historical Records of the 40th (2nd Somerset) Regiment. R. H. Raymond Smythies, 1894
History & Campaigns of the Rifle Brigade. Willoughby Verner (2 vols), 1912-19
The Reign of George III. J. Seton Watson, 1960
Wellington's Headquarters. S. G. P. Ward, 1957
Wellington in the Peninsula. Jac Weller, 1962

History of the 1st & 2nd Battalions, The Sherwood Foresters, 1740-1914. H. C. Wylly (2 vols), 1929

Part 4. *Other Works*
Details of the Rocket System. William Congreve, 1814
A Practical Guide for the Light Infantry Officer. T. H. Cooper, 1806
Principles of Military Movement. David Dundas, 1788
A View of the History & Actual State of the Military Forces of Great Britain. Charles Dupin. Tr: 'by an Officer' (2 vols), 1820
Report on the Manuscripts of Earl Bathurst. Historical Manuscripts Commission, 1923
Report on the Manuscripts of the 1st Earl Charlemont. Historical Manuscripts Commission, 1891
Report on the Manuscripts of the late R. Rawdon Hastings. Historical Manuscripts Commission, 1934
Report on the Manuscripts of Robert Graham of Fintry. Historical Manuscripts Commission, Supplementary Report, 1934
British Smooth Bore Artillery. B. P. Hughes, 1969
Military Dictionary. Charles James, 1810
The Regimental Companion. Charles James (4 vols), 1803-14
Military Miscellany. Charles Marshall, 1846
Recruiting the Ranks of the Regular British Army during the French Wars. T. H. McGuffie. AHR, xxxiv
The Raising and Organising of the King's German Legion. R. E. F. G. North. AHR, xxix
Weapons of the British Soldier. H. C. B. Rogers, 1960
General Regulations and Orders for the Army, Adjutant General's Office, 12 August 1810, to which are added such Regulations as have been issued to the 1st January 1816. Reprinted 1970
Field Exercises & Evolutions of the Army, 1833
Rules & Regulations for the Formations, Field-Exercises and Movements of His Majesty's Forces. 1803

Acknowledgements

I must record my thanks to many people who have helped me with this book, notably Mr Peter Booth, Mr Evan Davies, Mrs Adrian Digby, Dr Carlos Estorninho, Mr Geoffrey Saunders and, most particularly, Miss Sheila Gullick, whose patience and industry seem inexhaustible.

My daughter Stephanie contributed ideas, advice and encouragement. Most of all, I am indebted to my wife, whose active participation in the work, together with her comfort and encouragement, made the book possible.

The sources of the illustrations are given in the captions in abbreviated form as follows:
The Queen's Collection at Windsor: HM
National Portrait Gallery: NPG
National Army Museum: NAM

I regret that it has not been possible to include references to the quotations in the text but the hard economic fact is that, since there are more than 600 quotations, to identify all of them would have meant the sacrifice of the equivalent of a whole chapter if the book was to fit into the required length.

Index

Page numbers in italics refer to illustrations.

189

190